Laws of Desire

Laws of Desire

*Questions of Homosexuality
in Spanish Writing and Film
1960–1990*

PAUL JULIAN SMITH

CLARENDON PRESS · OXFORD
1992

Oxford University Press, Walton Street, Oxford OX2 6DP
Oxford New York Toronto
Delhi Bombay Calcutta Madras Karachi
Petaling Jaya Singapore Hong Kong Tokyo
Nairobi Dar es Salaam Cape Town
Melbourne Auckland
and associated companies in
Berlin Ibadan

Oxford is a trade mark of Oxford University Press

Published in the United States
by Oxford University Press, New York

British Library Cataloguing in Publication Data
Data available

Library of Congress Cataloging in Publication Data
Smith, Paul Julian.
Laws of desire : questions of homosexuality in Spanish writing and
film, 1960–1990 / Paul Julian Smith.
Includes bibliographical references and index.
1. Spanish literature—20th century—History and criticism.
2. Homosexuality in literature. 3. Motion pictures—Spain—History.
4. Homosexuality in motion pictures. I. Title.
PQ6073.H65S45 1992
860.9'353—dc20 92-13021
ISBN 0-19-811953-4
ISBN 0-19-812275-6 (pbk)

Typeset by Cambridge Composing (UK) Ltd

Printed and bound in
Great Britain by Biddles Ltd,
Guildford and King's Lynn

For E.

ani leyedidi veyedidi li

Oxford Hispanic Studies

General Editor: Paul Julian Smith

The last twenty years have seen a revolution in the humanities. On the one hand, there has been a massive influence on literary studies of other disciplines: philosophy, psychoanalysis, and anthropology. On the other, there has been a displacement of the boundaries of literary studies, an opening out on to other forms of expression: cinema, popular culture, and historical documentation.

The new *Oxford Hispanic Studies* series reflects the fact that Hispanic studies are particularly well placed to take advantage of this revolution. Unlike those working in French or English studies, Hispanists have little reason to genuflect to a canon of European culture which has tended to exclude them. Historically, moreover, Hispanic societies tend to exhibit plurality and difference: thus Medieval Spain was the product of the three cultures of Jew, Moslem, and Christian; modern Spain is a federation of discrete autonomous regions; and Spanish America is a continent in which cultural identity must always be brought into question, can never be taken for granted.

The incursion of new models of critical theory into Spanish-speaking countries has been uneven. And while cultural studies in other language areas have moved through post-structuralism (Lacan, Derrida, Foucault) to create new disciplines focusing on gender, ethnicity, and homosexuality, it is only recently that Hispanists have contributed to the latest fields of enquiry. Now, however, there is an upsurge of exciting new work in both Europe and the Americas. *Oxford Hispanic Studies* is intended to provide a medium for writing engaged in and taking account of these developments. It will serve both as a vehicle and a stimulus for innovative and challenging work in an important and rapidly changing field. The series aims to facilitate both the development of new approaches in Hispanic studies and the awareness of Hispanic studies in other subject areas. It will embrace discussions of literary and non-literary cultural forms, and focus on the publication of illuminating original research and theory.

Preface

I N the last five years lesbian and gay studies has emerged as a discrete discipline, particularly in the United States, where many major universities now have programmes devoted to this new field. Scholars have attempted to elaborate a theorization of homosexuality drawing on psychoanalytic and political frameworks. Rather than vindicating an essential homosexual identity I aim (like them) to discuss representations of lesbians and gay men as historical constructs which respond to both unconscious fantasy and political change. I argue that 'homosexuality' (if such a unitary phenomenon exists) is invariably inflected by factors such as gender, 'race', and class.

Homosexuality has been treated only in a fragmentary way in Hispanic Studies;[1] and most of that which is published shows no awareness of recent developments in lesbian and gay studies.[2] I therefore begin with a brief account of some non-literary Spanish works (medical, legal, and polemical texts) and of issues raised by the latest contributions to the field in English studies. The first chapter charts the varying representations of the feminist or gay 'self', an identity which must always remain precarious even as it claims to reveal itself to the reader. The next two chapters offer radically new readings of trilogies by the major novelists of homosexual desire in Spain (male and female) in the light of

---

[1] Emilie Bergmann of Berkeley and I are currently editing the first collection of scholarly essays on lesbian and gay studies/Hispanic studies. A large number of scholars are now working in the field (especially in the USA), but little has been published as yet. Those whose work I have seen include Sylvia Molloy, Oscar Montero, and Juan Gelpí. See also the pioneering account of a contemporary poet: Chris Perriam, 'Reality and the Angels: Luis Antonio de Villena and *La muerte unicamente*', *BHS* 67 (1990), 31–42.

[2] See e.g. D. Gareth Walters, ' "Comprendí. Pero no explico.": Revelation and Concealment in Lorca's *Canciones*', *BHS* 68 (1991), 265–79. This article contains no reference to lesbian/gay studies. The author does not question the opposition between concealment and revelation problematized by Foucault as far back as the 1970s. I take it as axiomatic that homosexuality is called into being by that power which obliges it both to conceal and to reveal itself. For a study of a contemporary English writer which examines the interaction of law and desire, see Alan Sinfield, 'Who Was Afraid of Joe Orton?', *TP* 4 (1990), 259–77. For Lorca and gay studies, see J. S. Cummins, 'Epoca lorquiana: Lorca, Buñuel, Dalí, and Spanish Machismo', *EGR* 1 (1986), 117–24.

French theorists (Hocquenghem and Wittig). The final pair of chapters draws on archival research at the Filmoteca Nacional to offer a broadly historical account of the two major gay *auteurs* of Spanish film, paying close attention to their uses of cinematic form (*mise en scène*, cinematography, editing).

This is not a history of Spanish lesbian and gay life as reflected in literature and film; nor is it an exhaustive survey. I am not concerned with the writers and film-makers themselves (and readers must not assume that they identify as lesbian or gay), but with those texts they have produced which raise the question of homosexuality in more or less direct fashion. Many more texts remain.[3] Two omissions should be mentioned. First, I do not give equal space to lesbian texts; this is a rich, but undeveloped area which I hope to return to. Secondly, I do not deal with responses to AIDS in Spain. However, I have written at length in a previous book on Goytisolo's important novel on this topic.[4]

This book was written between summer 1990 and summer 1991. I would like to thank the staff and students of the Hispanic Studies, French, and English departments in Queen Mary and Westfield College, University of London, for providing a rich and stimulating environment over the past seven years. A sense of support and of common intellectual enquiry has been indispensable for the development of my work. Most particularly, I would like to thank my research students, from whom I have learned so much: David Vilaseca, Josep-Anton Fernández, and Alan Stewart. I am grateful to the QMW Library (especially Liz Mailer); the Filmoteca Nacional (especially Dolores Devesa); the British Film Institute (especially Jim Hillier and Roy Stafford, whose classes I attended); the British Library (but not the 'Special Table' where I was obliged to read many of the books I cite here); the University of London Library at Senate House; the Biblioteca Nacional, Madrid; the Ministerio de Cultura in

---

[3] See e.g. the important early autobiographies by former priest Antonio Roig Roselló, *Todos los parques no son un paraíso: memorias de un sacerdote* (Barcelona, 1977); *Vidente en rebeldía: un proceso en la iglesia* (Barcelona, 1979).

[4] The novel is *Las virtudes del pájaro solitario* (Barcelona, 1988), trans. *The Virtues of the Solitary Bird* (London, 1991). See my *Representing the Other: 'Race', Text, and Gender in Spanish and Spanish American Narrative* (Oxford, 1992), ch. 6. This volume shares with its predecessors the ambition of introducing into Hispanism theoretical debates of which Hispanism is not fully aware; see my *Writing in the Margin: Spanish Literature of the Golden Age* (Oxford, 1988); *The Body Hispanic: Gender and Sexuality in Spanish and Spanish American Literature* (Oxford, 1989).

Madrid (especially for the PIC). Professor Malcolm Bowie kindly sponsored the first international conference on Questions of Homosexuality in the UK at the Institute of Romance Studies (of which he was Director) in May and June 1991. My thanks to all those who helped to make the conference such a success, especially Administrative Secretary Simona Cain.

Jonathan Dollimore kindly sent me the proofs of *Sexual Dissidence* before publication; John Hopewell gave me invaluable advice on film in Madrid; Peter W. Evans was exceptionally generous with both videos and bibliography, as were his students Nùria Triana and María Delgado, who work on Almodóvar and Saura respectively. I received support and encouragement from several people on a visit to Duke University, North Carolina. Jonathan Romney kindly gave me the chance to write on and review Spanish-language cinema when he was editor of the *City Limits* film section. James S. Williams helped with bibliography, especially in French.

Material from Chapter 2 was given as a paper at the Conference on Sexuality in Hispanic Writing and Film organized by Pamela Bacarisse and held at the University of Pittsburgh in 1991; from Chapter 3 in the Conference on Hispanic Women Writers at St Andrews organized by Catherine Davies in the same year; from Chapter 5 in seminars at the QMW English Department and New Hall, Cambridge, and at 'The Body in the Text' conference held in 1991 in Gregynog, organized by Valerie Minogue. The Coda was read at the MLA, San Francisco, 1991.

Finally, Juan Goytisolo took the trouble to read and comment on Chapter 2. I am very grateful to him for encouraging me at an early point in the writing of this book.

I am happy to make formal acknowledgement of a grant from the British Academy which enabled me to carry out research on Spanish cinema in Madrid, 1990.

P.J.S

London, 1991

Half of the author's royalties from this book will be donated to the Globe Centre, a centre for those affected by HIV and AIDS in the City and East London.

Acknowledgements

I am grateful to the following for permission to reproduce extracts:

ROSA CHACEL: *Desde el amanecer*, © 1985 by Rosa Chacel. Reproduced by permission of Agencia Literaria Carmen Balcells, SA.

JUAN GOYTISOLO: *Señas de identidad*, © 1966 by Juan Goytisolo. *Reivindicación del conde don Julián*, © 1970 by Juan Goytisolo. *Juan sin tierra*, © 1975 by Juan Goytisolo; *En los reinos de Taifa*, © 1986 by Juan Goytisolo. All reproduced by permission of Agencia Literaria Carmen Balcells SA. *Marks of Identity*, © 1966 by Juan Goytisolo, English translation © 1974 by Viking Press. *Count Julian*, © 1970 by Editorial Joaquín Mortiz, English translation © 1974 by Viking Press. *Juan the Landless*, © 1975 by Juan Goytisolo, English translation © 1975 by Viking Press. All reproduced by permission of Serpent's Tail. *Realms of Conflict*, © 1986 by Juan Goytisolo, English translation © 1990 by Quartet Books. Reproduced by permission of Quartet Books.

ESTHER TUSQUETS: *El mismo mar de todos los veranos*, © 1978 by Esther Tusquets; *El amor es un juego solitario*, © 1979 by Esther Tusquets; *Varada tras el último naufragio*, © 1980 by Esther Tusquets. All reproduced by permission of Esther Tusquets and Editorial Lumen. *The Same Sea as Every Summer*, © 1978 by Esther Tusquets, English translation © 1990 by Margaret E. W. Jones. Reproduced by permission of University of Nebraska Press. *Love is a Solitary Game*, © 1979 by Esther Tusquets, English translation © 1985 by Bruce Penman. Reproduced by permission of Calder Publications.

TERENCE MOIX: Plaza y Janés did not reply to my request to reproduce an extract from *El peso de la paja*.

Contents

List of Abbreviations

The following abbreviations have been used both in the footnotes and in the Bibliographies:

ALEC	*Anales de la literatura española contemporánea*
BHS	*Bulletin of Hispanic Studies*
CaC	*Cahiers du Cinéma*
CC	*Comparative Criticism*
CH	*Crítica Hispánica*
EGR	*European Gay Review*
EL	*Estudios de Lingüística*
FMLS	*Forum for Modern Language Studies*
FC	*Film Comment*
FQ	*Film Quarterly*
FR	*Feminist Review*
GLAN	*Gay and Lesbian Academic Networking*
HR	*Hispanic Review*
HuR	*Hudson Review*
LD	*Letras de Deusto*
LF	*Letras Femeninas*
LP	*Letras Peninsulares*
MLR	*Modern Literature Review*
PMLA	*Publications of the Modern Language Association of America*
RC	*Revue du Cinéma*
RFH	*Revista de Filología Hispánica*
RHM	*Revista Hispánica Moderna*
RR	*Romanic Review*
SS	*Sight and Sound*
TJ	*Theatre Journal*
TLS	*Times Literary Supplement*
TP	*Textual Practice*
YJC	*Yale Journal of Criticism*

List of Plates

I have been unable to contact Eloy de la Iglesia to discover who owns the copyright to Plates 1 and 2.

Introduction: Desiring the Law

WHILE visiting relatives in the Brazilian rainforest, a formerly timid young woman experiences a 'transformation' and is suddenly inspired by a new 'way of being'. Out riding her horse, she almost tramples a teenage girl she passes on the forest path. The girl has a feline face and 'diabolical' blue eyes. The first woman pursues the second, guiding her into marshy ground, the dangerous place which (we are told) she knows so well. She dismounts, forces the younger woman to stop, and leans her shoulder a little on hers. As the couple move ever deeper into the marshland, the girl's hair shines amongst the emerald plants, like the pink lilies at the water's edge.

'Since I became a dyke ["tortillera"] I see life in a different way . . .' A grand Catalan lady is addressing a vulgar Andaluza in the first-class cabin of a plane flying from New York to Madrid. The first woman is tall, painfully thin, and as blonde as a Valkyrie. She is dressed in mourning and sports a hat with an improbably wide brim. The second is small and squat. She resembles a 'travelling sacristy', her ample bosom weighed down by devotional images; Saints Justa and Rufina, patrons of Seville, dangle from either earlobe. The Valkyrie is returning from a wake for Greta Garbo, organized by the League of Tyrolese Lesbians; the 'sacristy' from a sell-out tour of Spanish America with the miraculous Copper Virgin and her fellow performers. The two have more in common than they at first think.

The first text is 'Transfiguración', a short story by Rosa Chacel, first published in Mexico in 1961.[1] The second is the opening scene of *Garras de astracán* ('Astrakhan Claws') by Terenci Moix, one of the bestselling novels of 1991.[2] In Chacel we find ambiguity and understatement: at the very moment of what is coded as a sexual encounter, the narrator 'cuts away' to a frightened bird flying out of the marsh. In Moix everything is

---

[1] Text from *Icada, Nevda, Diada* (Barcelona, 1982), 145–64 (p. 162).
[2] Pub. in Barcelona (p. 5).

patently, even excessively, clear: his meeting of two remarkable women is presented in indulgently camp and outrageous style. This very first page of the novel features a rather tired pun on 'polvo' (meaning both 'dust' and 'fuck'). The 'different way of being' celebrated by both writers is thus very different in each.

How can we account for the change in tone between the two texts over a period of thirty years? It is not simply a case of greater explicitness in the depiction of lesbian desire. As we shall see when we examine the autobiographies of Chacel and Moix in Chapter 1, it cannot be taken for granted that sexuality somehow precedes its expression in language and stands mutely waiting to be revealed as the truth of the subject. On the contrary, it may be that it is the tension between concealment and display that calls homosexuality into being. What both of these passages share, however, is a stress on the encounter: on lesbianism as intersubjectivity, not existential isolation. Neither of these encounters lead to genital sex;[3] but both suggest a model of homosexual desire which will recur in writers such as Goytisolo: 'cruising' as a relation with the other in present time. However, there are added questions of gender and sexuality at stake here: Chacel (a heterosexual woman) presents female seduction as the final result of a masculine identification: we have been told that her unnamed heroine is possessed by the spirit of a fearless man of the jungle;[4] Moix (an openly gay man) impersonates a 'vocational' lesbian, lending her a camp sensibility normally gendered as masculine. Can the lesbian body transcend heterosexist norms? Do gay men's representations of lesbians serve merely as a screen for their own cultural concerns? I discuss these problems in Chapters 3 and 5, on novelist Esther Tusquets and film-maker Pedro Almodóvar respectively.

There is no social history of homosexuality in Spain from 1960–90, no work comparable to that of Jeffrey Weeks for Britain.[5] The relation of the texts I treat to the complex historical

---

[3] As the novel develops we learn that neither of Moix's 'ladies in the air' show much enthusiasm for sex of any kind.

[4] The expression 'way of being' recurs in Chacel's autobiography with reference to her father (see Ch. 1); it may also have homosexual resonance, as is suggested by the title of Juan Gil-Albert's important apology for homosexuality, *Heracles: sobre una manera de ser* (Madrid, 1975) (written in 1955).

[5] See Weeks, *Coming Out: Homosexual Politics in Britain from the Nineteenth Century to the Present* (London, 1977); and for an earlier period, his and Kevin Porter's oral history, *Between the Acts: Lives of Homosexual Men 1885–1967* (New York, 1991).

background in which they were produced is a task I do not attempt here. Occasionally, direct links become visible. Thus Eloy de la Iglesia claims that it was the banning of his film *Los placeres ocultos* ('Hidden Pleasures', 1976) that precipitated the first openly gay demonstration in Spain, on the streets of Barcelona.[6] Generally, however, it is not possible or indeed fruitful to seek such direct links. Several of the artists discussed in this book were in exile for part of the period (Chacel, Goytisolo, Moix); several of them do not identify as lesbian or gay writers or film-makers. My answer to the thorny question 'What is lesbian and gay writing and film?' is thus to consider not the producer but the product: I examine texts which raise the question of homosexual desire and consider the figure of the author only in so far as it affects the text's historical reception. This is particularly the case in Chapter 1 on autobiography and Chapters 4 and 5 on cinema. For example, it seems clear from the study of press clippings that the public image of a film-maker such as Almodóvar helps to create the conditions under which his films are consumed, tends actively to produce an audience for those films.

This is not a historical study, then, in any empirical sense; though it is one which will pay close attention to material questions of gender, class, and national identity. And nor is it an exhaustive survey. Rather I have chosen to concentrate on the work of six writers and film-makers during the period 1960–90 and submit their texts to close analysis. Once again, they are very different from one another. Rosa Chacel was born in Valladolid in 1898 and moved to Madrid as a child. Before the Civil War, she lived in Italy with her husband Timoteo Pérez Rubio. In 1939 she left Spain for Latin America, where she settled in Rio, returning after the death of Franco. She is best known for her fiction, which includes the novel *La sinrazón* (1960), and the autobiography of her childhood, which I discuss in Chapter 1. Her work is woman-oriented but not explicitly lesbian in nature. Juan Goytisolo is the major novelist of contemporary Spain. Born in Barcelona in 1931, he has lived in Paris since 1956. The author of many novels and collections of essays, he is perhaps best known for his two volumes of auto-biography (Chapter 1) and the fictional 'trilogy of treason'

---

[6] See George De Stefano, 'Post-Franco Frankness', *FC* 22 (June 1986), 58–60.

which appeared between 1966 and 1975 (Chapter 2). Esther
Tusquets was born in Barcelona in 1936. She has directed the
Lumen publishing house since the early 1960s. Her trilogy of
novels with a lesbian theme (Chapter 3) was published just
after the death of Franco at the end of the 1970s. Terenci Moix
was born, also in Barcelona, in 1942. A prolific novelist, first in
Catalan and more recently in Castilian, he is also a journalist,
travel writer, and television 'personality'. The first volume of
his memoirs was published in 1990 (see Chapter 1). Eloy de la
Iglesia (Chapter 4) is a Basque, born in Zarauz (Guipúzcoa) in
1944. He has made some nineteen films since the 1960s, specializing in exploitation movies which feature teenage gangsters.
During the transition to democracy in the late 1970s the films
he made on gay themes such as *El diputado* ('The MP', 1978)
were the most popular (and profitable) in Spain. Pedro Almodóvar (Chapter 5 and Coda) was born in the small town of
Calzada de Calatrava (Ciudad Real) in 1949 and is the best
known film-maker of the *desencanto* (post-democracy 'disillu-
sion'). His nine features include the most successful Spanish
film of all time: *Mujeres al borde de un ataque de nervios* ('Women
on the Verge of a Nervous Breakdown', 1988). *Tacones lejanos*
('High Heels'), with Victoria Abril and singer Miguel Bosé, was
released in late 1991.

Immediately evident from the summary above is a bias
towards the autonomous regions of what is now a loosely federal
Spanish state. As we shall see in a moment, the emphasis on
Catalunya is also justified by the history of the lesbian and gay
movement in Spain in the period, which began in Barcelona.
Thus one surprise for English-speakers is the way in which
lesbian and gay identities were, from the very beginning, inseparable from the historical and political questions of national and
ethnic identities. It is the gay character in de la Iglesia's *El pico*
('The Shoot', 1983) who articulates the film-maker's problematic
conception of Basque autonomy; and in Tusquets, Goytisolo,
and Moix a complex and variable engagement with bilingualism
and biculturalism is inseparable from the construction (the
assertion) of a sexual self. It seems likely, moreover, that the
Spanish gay movement (like the French and unlike the British
and North American) understood the first stage of liberation to
be the critique, rather than the celebration, of homosexual

identity.[7] Many Spaniards do not seem to believe that homosexuality can be the basis for a political community. It is perhaps
significant that novelists such as Tusquets and Goytisolo, film-
makers such as Almodóvar, rarely address the relation between
gay and straight society, the problematics of the closet and of
coming out that are so much discussed in English-speaking
countries. It is also noticeable that their representations of
lesbian or gay relationships rarely coincide with what was until
recently the ideal of many Anglo-Saxon gays: a reciprocal
relation between two partners of more or less equal status.

Let us look, briefly, at some non-fictional texts which appeared
in the crucial decades of the 1970s and 1980s, between Francoism
and a full consolidation of liberal democracy. Such texts can be
loosely divided into three categories: homophobic; disciplinary
(medico-legal); and contestatory. Typical of the first category is
the popular work attributed to the pseudonym 'Mauricio Karl',
first published in 1956 but reprinted in its twelfth edition in
1973: *Sodomitas: homosexuales políticos, científicos, criminales, espías,
etc.* (no place of publication given).[8] 'Karl' (who also claims to
be the author of books on Communism and masonry in Spain
and on 'the mystery of the state of Israel') divides his work into
three parts: 'Sodomy and Communism'; 'Sodomy and "Sci-
ence"'; and 'Sodomy, Politics, and Espionage'. The first section
traces the supposed common history of homosexuality and
Communism from their birth in Crete and Sparta, through
Platonism and Kabbalah, to Protestantism, Jacobinism, and the
'fraternity' of Marx and Engels (pp. 14, 16, 20, 44, 61). The
second section attacks 'criminal writers' such as Gide and Proust,
Spanish doctor and sexologist Gregorio Marañón, and Jews such
as Freud, held to be the founders of the 'sodomitic school' of
psychoanalysis (pp. 71, 74–118, 98). The final section has a
lengthy diatribe against Azaña, former President of the Spanish
Republic, and accuses Jews in the International Brigades of

[7] See the preface to the Spanish trans. of Jean Nicolas, *La cuestión homosexual*
(Barcelona, 1978), in which Lubara Guílver and Roger de Gaimon of the FAGC
(Front d'Alliberament Gai de Catalunya) state that 'the critique of homosexual
identity' is the first priority of a 'revolutionary' gay liberation (p. 15).

[8] 'Karl' also published under the name Mauricio Carlavilla del Barrio. For
homosexuality as crime, vice, and sickness see *Biografía de la homosexualidad* (Barcelona, 1976), by Enrique Martínez Fariñas (also known as 'Helmuth von Sohel' and
'Irving Smutty'); compare the sensationalist *Fronteras de la homosexualidad* (Barcelona,
1976) by Enrique Sánchez Pascual ('Ludwig Wasserman').

wishing to restore 'Sefard'[9] (*sic*), before proposing a solution to the problem: as homosexuality flourishes in the city, urbanization must come to a halt (pp. 131–54, 191, 295). Only then can the 'Satanic' cult be extirpated (p. 299).

It would be easy to dismiss *Sodomitas* as a catalogue of paranoid delusions. However, to do so would be to neglect the power of fantasy to effect material change in the world. As Jacqueline Rose has repeatedly warned,[10] there can be no simple distinction between psychic and political life. Moreover, in his obsessive reiteration of the supposed connection between homosexuality, Judaism, and Communism, 'Karl' inadvertently coincides with radicals such as Goytisolo, who also seek to examine the common history of dissident minorities opposed to Spanish orthodoxy. Finally, we cannot be sure what the readership of 'Karl''s work was. It seems possible that at a time when no favourable accounts of homosexuality were permitted,[11] homosexual readers may have found material in such diatribes which allowed a 'reverse reading': the vindication of a gay (if not lesbian) history and identity which have existed at all times and in all places. Such a reader would have discovered that (according to 'Karl'), far from being an isolated anomaly, men like himself were proliferating, especially in the metropolis. Homophobia would thus call into being that very identity it sought to disavow and to repress: the 'etc.' at the end of 'Karl''s title marks the space of an uncontrollable dissemination of sexual dissidents, all the more potent because of their invisibility.

As his use of the archaic 'sodomy' suggests, 'Karl''s discourse is based on the religious model of homosexuality as sin. Later texts invoke the more contemporary disciplinary models of medicine and the law. One particularly unselfconscious example of this genre is Alberto García Valdés's *Historia y presente de la homosexualidad* (Torrejón de Ardoz, 1981). The author, a doctor and criminologist, states that the motive for the book came from his observation of gay men on professional visits to prisons,[12] and

---

[9] The Hebrew word for 'Spain' is, of course, 'Sefarad'.

[10] Most recently in *The Haunting of Sylvia Plath* (London, 1991).

[11] In 1972 the censor refused Enrique Núñez permission to publish his anodyne medical dissertation; it appeared five years later as *Homoeróticos* (Madrid, 1977) with the censored lines printed in italic type face.

[12] Cf. Baldomero Montoya's *Los homosexuales* (Barcelona, 1977), which claims to be written from '14 years of psychiatric experience'; and Marciano Vidal's normative and biologist *Homosexualidad: ciencia y conciencia* (Santander, 1981).

from his discovery that there was a complete lack of material on homosexuality in Spain (pp. 9–10). García Valdés gives a historical account of homosexuality based on the three models noted above: sin, crime, and sickness. He shows that the legal position of gay men in twentieth-century Spain had continued to deteriorate until the establishment of democracy in 1976. Since the Penal Code of 1932, in which homosexuality was not cited as a crime unless it was accompanied by additional factors such as 'public scandal' or corruption of minors, a series of anti-gay laws had culminated in the 'Ley de peligrosidad social' of 1970 which set a maximum prison term of three years (pp. 109–22). García Valdés's conclusions are impeccably liberal: in spite of repression, homosexuality has always existed, even in nature; it has no basis in physiology or pathology, but may have its 'origin' in parental factors (pp. 345–9).

García Valdés's stress on the ubiquity of homosexuality is thus curiously similar to 'Karl''s, although he writes from a very different vantage-point. And he does not think to ask himself whether his 'experimental data' might be compromised by the subjects he chooses for investigation: youthful delinquents. In order to prove his hypothesis that homosexuality has no physiological component, García Valdés reproduces colour photographs of his subjects in the nude, sometimes with closeups of the genital organs. As in the case of *Sodomitas*, it is not difficult to see how such a text (for all its protestations of scientific dispassion) offers itself up for quite another reading. Thus if 'Karl' tends to promote that very sexuality he sought to destroy, García Valdés discloses in spite of himself that there can be no discipline without desire, no rationality untroubled by affect.

The third and final text I consider is Antoni Mirabet i Mullol's *Homosexualitat avui* (Barcelona, 1984), translated into Castilian the following year.[13] Mirabet's original text is published by the Insitut Lambda, a lesbian and gay research centre founded by Armand de Fluvià.[14] An impressive and wide-ranging survey, the

[13] *Homosexualidad hoy* (Barcelona, 1985); reviewed by J. S. Cummins in *EGR* 2 (1987), 126–9.

[14] Another contestatory text pub. by the Institut is the collective work, *Perspectives actuals de l'homosexualitat* (Barcelona, 1985), which also advocates 'homosexualities' and attacks the idea of a single 'homosexual identity'. Earlier books include (in order of publication) Miguel Gámez Quintana, *Apuntes sobre el homosexual* (Madrid, 1976), a liberal apology; José Ramón-Enríquez (ed.), *Los homosexuales ante la sociedad enferma* (Barcelona, 1978), an important collection which includes an essay by a lesbian

book begins with a round up of the contribution of various fields of knowledge (psychoanalysis, anthropology, sexology, sociology) to the study of homosexuality (pp. 21–78). It continues with an account of homophobia in the church, state, and medical profession (pp. 79–166) before moving on to various modes of resistance to that repression, including a history of the Spanish gay movement (pp. 167–91). The last section offers an invaluable history of gay liberation in Catalunya and establishment responses to it (pp. 255–360). Unique here is the chapter on GLAL, the Catalan lesbian liberation group (pp. 276–87).[15]

Although now somewhat dated, Mirabet's book remains the principal source-book for the study of 'homosexuality today' in Spain. Yet, even here, in a text which allows 'gays [to] speak for themselves' (p. 167), there are disturbingly institutional or disciplinary touches. Thus the author takes pains to insist that, as a priest and a doctor, his interest in the topic is professional: his motive in writing the book was the suicide of a teenage patient whose pathetic note to his parents is reproduced as an appendix (pp. 15, 383–4). Similarly, the jacket informs the browser that the book is 'indispensable for professionals and informative for all types of readers'. It is thus not directed explicitly to a lesbian and gay readership who are presumed to constitute a more or less homogeneous community. Moreover, although scholars will appreciate the invaluable bibliography and foreigners may well envy Spaniards the incorporation of the EEC's anti-discrimination charter into the *autonomías*'s constitutions, the consistently worthy tone offers little to excite the libido. Ironically, the satanic visions of *Sodomitas* and the dubious medical investigations of *Historia y presente* provide 'all kinds of readers' with more of an incitement to sexual dissidence.

After this brief account of Spanish studies of homosexuality it

---

collective and an interview with poet Jaime Gil de Biedma; FHAR (Frente Homosexual de Acción Revolucionaria), *Documentos contra la normalidad* (Barcelona, 1979); and Héctor Anabitarte Rivas and Ricardo Lorenzo Sanz, *Homosexualidad: el asunto está caliente* (Madrid, 1979), a collection of short pieces from a liberationist viewpoint with some reference to Deleuze and Guattari and the critique of reproduction and the family. The Spanish trans. of Mario Mieli's more developed and theorized work appeared in the same year: *Elementos de crítica homosexual* (Barcelona, 1979).

[15] See also Ramón-Enríquez (n. 14 above). I have not seen Victoria Sau, *Mujeres lesbianas* (Madrid, 1980).

will not come as much of a surprise that, in spite of the wealth of writing and film on the topic in contemporary Spain, there has as yet been little response to the burgeoning of the field known as 'lesbian and gay studies' in the USA and, more recently, the UK. One aim of this book (like its predecessors) is thus to introduce a new and challenging subject area into Hispanic studies. The questions raised by the current debate (which derives in part from French texts of the 1970s by Monique Wittig and Guy Hocquenghem) include: is homosexuality an unchanging essence or a material construct? How can we hold on to the specificity of the lesbian body and homosexual desire without confining them to a minoritizing ghetto? What is the relationship between homosexuality, class, gender, and 'race'? How is that relationship articulated in popular media, such as film? In raising such questions I draw throughout this book on work published very recently in the USA by scholars working in fields as diverse as feminist philosophy (Diana Fuss, Judith Butler) and classical anthropology (David Halperin, John J. Winkler). In the chapters on film I rely on Britons Richard Dyer and Andrew Ross.[16] Clearly, the field is already a very large one. But it may be useful at this preliminary stage to give a brief account of some issues raised by two major books published this year, paying particular attention to their accounts of 'law' and 'desire'. The books are Eve Kosofsky Sedgwick's *Epistemology of the Closet* (New York, 1991);[17] and Jonathan Dollimore's *Sexual Dissidence: Augustine to Wilde, Freud to Foucault* (Oxford, 1991). Both tend to confirm what we learned from the Spanish texts: that power carries resistance within it, that discipline both polices and produces the territories of homosexual affect.

Sedgwick begins by suggesting that homosexuality is no minority concern. Rather 'Western culture is fractured by . . . [the] crisis of homo/heterosexual definition dating from the end of the nineteenth century'; it follows that the understanding of any aspect of this culture will be deficient if it fails to take account of this crucial distinction (p. 1). The initial binary is repeated in the related oppositions of secrecy/disclosure, knowledge/ignorance, private/public, masculine/feminine, etc.

---

[16] Ross teaches in the USA and works on North American popular culture.

[17] Sedgwick's earlier *Between Men: English Literature and Male Homosocial Desire* (New York, 1985) is generally thought to have inaugurated a theoretically informed body of lesbian and gay studies.

(p. 11). In the title essay, Sedgwick explores the paradoxes of the closet, the double binds through which 'disclosure is at once compulsory and forbidden' (p. 70). But if homosexuality brings with it a 'metonymic chain of . . . binarisms' in which 'knowledge' and 'sex' are conceptually inseparable, then the homo/hetero distinction cannot be collapsed into other differences. Sedgwick contrasts the biblical story of Esther with the coming out of a modern lesbian or gay man. For example, when Esther reveals her Jewishness to her Gentile husband in an effort to save her people, there is 'no suggestion that that identity might be debatable, porous, mutable'. Gays, on the other hand, must expect to be asked, 'How do you know you are one?' or 'Isn't it just a passing phase?' (p. 79). Likewise, Esther expects her husband to be surprised by her revelation and he is. A closeted lesbian, however, can never be certain who has already penetrated her secret when she chooses to reveal it. Finally, unlike the emergent homosexual, the Jewess already knows who her people are and is directly answerable to them (p. 81).

I have suggested earlier that the idea of the 'closet', even when framed in Sedgwick's deconstructive terms, has less resonance in Spain than in the English-speaking world; indeed, there is no single equivalent for the term in the Spanish language. However, Sedgwick stresses that 'coming out' is no single event, but rather an interminable process. And the force of her argument is to shift analysis from homosexuality as a discrete identity to homosexuality as a discursive construct: from ontology to epistemology. It is a move also made by Spanish writers and filmmakers, already sceptical of the claims of homosexual selfhood. By mapping the incompatibility of competing definitions of homosexuality (based as they are on separatist or integrative criteria, on sexual and gender distinctions)(p. 88) Sedgwick thoroughly denaturalizes lesbian and gay desires. But she also suggests that those same desires and their literary expression are bound up with the disciplinary laws that they appear to trangress: 'the indisseverable girdle of incongruities under whose discomfiting span, for most of a century, have unfolded both the most generative and the most murderous plots of our culture' (p. 90).

Sedgwick restricts herself for the most part to turn-of-the-century fiction in English and French (Wilde, Melville, James, and Proust). Jonathan Dollimore is more ambitious, ranging beyond the literary into the philosophical and psychoanalytic and treating Latin, French, German, and Italian material (albeit in translation). Dollimore begins with an encounter, contrasting the 'decentred desires' of Wilde's cult of the surface with Gide's more earnest quest to reveal 'true' sexual identity as the deep centre of subjectivity (pp. 3–18). Like Sedgwick, Dollimore elaborates a series of binaries, but with the twist that here they operate not between gay and straight but within competing definitions of homosexuality (p. 15). Thus Wilde's 'perversion' of the dominant order is opposed to Gide's 'inversion' of it, which keeps faith with bourgeois notions of authenticity (p. 18). But even Wilde is not outside the society whose doxa he disrupts. On the contrary his 'transgressive aesthetic' is contained within that society and exploits its contradictions. This is what Dollimore calls the 'perverse dynamic' in which 'the antithetical inheres within, and is partly produced by, what it opposes' (p. 33). The 'proximate' nature of deviance (of homosexuality), its very closeness to the heterosexuality that seeks to exclude it, enables it to 'track back' in a 'transgressive reinscription' as an anti-essentialist agency freed from the humanist illusions of autonomous selfhood. This is a 'dissidence within sexuality which is not . . . confined to sexuality' (p. 33).

Dollimore develops this argument at great length and with great subtlety throughout his book; and I cannot do it justice here. But his 'decentring' of desire suggests (like Sedgwick's generalization of the 'closet') that homosexuality cannot be confined to a narrow libidinal sphere; and the fact that it is discursively produced does not make its material consequences any less violent. As Dollimore reminds us, Wilde did not long survive his proposal of a transgressive aesthetic. And just as Sedgwick stresses that there can be no simple opposition between knowledge and ignorance, so Dollimore does not set up Wilde as the good (anti-essentialist) pervert and Gide as the bad (essentialist) invert. Indeed, he argues that it was the very 'proximity' of the latter's confessional ethic to Christian doctrine that made the Catholic Church ban his books (p. 18). The shifting configurations of law and desire are complex indeed.

It seems likely that the impetus for gay liberation in Spain came from the threat of increased legal penalties for homosexual-

ity.[18] But it is not enough to argue that there is a desiring relationship between power and resistance. We should also ask how Sedgwick's and Dollimore's models, which fail to account for the diversity of nationalities in 'our culture', might be modified by an awareness of cultures such as the Hispanic which cannot be confined to the straitjacket of a Euroamerican same. To take a specific example, the figure of Lorca (a dramatist who embraced both essential identity and gestural performance)[19] would further complexify Dollimore's Gide/Wilde antinomy. But here again the case of Spain is anomalous, containing as it does national identities, such as the Basque or Catalan, which are defined by their transgression of prevailing state boundaries. We shall see in this book what happens when 'proximate' nationalities and sexualities 'track back' into the dominant cultures with which they are coterminous.

I end this introduction with two stills taken from films by Pedro Almodóvar (Plates 5 and 3). In the first, Antonio Banderas as the obsessive lover in *La ley del deseo* ('The Law of Desire', 1987) stares out through a grille in extreme close up. His hand clutches the metal, as he looks moodily down and out of the frame. This might seem to be an image of a victim of heterosexist law: a man behind bars. Banderas's melancholia is also reminiscent of the 'sad young man', a stereotypical movie image of the sensitive gay. However the grille belongs not to a prison but to his mother's elegant house in southern Spain. Its role is not functional but ornamental. The picture thus signals not a generalized alienation (the intrinsic or essential condition of homosexuality) but a specific geographical and class location (provincial bourgeoisie). This is why I speak of 'laws' in the plural in my title: to remind the reader that there is no monolithic struggle between power and pleasure, but rather a multiple, capillary network inflected by regional and ethnic differences.

The second image is from *Entre tinieblas* ('Dark Habits', 1983). Homely Chus Lampreave as Sor Rata is shown in a medium long shot (*plan américain*). She has picked up the red lurex gown belonging to Yolanda, the glamorous nightclub singer who has taken refuge in her convent. Holding it to her, over her dark

---

[18] The introduction of the 'Ley de peligrosidad y rehabilitacion social' in 1970 stirred the first movements in Barcelona which subsequently spread through Spain (*Homosexualitat avui*, 184–5).

[19] See my account of Lorca in *The Body Hispanic* (Oxford, 1989), ch. 4.

robes, she looks upward out of frame. The image is ambiguous: does it suggest Sor Rata's love for Yolanda or her desire to appropriate to herself the younger woman's seductive feminine masquerade? Whatever the case, it forms part of a lesbianization of Catholic imagery central to the film: as a very worldly nun (the writer of sleazy crime novels) Sor Rata both embodies and remotivates the ready-made iconography of the aspirant woman of God.

As we shall see in the Coda to this book, the image points forward to Almodóvar's subsequent *¡Atame!* ('Tie Me Up! Tie Me Down!', 1990) in its suggestion that desire is like a habit or costume. As Andrew Ross[20] says of pornography: 'for the individual consumer . . . pornography provides more or less a fit between the set of images it can offer and the demands of an individual libidinal economy. A temporary fit is arranged, which also generates a future desire for something more exact' (p. 202). The still of the plain, older woman clutching to herself the dress to which she aspires and which could never fit her, says much about the consolations of the image and the displacements of desire in the quest for 'something more exact'. It is an image at once humorous and moving, typical of Almodóvar's use of conflicting levels of association.

In the passage I cite Ross is drawing, discreetly, on the psychoanalytic definition of desire as that unfillable gap which opens up between demand and need: between the absolute and the particular, between ideal love and material gratification.[21] This is the space of my book also, as it weaves backwards and forwards between a general discussion of homosexuality and a more local analysis of individual works, passages, or cinematic sequences. As we shall see in Chapter 1, this is the provisional and unstable territory mapped out by those who run the risk of writing feminist or gay autobiography.

---

[20] *No Respect: Intellectuals and Popular Culture* (New York, 1989).
[21] See my discussion of Lacan's version of desire in *The Body Hispanic*, 73.

I

Writing the Self in Feminist and Gay Autobiography

1. THE RISK OF ESSENCE

Is homosexuality a discursive position or a personal identity? Is it constructed by and in history or is it relatively autonomous of the social formations within which it is expressed? The long running debate between constructionism and essentialism may now seem something of a blind alley. However, the questions raised in that debate (of historicism and idealism, of determination and agency) are posed most urgently in the case of autobiography. For as Bill Marshall notes, autobiography is conventionally understood as that genre in which the coherence of the individual guarantees the authenticity of the text, in which linguistic transparency is the effect and instrument of unmediated personal testimony.[1] Autobiography also tends to reconfirm the binaries of public and private, subjective and intersubjective, which social constructionists most bitterly contest. The autobiographical text would thus stand as a test case for poststructuralist theories of the linguistic constitution of the

---

[1] 'The Autobiographies of Daniel Guérin and Yves Navarre', unpub. paper read at the Conference on 'Questions of Homosexuality' at the Institute of Romance Studies in the University of London (June 1991). Two other papers on male gay autobiography read at the same session were Murray J. Pratt, 'Reading AIDS: Questions of Identity in Guibert's Autobiographies'; and David Vilaseca, 'Homosexuality and the Rejection of the Double in Dalí's Autobiographical Writings'. For lesbian autobiography, see The Hall Carpenter Archives, *Inventing Ourselves: Lesbian Life Stories* (New York, 1989); for feminist autobiography, see Liz Stanley, *The Auto/Biographical I: Theory and Practice of Feminist Auto/Biography* (Ann Arbor, Mich., forthcoming (1992)). For gay autobiography, see The Hall Carpenter Archives, *Walking after Midnight: Gay Men's Life Stories* (New York, 1989) and Kevin Porter and Jeffrey Weeks (eds.), *Between the Acts: Lives of Homosexual Men 1885–1967* (New York, 1991); for Spanish language autobiography, see Nicholas Spadaccini and Jenaro Talens, *Autobiography in Early Modern Spain* (Minneapolis, 1988). Carla Trujillo (ed), *Chicana Lesbians: The Girls Our Mothers Warned Us Against* (Berkeley, Calif., 1991) contains much autobiographical material. There is no comparable collection for Spain. Recent collections on autobiography include *FMLS* 26/3 (1990); *CC* 12 (1990).

subject: if the narrative of confessional interiority is compromised by the insistence of the letter (of symbolic law), then so too must be the more public forms of novel and film which are overtly marked as 'fictional'.

Following Diana Fuss's *Essentially Speaking* (New York, 1989), I argue in this chapter that the opposition between essence and construction is at once unavoidable and mistaken.[2] The object of critical enquiry is not to award prizes to those texts that are astute enough to avoid essence and black marks to those that are not, but rather to ask the strategic questions: what is the motive of essence (of construction) in this text? What work does it do in the specific context in which it is deployed? If critics are willing to run 'the risk of essence' they may be able to produce rich and complex readings of texts hitherto dismissed as banal or ingenuous.

In this opening chapter I treat three very different autobiographical narratives published over a period of twenty years. Rosa Chacel's *Desde el amanecer* (*Since Dawn*) (written in Rio in 1968)[3] documents in great detail a childhood spent in Valladolid and Madrid in the first decade of the century. It is explicitly feminist and woman-oriented, but not lesbian. Juan Goytisolo's *Coto vedado* (*Forbidden Territory*)(1985) and *En los reinos de Taifa* (*Realms of Strife*) (1986)[4] recount the narrator's childhood in post-War Spain, his exile in Paris, and his ultimate sexual and textual self-realization in North Africa. Less self-confident than Chacel, Goytisolo interrupts his first person narration of the past with a second person commentary on the nature of autobiography which calls into question the linear narrative of the life. Finally, Terenci Moix's *El peso de la paja* (*The Weight of Straw*)(1990)[5] intersperses adult adventures in the Rome of the 1960s with reminiscences of a childhood in drab Francoist Barcelona where

[2] See also the collection of essays edited by Fuss, *Inside/Out: Lesbian Theories, Gay Theories* (New York, 1991). For a clear account of the essentialism/constructionism debate, see David Halperin, ' "Homosexuality": A Cultural Construct' in *One Hundred Years of Homosexuality* (New York, 1990), 41–53. See also Celia Kitzinger, *The Social Construction of Lesbianism* (London, 1987); and Pat Caplan, *The Cultural Construction of Sexuality* (New York, 1987).

[3] First pub. 1972; my edn. 1985. I have also referred to the collection of interviews by Alberto Porlán, *La sinrazón de Rosa Chacel* (Madrid, 1984). For a more recent interview see Kathleen Glenn, 'Conversación con Rosa Chacel', *LP* 3 (1990), 11–26.

[4] Both pub. in Barcelona. Trans. by Peter Bush as *Forbidden Territory: Memoirs 1932–56* (London, 1989) and *Realms of Strife: Memoirs 1957–82* (San Francisco, 1990).

[5] Pub. in Barcelona. This is the first of a projected four vols. of memoirs.

Hollywood cinema is a dominant, indeed constitutive, image repertoire for the emergent gay self.

It would be easy to construct a teleological narrative of my own from these texts. Thus Chacel focuses on female friendships both inside and outside a family dominated by women; and on infantile fantasies of womanly eroticism which do not achieve genital expression. Goytisolo relates the story of his enduring love for Monique Lange, the woman who became his wife; but he also gives an extended account of his struggle to acknowledge and give voice to his same-sex affairs. Finally Moix, a self-proclaimed narcissist and fantasist, describes a life wholly given up to homoerotic reverie. But to focus on this tendency towards increasing explicitness in the representation of homosexual desire would be mistaken. Rather than colluding with that practice of confession which is already implicated in the subject of both (homo)sexuality and autobiography, my aim is to question the doxa which makes of sexual preference the innermost truth of the subject, the essence of individual identity. As David Halperin notes in *One Hundred Years of Homosexuality* (New York, 1990), we need not subscribe to the modern belief that 'sexuality holds the key to unlocking the deepest mysteries of the human personality [or] that it lies at the centre of the hermeneutics of the self' (p. 26).

But when these three autobiographical texts are considered in turn, another, more complex progression appears. This is a movement from an unquestioning faith in the permanence and self-sufficiency of the subject (Chacel), through an anxious critique of subjective integrity and of the split between private and public selves (Goytisolo), to a defiant pleasure in fragmentation and superficiality, in the constitution of a self through *bricolage* and mechanical reproduction (Moix). This movement, then, is not a progressive revelation of the true self, but on the contrary a drift from a strong, unified ontology to a 'weak' and fragmented epistemology, in which representation is not the effect but the cause of being.[6] It is a shift, in other words, from identity to positionality, from essence to construct.

At this stage it is worth looking more closely at Diana Fuss's

---

[6] For 'weak thought', see Gianni Vattimo, *La Fine della modernità: nichilismo ed ermeneutica nella cultura postmoderna* (Milan, 1987), 19; discussed in ch. 5 of my *Representing the Other*.

discussion of 'Lesbian and Gay Theory: The Question of Identity Politics' (pp. 97–112). Fuss begins by asking the question I posed at the beginning of this chapter: is lesbian or gay identity an empirical fact or a political fiction? Is it natural or discursive (p. 97)? If the assertion of any identity is problematic then how much more so is that of the *homo*, the sameness which some feminists have identified with the great One of the phallus? Fuss suggests, however, first that identity is not identical to itself, that it may be multiple and contradictory; and secondly, that identity need not be collapsed into essence, that a distinction between the two can be observed in and preserved by lesbian and gay theory (p. 98). Even in the most vigorous of the proponents of identity politics, Fuss finds a tension between an identity that has been repressed (and thus waits meekly for its owner to discover it) and an identity that is still to be developed (and must thus be invented by the subject who wishes to proclaim it)(p. 100). This tension suggests that the personal cannot simply be identified with the political, that the coimplication of the two terms must constantly be examined (pp. 101–2).

How, then, are we to theorize identity? Fuss suggests we reject both the reassuring fantasy of a unitary, stable identity outside history and the bleakly historicist vision of identity as a wholly political construct. Making a detour through analytic philosophy and Aristotelian logic, she proposes that identity be read as an effect of essence (p. 102). Emphasis would then shift from the discrimination of differences between identities to the exploration of differences within identities, from an understanding that identities are contingent to an acknowledgement that identity itself is contingent (pp. 103–4). It is symptomatic that identity politics cannot address the unconscious or admit that the field of politics itself might be troubled by psychic conflict or disorder. 'Politics', in an unexamined sense, is thus no longer admissable as a final measuring stick for theories of gay identity (pp. 105, 106).

Having dismissed this 'essentialism of the political', Fuss discusses the 'invention theories' of homosexuality associated with Foucault, to which she herself is more sympathetic. Here homosexuality is claimed as a historical development contemporaneous with industrial capitalism. While same-sex behaviour is assumed to have taken place at all times and in all societies, lesbian and gay identities are specific and have been produced under historically variable conditions. Fuss sees a number of advantages in invention theory: it is not ethnocentric, stressing as it does differences within the global term 'homosexuality'; it facilitates the analysis of heterosexuality as a discrete production itself; it enables us to read identities as categories of classification, not essence; it permits the analysis of lesbian and gay male identities in their specificity; and, finally, it shifts critical attention from ontology to epistemology, from being to knowledge (pp. 108–9).

However, identity politics and invention theory (apparently so different from one another) share a common blind spot: the elision of the psychic. For identity cannot only be a social construction; it must also be a question of desire. In its failure to address psychoanalysis (dismissed as just another of those disciplines that subtend subjectivity), invention theory ignores the psychoanalytic discovery that homosexuality is already within heterosexuality as that which must perpetually be disavowed (p. 110). For Fuss, then, gay oppression cannot wholly be accounted for either as repressed desire (homophobia) or as a superstructural effect of cultural processes (heterosexism). The workings of both the libido and the polity must be considered simultaneously.

Fuss thus offers not an 'either/or' but a 'both/and'. And this supplementary logic is particularly helpful for autobiography, as it is for homosexuality. As the site of transition between the personal and the social, the private and the public, the subject of autobiography is necessarily liminal, caught at the crossroads between individual identity and cultural determination. But this double movement applies to readers as well as writers. Thus for Wayne Koestenbaum, Oscar Wilde's autobiographical texts not only serve to create a gay male readership; they also give birth, in a reverse movement, to 'gay reading' as a historically specific hermeneutic strategy.[7] Biddy Martin has gone further, arguing that superficially 'straight' autobiographies may be transformed by lesbians who read them out of a concern for the identity of the author, the mimetic function of the text, and their own wish

[7] 'Wilde's Hard Labour and the Birth of Gay Reading', in *Engendering Men: The Question of Male Feminist Criticism*, ed. Joseph A. Boone and Michael Cadden (New York, 1990), p. 176–89. See also Koestenbaum's *Double Talk: The Erotics of Male Literary Collaboration* (New York, 1989).

to identify with that text.[8] As Joanne Glasgow and Karla Jay suggest, to pay attention to lesbian readers' sensitivity, to their desire, is to acknowledge a radical alteration in such texts.[9] I would argue, then, that it is possible both to preserve the desire for identity (for recognition of oneself in the text) and to acknowledge that that desire is itself a performative (that it transforms the text in which it seeks to see itself reflected). In the models of lesbian reader-response suggested by Martin, Glasgow, and Jay, identity is both asserted (as preexisting) and discovered (as newly produced). Each of the texts I treat in this chapter has moments in which the subject seeks to recognize him or herself in the phantasmal reflections of mirror, photograph, or printed text, moments in which a sense of self is at once reaffirmed and undermined. In my reading of Chacel (a feminist-but not lesbian-identified woman) I draw on recent accounts of women's 'life/lines' which acknowledge similar dualities.

One of Fuss's priorities for future research is the historical relation between the state and identity formation:

What does it mean to be a citizen in a state [such as the United States] which programatically denies citizenship on the basis of sexual prefer-ence? . . . Do gay and lesbian subjects escape the objectification and commodification associated with the sexual marketplace, or are we fully inscribed within the terms of sexual exchange? (p. 112)

One recent attempt to explore the political and historical implications of Spanish-language autobiography is Jo Labanyi's 'The Construction/Deconstruction of the Self in the Autobiogra-phies of Pablo Neruda and Juan Goytisolo'.[10] For Labanyi, the crucial discourse mediating here between self and state is Marx-ism. Neruda, the self-proclaimed advocate of political commit-ment, constructs a self in the bourgeois humanist mode: coherent, unified, and stable. He casts others (celebrities, work-ers, and most particularly women) as bit players whose role is

---

[8] 'Lesbian Identity and Autobiographical Difference(s)', in *Life/Lines*, ed. Bella Brodski and Celeste Schench (Ithaca, NY, 1988), 77–103 (p. 77).

[9] *Lesbian Texts and Contexts: Radical Revisions* (New York, 1990), 6.

[10] *FMLS* 26 (1990), 212–21. See also Elsa Dehennin, 'Relato en primera persona: novela autobiográfica versus autobiografía: el caso de Juan Goytisolo', in *Homenaje al profesor Antonio Vilanova*, ii (Barcelona, 1989), 149–61; Sixto Plaza, 'Coto vedado, ¿autobiografía o novela?' in *Actas del IX Congreso de la Asociación Internacional de Hispanistas*, ii (Frankfurt, 1989), 345–50; and Randolph D. Pope, 'Theory and Contemporary Autobiographical Writing: The Case of Juan Goytisolo', *Siglo XX/ 20th Century* 8 (1990–1), 87–101.

merely to support a star performance which transcends internal contradiction and historical development. Goytisolo, on the other hand, narrates a loss of political commitment, which enables him to deconstruct a self which is now wholly fragmented and discontinuous, riven by historical and cultural difference. As Labanyi concludes:

A Marxist autobiography would surely be one which recognized that both personal and public history are made of contradiction, and that the self can never be 'natural' or 'whole' because it is inevitably the product of the 'other'. It is the ex-Marxist Goytisolo, and not the Marxist Neruda, who has written such an autobiography. (p. 221)

But as Labanyi notes (p. 216), for all his stress on the other, Goytisolo does not give voice to his (mainly Arab) sexual partners. Like Neruda's numerous and frequently exotic female lovers, they remain mute and dispossessed. Hence in Hispanic as in Anglo-American contexts homosexuality is no guarantor of unique insight into the sexual marketplace or the ideologies of national identity.

Yvonne M. Klein laments the loss in the 1980s of that confident sense of the 'lesbian nation' that she identifies in lesbian autobiographical fiction of the previous decade.[11] One aim of this book is to remind its readers that the experience of English-speaking nations since the Sixties cannot be generalized to other cultures: Spain has not suffered the homophobic excesses Klein identifies with a Bush, Thatcher, or Mulroney (p. 330). It remains the case, however, that feminist or homosexual autobiographers in both cultures must choose whether to stress the subjective integrity of a personal identity or the intersubjective network of a common cause. Rosa Chacel is amongst those who have chosen to run 'the risk of essence'.

2. ROSA CHACEL: THE REPUDIATION OF FEMININITY

Rosa Chacel's signature is reproduced on the cover and title page of her autobiography. It is symptomatic of a text which, offers itself quite explicitly as the authentic testimony of a unique individual. Chacel's identity is one of pure presence, outside temporality. And it is one that is based on desire or will. Thus of

---

[11] 'Myth and Community in Recent Lesbian Autobiographical Fiction', in *Lesbian Texts and Contexts* (see n. 9 above), 330–8.

her birth in 1898 (the year in which Spain lost its last colony, Cuba) she states that she would not have been born at this historically significant moment had she not willed it herself: for desire and being ('querer' and 'ser') are inextricable (p. 9). As the title of the volume suggests, Chacel believes she has remained the same from birth ('since dawn'); indeed, since even before birth. She chooses as her epigraph an enigmatic quote from Quevedo: 'I have desired since I was a child; or before, if that is possible.' The words 'if that is possible' (for desire, identity, and memory to precede physiological birth) will be repeated mantra-like throughout the three hundred pages of text. Like Salvador Dalí,[12] Chacel claims that her very first memories (of her maternal grandparents in Venezuela) derive from a time when she herself had not yet come into existence.

Chacel's narrative, then, is one of insistent repetition of the same, of self-present identity: she claims that in her childhood 'I was *I* as I am: just as I always will be as long as I am' (p. 14). The distinction between narrator and actor (subject of *énonciation* and *énoncé*) is here collapsed into a transcendent One who communicates to the reader '*What was, as it was*' (Chacel's emphasis; p. 13). Language is thus taken to be a wholly transparent medium, the vehicle of authenticating personal testimony.

However, this vigorous assertion of essential identity raises more questions than it answers: if the subject has access to 'innate experience' deriving from fifteen or twenty years before her birth, how can her origin be fixed in time or space? And if family history is already imprinted in the consciousness of the unborn child, how can that child be as self-sufficient, as parthenogenetic as she claims? Thus Chacel says of her 'memories' of an exotic Caribbean which she had never visited herself, that they were not *in her*; rather she was *in them*. Her origin is in that distant place (p. 10). Already, then, the assertion of individual autonomy slips imperceptibly into an acknowledgement of communal constitution: the 2-year-old Rosa, precociously aware of her family history, already knows herself to be a product of that history (p. 13).

As the narrative develops, the fantasy of subjective integrity comes face to face with the first of the irreducibly material

---

[12] I am grateful to David Vilaseca for bringing this coincidence to my attention.

determinants it must encounter: sexual difference. Thus it is Chacel's overbearing father who quite literally makes her speak, forcing her to make the connection between word and thing (p. 14). In a household of women in provincial Valladolid, it is the father who enforces law: he scrubs his wife's face with a wet cloth in order to prove she is not wearing cosmetics, as a malicious relation had claimed (p. 20); he jealously torments his wife in public, causing her to tear apart the fan she is carrying (p. 35); he indulges his love of vulgarities (*estilo quevedesco*), of that smutty humour whose purpose is to exclude women and to cement the bonds between men (p. 44). Each of these domestic 'scenes' reveals that heterosexual love is socially mediated: male access to women is not direct, but is rather rerouted through a communal awareness of female shame and vulnerability. Significantly, however, the father (like the daughter) is represented by Chacel as pure presence: unlike his wife he does not *have* ideas; he simply *is* his ideas, his unique 'way of being' ('modo de ser')[13](p. 25). Yet this apparently secure paternal identity is shown to be dependent on the reputation of the female members of the family. The father who has a typewriter, carbon paper, and duplicator (who has reserved for himself the rights of reproduction) forbids his wife and daughter to touch the writing instruments, lest they 'stain' themselves. Mother and daughter dare not even touch an ashtray: for a woman to smell of smoke is as if she had 'rolled in mud' (p. 42). I return to these motifs (of abjection and touching) in a moment.

Forced to address the gendering of an identity which has been initially presented as pure transcendence, Chacel's position becomes confused. An early scene is significant here. Walking in the park with her parents, Chacel catches sight of an uncle with his goddaughter, whom she has never seen before. Carmencita is 'a beautiful blonde child with a torrent of golden curls', contrasting with the black mourning dress worn in memory of a recently deceased mother. Chacel is 'dazzled' by her. She runs towards the couple and embraces not the girl but her uncle. Suddenly

---

[13] This is the same phrase used to describe the newfound virility of the female narrator of Chacel's story 'Transfiguración'. See Introd., pp. 1–2. As Jo Labanyi suggested to me, the phrase has Ortegan overtones; see Ana Rodríguez, 'El magisterio de Ortega en Rosa Chacel', in *Homenaje al profesor Antonio Vilanova*, ii (Barcelona, 1989), 567–77. For Chacel on her family, see Abigail Lee Six's unpub. paper 'Perceiving the Family: Rosa Chacel's *Desde el amanecer*'.

Carmencita is rolling in the thick dust, rubbing her golden curls and pink face into the ground, twisting over and over 'like a panther' (p. 34). The adults explain that Carmencita is jealous of Rosa, who feels both admiration and scorn for this beautiful girl who can so degrade herself. This scene leads (by a train of association) to one which took place at another time: the walk during which Chacel's mother, humiliated by her husband's jealous tirade, pulls apart her fan in silent despair (p. 35). Chacel resents her mother's weakness: unable to resist male violence, she can only displace her rage on to an inert object. Even as she proclaims a feminine identity founded on autonomous desire and will, Chacel will repudiate the femininity represented by the glamorous Carmencita and her tormented mother: both are passive, vulnerable, and impotent.

I use repudiation here in the technical sense of 'foreclosure' (*forclusion, Verwerfung*).[14] In Chacel's infantile hallucinations we find evidence of a primordial rejection which returns not inside the subject's mind, but outside her in the real. Thus one fantasy is of a thread ('hilo') of glass, standing vertical in front of her, so close that she cannot separate it from herself. Even at age four or five, this is an 'ancient' memory evoking the response 'It's here again; the thing that always is ["lo de siempre"]' (p. 16). Like the later hallucination of a train hurtling out of the bedroom wall, this is clearly an image of the phallus, the primordial signifier that the child can neither internalize nor escape. The terror of the thread or train is that of the young woman caught between her identification with the phallus (with Law, with language, with the father) and her repudiation of the feminine (of castration, of impotence, of the mother). But although this conundrum is presented to the reader as the personal problem of a private individual, it is revealed by the text itself to be a social question inflicted on women by the violent hierarchy of sexual difference.

Chacel, then, at once repudiates the image of the feminine that is offered to her and rejects the identification with the masculine that she intermittently desires to embrace. But in play and fantasy she is able to act out a number of different gender positions which do not require her to make that definitive choice

[14] For this Lacanian term, see Jean Laplanche and J. B. Pontalis, *The Language of Psychoanalysis* (London, 1983), s.v. 'foreclosure'.

to which she is led by her voluntarism. Thus on the one hand, Chacel scorns simulation: to recite a devotional verse in church is to imitate a saint and thus to be inauthentic: she would rather *be* an offering to God than impersonate one (p. 63). And after dressing as an odalisque for the photographer, she remains unconvinced by the picture which results, a travesty of the oriental grace she had hoped to duplicate (p. 67). But, on the other hand, the house of women in which Chacel lives lends itself to games and fantasies which are also simulations of the real: Chacel plays at 'visiting' with a favourite aunt, who reads out a letter from her imaginary husband 'in a gruff voice'; or she fantasizes a tiger hunt with the same aunt, in which both women play the role of men (pp. 55, 58). These games can be read not (or not merely) as an identification with roles gendered as masculine in the period; they are also testimony to the space provided by the bourgeois family for women of different generations to explore fantasy and role-play together.

What is more, these womanly games are underwritten by erotic fantasies which (like the games) are inspired by illustrated books or magazines. For Chacel, 'erotic emotion' in women is an 'innate' and primordial experience: it is impossible to specify the age at which it begins. The child is enraptured by images of couples hidden amongst the branches, of young women pursued by men or swept off on a galloping horse (p. 85). Later archetypes of fantasy are the goddess of water, pictured wearing a 'skimpy tunic' in a magazine; and the Virgin Triumphant, far more attractive to Chacel than the Virgin of the Sorrows, who embodies the image of women's 'slavery' (pp. 86–8).

Chacel extends this erotic feminine space to include aspects of the aesthetic and the ethical: she cannot distinguish between the three. And one story which (she says) stands out from the erotic zone without taking leave of it, is that of the fairy who is frying fish: when she touches them they come to life in the frying pan and begin to speak. What disturbs (and delights?) the child, however, is not the resuscitation of the dead, but a linguistic vulgarism committed by the teller of the tale. Instead of the normal verb to touch ('tocar') the narrator uses the Valladolid regionalism 'tropezar' (literally 'to stumble'). Chacel feels 'shame' at this improper usage. But it is perhaps significant that the child focuses on this word. For Chacel also 'stumbles' when it comes to the feminine-erotic, tends at once to assert and to deny its potency. Thus her example of the interconnection of erotics and ethics is a 'naked or dressed' woman with a protuding stomach (p. 86). The child's desire is thus at once attracted and repelled by the woman's body, must summon it into being only to dismiss it as shameful and ugly.

Chacel's erotic fantasies are presented as authentic experiences distinct from the alienating images of socialized femininity. But her fantasies are themselves the product of mechanical reproduction: of images in books and magazines. However, Chacel's commitment to voluntarism and to female autonomy reconfirms Fuss's suggestion that women's experience is not only a construct, but something that constructs (p. 25). In other words, we need neither concur with Chacel's claim that she is a unique and self-sufficient individual, nor dismiss that claim as an ingenuous fantasy. Rather we can suggest with Fuss again that 'the poststructuralist objection to [women's] experience is not a repudiation of grounds of knowing *per se*, but a refusal of the hypostatization of experience as *the* ground . . . of knowledge production' (p. 27). Hence, Chacel's defiant essentialism (her constant appeal to experience) should not be dismissed as naïve: rather it forms one of the ways in which a young woman can stake out a place from which to speak.

And here the word 'place' is of the essence. Chacel shows an acute sensitivity to place and an astonishing ability to recall details of each house or locale she visits.[15] And, as in the story of 'The Transfiguration' which I analysed in the Introduction, the space of womanly desire is where land and water merge. When the sickly Rosa is taken for the first time from Valladolid to the country she goes on a picnic by the river. An older peasant girl, Marcela, leads her through the shallow water. As she points out where the birds nest, she frightens one and (as in the short story) it flies off. This is a dangerous place with treacherously deep water. Later, the same Márcela, described (like the infant Carmencita) as a blonde in a black dress, comes to visit Chacel's family in Valladolid. Marcela walks with her from the park. Holding hands, once more, Rosa feels a sticky pebble attached to the older girl's palm. She connects it in her imagination with

---

[15] See Daniele Miglos, 'El pequeño mundo de Rosa Chacel', *RFH* 6 (1990), 245–307. For memory see Shirley Mangini, 'Worshipping Mnemosine: The Prose of Rosa Chacel', *LP* 3 (1990), 27–40.

the little droppings of her pet lamb. It turns out to be a ball of nasal mucus (p. 172). Chacel tells us that the 'repugnance' she felt could not be erased 'in centuries'. In this scene, then, we find once more a fascination with and a repudiation of the feminine. The fluid delight of the river bank (which is 'tattooed' on Chacel's memory) becomes the nauseous viscosity of bodily discharge. But unlike in the cases of Carmencita or the mother, here we find the added factor of class. While in her native landscape, the bucolically named Marcela[16] inspires only wonder, in the city she provokes anxiety, even disgust: in spite of her smart dress, her 'quality' remains unchanged. Like the pet lamb, Marcela is natural, seductive, and disturbingly physical. Once more, the Chacel who wished to 'touch' the countryside (p. 106) stumbles over its materiality, here gendered as feminine. And if the marsh or forest is a space of womanly desire in Chacel's fiction and autobiography, it is by no means untouched by the perverse pleasures of mechanical reproduction: the landscape that 'tattoos' itself on the child, inserting its 'needles' into her virgin flesh (p. 107) reminds Chacel of engravings she has seen in the magazines kept in the family home (p. 110).

Even as it proclaims its autonomy, experience is thus inextricable from representation. But it is possible that in such cases Chacel has adopted the feminist strategy recommended by Fuss to subaltern groups: that of miming élite forms, undoing them by overdoing them (p. 32). We have seen that Chacel almost parodies the self-sufficiency of the bourgeois subject by insisting that she has remained the same since before her birth. And she does this even as she documents the ravages of gender and class in a rigidly hierarchical society. It is significant, then, that the second half of her autobiography (which charts her discovery of an artistic vocation) would also be in the mode of imitation. Thus while still in Valladolid she is suspended in wonder before a Greek sculpture,[17] possibly of Apollo (p. 191). Its unique power is its pure presence, its identity-to-self: 'it is as it is; and has to be as it is.' Encouraged by her father once more, Chacel learns to draw by copying plaster models of body parts and plates of great paintings (p. 142). She laboriously reproduces an engrav-

---

[16] Marcela is the name of the lover of Grisóstomo in a pastoral episode of *Don Quijote* i.

[17] Cf. the effect of the classical statue on the child narrator of Tusquets's *El mismo mar* (see Ch. 3, p. 98).

ing of a plaster ivy leaf (p. 146). Far from 'touching' the real
(Chacel's professed aim), such artistic activity highlights the
multiple mediations which intrude between subject and world.
And this external space of the vocation becomes the touchstone
by which the subject authenticates her inner being: once her
father has touched up her drawing, Chacel has no interest in a
work that is no longer uniquely hers. Art is thus the origin of the
child's nature, her access to the ultimate truth of her self: 'My
honour consisted in my relation to truth' (p. 151).

At the age of 10 Chacel moves with her family to Madrid.
With her father absent in Valencia in a vain quest for work,
Chacel is left in a wholly female environment from which she
escapes to further her exploration of the masculine world:
drinking beer with one uncle in an establishment 'where women
are not allowed'; practicing metalwork with another, who speaks
to her as if to another man (pp. 224, 244). But she also continues
her passionate engagements with women, learning with her new
friend Inés the companionship girls can feel in their common
'femininity, slavery, and vulnerability' (p. 253). Meanwhile she
conceives a hatred of her maternal grandmother. Reduced to the
metonym 'the voice', the latter seems at first to embody ultimate
power and presence-to-self (p. 236). But even this terrifying
figure is compromised by mimicry: the grandmother tells a story
in which she imitates the black maids she had in America and
the way they addressed her as 'niña' ('little girl')(pp. 292–3).
Chacel now understands her grandmother's dependence on
theatricality, even ventriloquism. The 'voice' is but a mask (p.
291). Overcome by a horror of slavery (which, as we shall see, is
shared by the young Goytisolo), Chacel is forced to confront
'race' as previously she has confronted gender and class. And
once more it is at the level of language that the revelation occurs.
The specific value of 'niña' in a Caribbean context lays bare the
constitutive force of language which is no longer transparent but
is rather opaque with cultural signification.

But let us go back to a scene which takes place just before the
10-year-old leaves for Madrid. Normally friendless, she has
recently been taken up by some girls of her own age.

Jugaban a tener un niño: la pequeña era la que iba a tenerlo y la mayor
era el médico. El niño era un muñeco de celuloide, de los que estaban
de moda, casi tan grande como un recién nacido. . . . Lo extraordinario

—podría decir, lo encantador, lo adorable— era que no había en nada de aquello picardía y sí acción: una emoción imperecedera, que hoy compruebo con el criterio de hoy y que nunca, cuando mi cultura se extendió hasta conocer el sentido de la palabra picardía, vi empañada por él.

Inesperadamente, ese fenómeno que afecta al tiempo, esa detención o dilatación, que parecería que no pudiese ocurrir más que a solas, en el sueño o el ensueño, se impuso vivido por las tres. Lo maravilloso no era más que el momento de la espera. La chica estaba metida en la cama, venía el medico, la tomaba el pulso y decía: —El niño va a llegar en seguida. No recuerdo si la pequeña hacía un poco de comedia, creo que sí; repetía frases pescadas en las conversaciones de las señoras, pero el caso es que durante un par de minutos —tal vez de segundos— nuestros corazones se agitaban al unísono, con la seguridad de estar en aquello, libres, ignoradas, envueltas en un secreto, en un clima que perfumaba el olor a vainilla de las galletas María, en un silencio y una penumbra porque empezaba a ponerse el sol y nosotras seguíamos allí esperando que llegase el niño. Y el niño llegaba y volvíamos a esperar, tal vez cien veces, tal vez una sola. Y tal vez esto mismo lo he dicho ya cien veces o no lo he dicho ninguna, porque el éxtasis es el río en que navego desde el primer día de mi vida. Extrema paradoja, río-éxtasis, que antes que la palabra, antes que la conciencia brotaba ante mí —o en mí— como un hilo inmóvil y fluyente. Era mi fórmula, era mi mismidad, que hasta tanto sólo se había ejercitado en sus juegos singulares y que en aquella tarde se dilataba en una especie de lazo o de ronda . . . (p. 208)

They used to play at having a baby: the small girl was the one who would have it and the older one was the doctor. The baby was a celluloid doll, of the kind fashionable at the time, almost as big as a newly born child . . . The extraordinary thing (one might say, the enchanting or adorable thing) was that there was no sense of *picardía* in any of this; yet there was action: we felt an undying emotion, which I can check today against adult criteria and which, after I came to know the meaning of the word *picardía*, I never felt was tarnished by that meaning.

Unexpectedly, that phenomenon affecting time, that sense of arrest or expansion, which I had thought could occur only when I was alone and asleep or half-asleep, was experienced by all three girls. The marvelous part was the moment of waiting. The girl was in bed, the doctor came, took her pulse and said, 'The child is arriving right away.' I don't remember if the little girl made believe a little, I think so; she repeated phrases she'd heard in ladies' conversations, but the fact is that for a couple of minutes, perhaps seconds, our hearts were beating as one, secure in the knowledge that we were free, unobserved, enveloped in our secret, in an atmosphere perfumed by the vanilla scent of the Marie biscuits, in silence and half-light, because the sun was starting to set, and we went on waiting there for the child to arrive. And the child would arrive and we would wait once more, perhaps a hundred times, perhaps just once. And perhaps I have told this story a hundred times already or I have not told it once, because ecstasy is the river in which I have been sailing since the day I was born. It is an extreme paradox, this ecstasy-river which gushed forth in front of me (or in me) before language, before consciousness like a motionless, flowing thread. It was my principle, my essence, which until then had expressed itself only in its own particular games and which that afternoon extended into a kind of bow or ring . . . (*translation mine*)

The passage takes place in a privileged space of feminine desire: a metaphorical 'ring' or 'river'. It is a scene which Chacel herself would no doubt classify as aesthetico-erotic. But what is unusual here is that the essential self (which is held to preexist language) opens out onto the intersubjective arena of play: Chacel's autoerotic fantasies are suddenly shared by her two female companions. The little girls are re-enacting the birth of the subject: the entrance of the child into history. But by repeating that birth indefinitely they achieve a suspension or deferral of linear time. This fantastic motherhood is a process by which the child's singularity accedes to universality, to a 'woman's time' beyond numerical calculation.[18]

But is the passage merely an example of the 'reproduction of motherhood' under the auspices of heterosexism? On the next page Chacel herself says that the game's 'flow of maternity' anticipates the girls' future as childbearers. The (male) baby would then be seen as the phallus, the centre of the female 'ring', a concrete equivalent of the phantasmal 'thread' with which it is associated by Chacel. However lesbian readers have suggested we look for the 'overtones' in heterosexual texts, that we attend to their 'fault lines', 'ellipses', or 'symptoms'. One key term here is 'picardía', a word I have left untranslated. It can mean both 'an innocent joke' and a 'shameful action'. Here, it seems to refer not to childish naughtiness, but on the contrary to self-conscious sexuality. In a characteristic gesture of 'negation' (*Verneinung*),[19]

---

[18] See Julia Kristeva, 'Woman's Time' in *Signs* 7/1 (1981), 13–35.

[19] See Laplanche and Pontalis (n. 14 above), s.v. 'negation'. The difference between repudiation and negation is that in the former the repressed returns as hallucination in the real, while in the latter the repressed is formulated by the subject while s/he continues to deny its existence.

Chacel at once evokes a powerful scenario of infantile, feminine sexuality (of *jouissance* without end) and denies that she and her friends had any knowledge of their actions. Symptomatically, this is one of those rare moments in Chacel's autobiography when a gap or 'fault line' opens up between narrator and protagonist, present and past, *énonciation* and *énoncé*.[20] The fear that the scene will be branded as sexually precocious forces the adult Chacel to validate her experience as a child, to insist on its innocence. However the impossibility of divorcing innocence and experience is implied none the less by the twin, irreconcilable meanings of the word that Chacel invokes, considers, and repudiates: 'picardía'.

Chacel's text thus acts out on a linguistic level the children's game of presence and absence (desire and denial). And at this crucial moment its syntax becomes muddy, convoluted. Just as the subject can no longer collapse past and present into a transcendent Same (with Chacel insisting here that the adult is different from the child) so language can no longer be transparent, the mere vehicle of authenticity. For, in spite of Chacel's denials, the birth game is not creation but imitation. Indeed, one of the girls mimics adult women's conversations. But there is another telling ellipsis in Chacel's argument. For she does not attend to the fact that one of the girls is playing the masculine role of the doctor, and is thus not anticipating the supposed female destiny of motherhood. If, unlike Chacel, we choose to acknowledge the theatricality of this scene, we can read it (in Marilyn R. Farwell's[21] words) as a 'disruptive space of sameness' which offers a 'new positioning of female desire' (pp. 93, 95). For the acting out of the scene (which is 'lesbian' in Farwell's extended, metaphorical sense) undoes the dominant order by overdoing it, by repeating it until it is emptied of meaning. Time and space are thus rendered indeterminate. For Elizabeth Meese,[22] the lesbian is a 'shadow', a subject who 'does not yet exist' (pp. 70, 71).

[20] For autobiography as a 'pact' which sutures the gaps between narrator, protagonist, and reader, see Philippe Lejeune, *Le Pacte autobiographique* (Paris, 1975).

[21] 'Heterosexual Plots and Lesbian Subtexts: Toward a Theory of Lesbian Narrative Space', in Jay and Glasgow (see n. 9 above), 91–103.

[22] 'Theorizing Lesbian: Writing—A Love Letter' [*sic*], in Jay and Glasgow (see n. 9 above), 70–88. For lesbian writing and reading as 'fault line' and 'ellipsis', see Shari Benstock in the same vol., 'Expatriate Sapphic Modernism: Entering Literary History' (183–203), esp. 188, 191; see also Diana Collecott, 'What Is Not Said: A Study in Textual Inversion', *TP* 4 (1990), 236–58. Cf. Chacel's statement that what is most important in her novels is that which is unsaid and left as an ellipse (*La sinrazón*, 77).

Similarly, in the half-light of the bedroom, Chacel's girls reach ecstasy together through a suspension of time, a deferral of subjecthood. And there is a final repetition here: one of the girls is called Marcela, the same as the peasant girl of the river and park.

This passage, then, acts out the social construction of the female subject even as it invokes an essential self that is irreducibly personal and private. Singularity meets communality in feminism: Chacel tells us that the girls 'dared to attempt a life of women—not of ladies—to live feminine friendship, which is like a secret of the body' (p. 209). I would suggest, then, that the ultimate value of Chacel's text lies in the way in which it juxtaposes, without explanation, role-play and *jouissance*, social determination and psychic autonomy.

Desde el amanecer ends, as it began, with an effort of the will: the ten-year-old Rosa determines her desires will never be frustrated like those of the women she has known. Outside the Madrid Art School she determines that it is through these doors that she will enter the world (p. 319). We have seen, none the less, that there is in Chacel a tension between the assertion of a pre-existing self (outside language and sociality) and the production of a new and singular self (within the constraints of gender, class, and 'race'). It is a tension that will recur in a much more complex and self-conscious form in the autobiography of Juan Goytisolo.

3. JUAN GOYTISOLO: THE TERRITORY OF HOMOGRAPHESIS

Where Rosa Chacel holds on to the same, Juan Goytisolo embraces difference. And as an epigraph from Montaigne suggests (*Coto*, 135), for Goytisolo the difference *within* a person is as great as that *between* persons. Thus, unlike Chacel, Goytisolo writes that his family origin is obscure: his ancestors left their native Basque country for Catalonia and his great-grandfather emigrated to Cuba for reasons that remain enigmatic (p. 9). The invention of a family coat of arms, would-be proof of nobility, is dismissed as a preposterous sham. In this opening section of first-person narration in the past tense, Goytisolo reproduces verbatim letters from slaves owned by his family (they will recur in his novel *Juan sin tierra*). But this apparently stable historicity is undermined by the section which follows. This is written in the second person and distinguished typographically by the use of italic face. Here Goytisolo invokes the horror he felt at a chance sighting of a photograph of himself in his youth; and retells in the present tense of immediate action two recent accidents (a car crash and tossing by a bull) in which he nearly lost his life. The motive of autobiography, then, is no longer a solemn quest for facticity; rather it is a desperate attempt to impose order on the random accident of sensory experience, an attempt which will inevitably empty and falsify that experience by imposing narrative structure upon it. Goytisolo remarks that it is impossible for him to verify even recent family history: the 'tangible reality' of the past cannot be recovered (p. 35).

This discontinuity of self, of experience, is associated from the beginning with language. The death of Goytisolo's mother in 1936, killed in Barcelona by a Nationalist bomb, robs the 5-year-old child of the 'mother tongue' of Catalan. From now on his marginal linguistic status (his engagement with an unyielding Castilian) will be as much a part of himself as that struggle to achieve 'true' sexual expression which parallels the linguistic battle. Both language and erotic orientation chose him 'without his agreement' (p. 37). We shall return to this interpenetration of language and sexuality (what Goytisolo oddly calls 'my literary and phallic orality') a little later.

After his mother's death, Goytisolo is raised by his father in the country. Soon after the end of the war, he is sexually abused by his maternal grandfather. What is extraordinary about the depiction of these unwelcome sexual encounters is that, already, the child seems to understand homosexuality within a social context. Thus the boy is angered not by his own suffering but by the gratuitous shaming inflicted on his grandfather: already dismissed from work, he is now obliged to quit the family home. The child's rage is thus diverted to his (heterosexual) father, who takes such pleasure in renewing the grandfather's humiliations (pp. 101–6).

But if the homosexual (or more properly pederast) is portrayed here as the victim of social injustice rather than of psychic or moral disorder, then his influence is also obscurely genetic. We are later told that, as if in answer to the father's greatest fears, this latent 'seed' in the maternal branch of the family has taken root in Goytisolo himself (p. 272). And if Goytisolo insists from the beginning on the presence of contradictions within the self, those contradictions do not appear to be socially constructed. Thus the adolescent's impulse towards masturbation is said to be a 'law': a vital source of energy that must be expressed (p. 121). Here, as elsewhere, Goytisolo relies on a classic opposition between an expansive, bodily nature and alienating, repressive culture. Yet he himself remarks how the sermons he heard inveighing against self-abuse and the practice of confession[23] imposed on him by a Catholic schooling were counter-productive, inspiring ever more intense bouts of autoeroticism (p. 123). The unwritten 'law' of desire is thus inseparable from that symbolic law which it claims, nonetheless, to precede and transcend.

The division of the self characteristic of Goytisolo's autobiography can therefore be mapped on to the traditional binary of the private and the public. But this division is reinforced by a perception of homosexuality as that which must repeatedly be expelled beyond the social sphere into a libidinal no man's land. Thus the grandfather is ejected from the family and forced to move with his ailing wife to another house. And some years later in Barcelona, a gay man is summarily excluded from a literary circle to which the young Goytisolo belongs. He accepts this scapegoating with the same resignation as the grandfather (p. 169). Unwilling to identify as gay himself at this point (unable to make a connection between his violent homoerotic fantasies and the stultifying Francoist society in which he lives) Goytisolo can articulate no resistance to these examples of homophobia. But more importantly perhaps, he fails (even retrospectively) to recognize that such exclusions do not simply serve to mark out the homosexual as an 'essentially' marginal subject; rather they suggest that s/he has always been at the centre of social structures (of the family, of the arts), and that such spectacular acts of expulsion serve merely to reinscribe the boundaries of those structures.

If homosexuality is expulsion from the social arena, it is also repeatedly described as a physiological addiction (for example, p. 230). But before the young Goytisolo achieves physical consummation with men, he associates homosexuality with writing. For example, he experiences the 'abyss' between public

---

[23] For the role of confessional practices in the shaping of the self, see Jeremy Tambling *Confessions: Sin, Sexuality, the Subject* (Manchester, 1990).

and private selves as a longing for authenticity (p. 140). But while this dualism is often represented in the humanist terms of face and mask, person and persona, it is also expressed in the identification of the self as 'homonym' (p. 150). Likewise, in his initial fumblings towards same-sex encounters, the young Goytisolo is unable to 'decipher' the signals he is given, unsure if they signify erotic invitation or renewed humiliation (p. 191). I would suggest, then, that rather than reading Goytisolo's narrative of sexual discovery as the revelation of an authentic corporeal identity, we take up these hints of textuality and read it as the production and performance of a new subjectivity which is of a thoroughly textual character.

For Lee Edelman, 'homographesis' is at once the putting into discourse of homosexuality and the deciphering of the homosexual as readable body.[24] It is based on the misrecognition of sexual preference as essence (or metaphor) rather than contingence (or metonym). A classic example, cited by Edelman, is *The Picture of Dorian Gray*. In this text, the newly produced invert comes to figure his own identity (to decode his innermost sexual secret) through the visual evidence of a portrait.[25] But this trope of legibility, in which 'vice' is written across a man's face, is counteracted by the homograph: the word which, although written the same as another, masks an unreadable difference within itself (p. 200). In a rather similar way, as Goytisolo comes slowly to recognize himself as a 'homosexual' and to decode his own innermost being, he inadvertently reveals that this assertion of an identity predicated on sameness carries with it a masked difference, which is much more difficult to read. As homonym (homograph), he achieves a stable sexual identity only as he repeatedly shatters and alienates that identity in writing.

The concept of homographesis will become clearer if we examine an important early episode in the autobiography: Goytisolo's chaste, adolescent love for Raimundo, a sailor in the port of Barcelona. Here it is the social 'abyss' between the bourgeois youth and the older proletarian which calls desire into being, creating that dissimilarity which (according to Goytisolo) is 'usually' provided by sexual difference (p. 224). One night

[24] See the article of the same name in *YJC* 3 (1989), 189–207. Edelman's book, also called *Homographesis*, is forthcoming from Routledge.

[25] Cf. Ed Cohen's reading of the same text 'Writing Gone Wilde: Homoerotic Desire in the Closet of Representation', *PMLA* 102 (1987), 802–13.

Goytisolo climbs into his bed on the quay. But his friend (he claims) is genuinely surprised: any such intimacy is 'unthinkable' to the sailor (p. 225). Hence, it is not merely that class difference creates the possibility of erotic desire. Rather, it is the lack of reciprocity between the two men that defines the role of each. The object has no desire and is thus consigned to animality: Raimundo snores loudly while the sleepless youth ponders the injustice of the social laws that prevent him from realizing his desire (p. 226). As love object, Raimundo will, characteristically, be put into writing: having served as the model for a character in one of Goytisolo's early novels, he subsequently serves only as 'proof of the authenticity' of the writer's fiction. The textual pleasure of the book thus anticipates and disables the sexual desires of the body: when Goytisolo sees Raimundo after he has written about him he is 'distanced' from his ex-love, no longer in a position of 'subordination'. It is a pattern that will be repeated in the later affairs which are physically consummated. According to the logic of homographesis once more, a metaphorical identification with the object cedes to a metonymic displacement of him into the contingencies of narrative sequence.

In the second volume of the memoirs homosexual desire comes increasingly into conflict with political commitment. Indeed, the narrative proceeds in such a way that the one is incompatible with the other. After taking up self-imposed exile in Paris, the young writer suddenly finds himself successful and fashionable as a readily exportable image of the young, committed writer that faithfully matches the French preconceptions of his native land (*Reinos*, 85). Goytisolo is amazed to recognize himself in the 'swollen balloon' of an inflated reputation. He thus resolves to 'wage war' on his image and burst the balloon (p. 87). In this process, writing and sex will mark out the authentic territory of the true self (p. 89). Once more, literary and homosexual vocations are linked in their common (physiological) nature of addiction (p. 104). As the blind imperative of the body, the homosexual addiction resists expression in the social arena. Horrified by the official persecution of lesbians and gay men he sees on a trip to Cuba in 1963, Goytisolo is lost for words (p. 176). A recurrent image at such moments is of libidinal 'lava' which fails to erupt, which dares not disturb the stable terrain of political commitment.

Goytisolo stakes out the boundaries between authentic and

inauthentic both within himself and between others: thus writers (such as Beckett) who soberly accept their destiny are contrasted with others (such as Yevtushenko or Cela) who like 'clowns' revel in their celebrity (p. 120). And this act of negation (of rejection of the literary as theatrical and inauthentic) is repeated in the lengthy and moving portrait of Genet.[26] For Goytisolo, Genet exemplifies the writer in his defiant nomadism, his refusal to settle down at a fixed address (p. 125). But, more disturbingly, Genet's scorn for his gay readership is also exemplary: he cannot tolerate the use of his books as masturbatory aids and takes great pleasure in humiliating a closeted gay reader (p. 127). As a 'falcon' amongst the 'peacocks' of the Parisian literary scene, he embodies a dangerous and merciless virility (p. 130). And his affairs with Arab youths anticipate Goytisolo's own sexual commitments. A new 'Pygmalion', Genet grooms his young lover Abdallah as a tightrope walker, overseeing his rehearsals and even designing his costume (p. 137). Inevitably Abdallah falls, both literally and metaphorically: ultimately abandoned by Genet he commits suicide. There is a curious reference here to the new 'blackness' of his skin, tinged by the poison he had swallowed. Much later, the putrefying body of Genet will also turn black, in symbolic reference to his 'adoptive land' of Africa (p. 154). According to Goytisolo, the friends who accompanied Genet's body to its burial in Morocco, proudly proclaim at the frontier that he is just another migrant Arab worker.

Genet is Goytisolo's only moral master (p. 153). But the account of his homosexuality and its relation to 'race' is disturbing. Firstly, Genet's authenticity is based on a disavowal of the 'feminine', whether it is located in bourgeois women or camp men. Secondly, it expresses itself through the medium of young men of colour. For Goytisolo, Genet has achieved transcendence in death: 'like the glow from a blazing fire' (p. 154). But it is simply not the case that a celebrated Parisian writer has the same status as a young migrant worker, even when both are dead. For, unlike his Arab lovers, Genet had chosen to adopt a life of marginality. What is more, the authenticity of Genet's homosexual desire is colonized by that alienating theatricality which he disavows elsewhere: Abdallah is made into a circus

---

[26] See Randolph D. Pope, 'La hermandad del crimen: Genet examina a Goytisolo', in *Estudios en homenaje a Enrique Ruiz-Fornells* (Erie, Pa, 1990), 514–18.

performer; a later lover becomes a racing car driver. Such relationships do not open out on to the symbolic. On the contrary, Genet demands that his lovers abandon their links with family and friends: Abdallah is made to perform 'without a safety net'; in Genet's prose poem to him he dances 'with his eyes closed' (pp. 136–7).

The other is thus reduced to the medium through which the self realizes his fantasies, transcends his own singularity. And while the white writer chooses to abandon his roots, the Arab lover is defined by them and must be returned to them: Abdallah (who has a German mother) returns none the less to his (African) 'origin' on his death. Just as the homosexual is thought to 'speak' through a body that is marked by his innermost essence, so the Arab is made to signify through a newly black skin, the mark of a 'true' identity bought only at the cost of death.

The reduction of 'racial' or ethnic difference to skin colour is what Diana Fuss (following Spivak) calls 'chromatism'. And before turning to Goytisolo's long delayed consummation of his desire for Arab men, it is worth asking how Fuss's account of essential and constructed identities applies to the question of 'race' (p. 92).[27] Fuss reminds us that 'race' cannot be defined by morphological criteria (p. 73). The 'black body' is the product not of biological determinations but of cultural over-determinations (p. 75). For example, the title of Fanon's *Black Skin, White Masks* suggests both that bodily characteristics are ineradicable and that ethnic identities can be assumed at will (p. 75). But if we deconstruct the 'racial' binaries, then must we deny the existence of black (or Arab) identities? Afro-Americans (like Arab migrants) begin from a position of fragmentation and dispersal: historically they have been denied access to the ego and cogito. The poststructuralist critique of identity may have less attractions for them than it has for Europeans who do not speak from a position of disempowerment (pp. 95, 96). Attempting to reconcile the demystifying critique of essence with the strategic demand for ethnic identity, Fuss suggests pragmatically that we 'work with "race" as a political concept *knowing* it as a biological fiction' (p. 91). To understand 'race' as fiction is not, of course, to deny the materiality of its effects in the world.

---

[27] For another account of Afro-American theorizations of 'race', see the intro. to my *Representing the Other*.

Goytisolo bravely acknowledges that his new-found political commitment to Arab causes is linked to his 'sexual debt' to the men he loves (p. 228). But he dare not admit that his 'innate attraction' (p. 207) to working class, Arab men is based on a physical desire that hypostatizes 'race' as a fixed and essential identity. Let us look at his first real affair. A chance meeting in a Barbès cafe leads to a brief relationship with migrant Mohamed. It is this 'bodily ideal' (eagle eyes, fleshy lips, wild moustache) which inspires the writer to 'delimit the imprecise boundaries of the exotic' and to become adept in the Arab community's language and culture (pp. 225, 226). However, the voyage of erotic discovery is also 'terrain' to be 'penetrated' in a conjugation of sexuality and writing. Indeed the act of writing repeats and reverses the erotic 'possession' Arab migrants have taken of Goytisolo's body: writing letters for his illiterate lovers, he 'counterbalances' physical submission with intellectual domination (p. 227). Thus in spite of his genuine concern for the well-being of his lovers, Goytisolo's desire tends to reiterate a binary divide between Europe, writing, and culture on the one hand and Africa, orality, and body on the other. Moreover, the attraction of white, bourgeois men to working-class migrants is no 'innate' disposition. Rather it is the historical disempowerment of the latter that makes them the perfect objects of a homosexual desire which (as we shall see) repeats and reverses the violent hierarchy of the world outside in the guise of sadomasochism.

Mohamed is married. He has left his wife and children at home and hopes, vainly, to support them from Paris. While for Goytisolo the relationship is an important stage on the path to a public avowal of homosexuality, for Mohamed (as for the sailor Raimundo) homosexuality simply does not exist: he never speaks of his desire. We are told, however that he treats Goytisolo as a 'wife', sometimes lying to him or cheating him of money (p. 226). As in David Halperin's account of pederasty in ancient Greece, here it is not the sex of the partners which is significant but rather their willingness to conform to roles gendered as 'male' and 'female'. As Halperin says of sex between men in modern American prisons:

Desire is sparked only when it cuts across the political divide, when it traverses the boundary . . . [that] distinguishes subjects from objects of desire . . . Sex [between men who do not consider themselves gay] does not so much implicate both partners in a common 'sexuality' as it articulates and defines the differences in status between them. (*One Hundred Years*, p. 39)

This would seem to be an accurate description of Goytisolo's desire. For the latter also sparks across (class and ethnic) divides, also implies no common ethos between the two partners. However, there is of course a twist. For while Mohamed is sexually dominant, the roles are reversed in writing. Goytisolo finds his pleasure in erotic submission; but unlike the Arab (unlike the Athenian slave or 'passive' prisoner) he can shake off his objecthood at will, and through homographesis, take loving revenge on the men who have so roughly disposed of his body.

We can now look at the final erotic 'scene' in the autobiography, in which spectacular violence is represented as the key to a renaissance of writing. While living in self-imposed exile in Tangier, Goytisolo takes up with a muscular, moustachioed farmhand he meets in a café terrace. One drunken, drug-fuddled night the 'wildman' beats him up, for reasons that remain obscure:

imágenes veladas, opacidad interrumpida por el fucilazo esclarecedor de la violencia, vuestra fulgurante comunicación energética, contundencia del golpe, caída, penosa incorporación, orden brutal de tenderte en la cama, . . . mientras él recorre la habitación como fiera enjaulada . . . se planta sin quitarte la vista de encima sabueso y torvo como un cancerbero . . . y, al despertar, le ves tumbado en el suelo, inerte, despatarrado, roncando, en medio del interior devastado, ropa esparcida, sillas volcadas, cama sucia y deshecha, percepción gradual del encuadre encrespado que te rodea, cruel agresión diurna, horario acusador y revuelto, desorden material y mental, esfuerzo trabajoso de levantarse, ir al baño mirarse con incredulidad en el espejo y descubrir un rostro que no es el tuyo, transmutado también el feroz remolino nocturno, incapaz de reflexionar aún y entender qué ha ocurrido, el chispazo casual de aquel brusco arrebato de virulencia
lavarse, afeitarse, ocultar la hichazón tras misericordiosas gafas de sol, abrir de par en par la ventana para que el aire entre y tu anublado cancerbero despierte, se incorpore a su vez, vaya a mear espaciosamente al lavabo, reaparezca con semblante azorado, bigotón desvalido y contrito como un niño que acaba de romper su juguete: musitando lamentos y excusas, ansioso de reconciliarse y hacer las paces con amigo tan formal y tan bueno, un verdadero hermano que cuida de él y le socorre cuando está sin dinero, más fino que el alquicel, más blando que

el algodón, presto a llegar al último confín del rebajamiento como el
amante pillado en falta tan bella y agudamente descrito por Ibn Hazm
pero tú quieres estar a solas, digerir lo acaecido, poner tierra por medio,
transformar humillación en levadura, furia en apoderamiento: llegar a
ese punto de fusión en el que la guerra emprendida contra ti mismo
simbólicamente trascienda, augure moral y literariamente una empresa,
vindique la razón del percance, del cataclismo buscado y temido: recia
imposición del destino cuyo premio será la escritura, el zaratán o la
gracia de la creación. (pp. 302–4)

veiled images, opacity broken by the glaring lightning flash of violence,
your stunning communication of energy, the bruising damage of the
blow, fall, painfully get up, brutal order to stretch out on the bed . . .
while he stalks the room like a caged beast, . . . stands there not taking
his eyes off you, grim alert like a brutal guard . . . and, when you wake
up, you can see him there lying on the floor, inert, spread-eagled,
snoring in the middle of the ravaged room, clothes scattered every-
where, upturned chairs, dirty unmade bed, gradual perception of the
tense scene around you, cruel aggression of day, accusing upside-down
time of day, mental and material disorder, painful effort to get up, go
to the bathroom, look at oneself incredulously in the mirror and find a
face that is not yours, transmuted as well into the fierce whirlwind of
the night, still incapable of thought, of understanding what has
happened, the chance spark that set off that sudden outburst of
virulence
get washed, shaved, hide the swelling behind merciful sunglasses, open
the window wide to let the fresh air in and wake up your befuddled
guard, he in turn gets up, goes for a lengthy piss in the bathroom,
reappears looking flustered, his mustache lank and contrite like a child
who has just broken his toy; mumbling pitiful excuses, wishing to make
it up, make friends with his friend who is so well-behaved, so kind, a
real brother who looks after him and helps him when he hasn't got any
money, daintier than lace, softer than cotton, ready to reach the bottom
of the pit of self-abasement just like the lover caught erring so
beautifully and sharply described by Ibn Hazm
but you want to be alone, to digest what has happened, distance
yourself, transform humiliation into yeast, rage into power: reach that
point of fusion in which the war waged against yourself symbolically
transcends, augurs in morals and literature a new departure, vindicates
the reason for the mishap, the cataclysm both sought and feared: stern
imposition of destiny whose prize will be the written word, the blight or
grace of creation. (pp. 255–6)

In the first few lines, there is no doubt who is dominant: the
anonymous Arab is defined as pure energy and animality; and

he incarnates (like a prison guard) the disciplinary structures of human law. But soon he is asleep. And Goytisolo rises to look at himself in the mirror. Like Dorian Gray, he is alienated from his own image, which seems to reflect back to him the bodily sign of his innermost condition. However, this metaphorical fixing of identity soon cedes to a metonymic displacement. Experience will be transmuted into writing, the written body into the writing of the body (into homographesis).

As the Arab awakes the binary is reversed. Castrated and infantilized (with droopy moustache and child-like demeanour) he must reassume the economic dependence implicit in the relationship, a social inferiority which is repeated and reversed in Goytisolo's decision to adopt the soft, receptive position gendered as 'feminine'. But already the writer is reinscribing the conflict within himself, assimilating the scene to text: the Hispano-Arabic love poems of Ibn Hazm. From the random and material chaos of this encounter Goytisolo will forge a transcendent identity or synthesis founded on writing. He does not tell us what became of the Arab, whose name is not given and who does not benefit from the resources of writing.

Goytisolo has claimed that sexual relations between men are commonplace in Arab countries; they are simply not talked about.[28] While his refusal to project 'gay identities' on to cultures in which they may not exist is no doubt to be admired, it also tends to reinforce the social and political deprivation of his lovers, who have no place from which to speak of their own desires and practices in their specificity. This is a case in which (as Diana Fuss suggests) disempowered subjects might benefit from the strategic adoption of a politics of sexual and ethnic identity. The more privileged Goytisolo can choose to do without such luxuries.

It seems likely, then, that in spite of the long and painful journey to homosexuality documented in the autobiography, Goytisolo does not conceive of himself as a gay man who shares a common identity or experience with other such men in the world. The letter in which, movingly, he confesses the homosexual 'truth' about himself (reproduced in *Reinos*, 238–42) is addressed to Monique Lange, the woman he was later to marry.

---

[28] In an oral response to a question at the Institute of Romance Studies in the University of London, Autumn 1990.

And it is perhaps significant that immediately after this letter, on a trip to the Soviet Union in 1965, it is Monique who asks their hosts about the status of gays in that country (p. 268). The long-delayed revelation of true identity (which Goytisolo had hoped would fill the 'abyss' between private and public selves) leaves him curiously indifferent to the sufferings of those who share the sexual preference he has finally come to proclaim as his own. It is not an irony of which he seems to be aware.

I noted at the beginning of this section that while Rosa Chacel asserts a single, unified self, Goytisolo embraces difference. We have seen, however, that Goytisolo's discontinuity derives from a struggle to reconcile the official territory of public life with the 'volcanic lava' of desire beneath its surface. In spite of his reservations about the authenticity of the autobiographical project, by the time he reaches its end Goytisolo claims to have achieved a transcendent synthesis of contradiction. But perhaps we have moved, in Fuss's words (p. 29), from 'the place of essentialism' (in Chacel), to 'the essentialism of place' (in Goytisolo). For as the titles of his two volumes remind us, what is intrinsic to Goytisolo's narrative of historical and cultural construction is the necessity of a terrain, however fragmented and depleted, on which the writing subject can take up a stand which can still be called 'moral'. This textual territory is an ethical 'ground' which will be undermined by Terenci Moix in his defiantly superficial and amoral autobiography.

4. TERENCI MOIX: SCREENS OF IDENTITY

Like Goytisolo, Terenci Moix defines himself as the writer of nomadism and hybridity. On the opening page of his first volume of memoirs, he claims to have abandoned 'many landscapes, many languages . . . many bodies' (p. 23). But unlike the exiled Goytisolo (who is also caught between Catalan and Castilian,[29] between old and new libidinal territories), Moix defiantly embraces superficiality. Thus the first section of the volume takes place in Rome in 1969. Man has just conquered the Moon; but the modish Moix (already a scandalously successful novelist

---

[29] For a discussion of bilingualism, see Moix's prologue to the 'definitive translation' of the early novel *El día que murió Marilyn* (Barcelona, 1984), 7–10. For struggle and division in the fiction see Gene Steven Forrest, 'El mundo antagónico de Terenci Moix', *Hispania* 60 (1977), 927–35.

in his late twenties) knows that technology is no match for fantasy. Having dyed his hair blond 'like Flash Gordon', he claims that the 'real' Moon is false, less authentic than its glittering and tawdry Hollywood version (pp. 24, 26). As the 'Great Decade' comes to an end, Moix describes a scene of group sex 'staged' by his flatmate Livio in a decor typical of the period's eclecticism and exoticism (p. 28). Refusing to take part, Moix retreats into onanistic, drug-induced reverie. For him, all beauty is the reproduction of the 'artificial paradises' of cinema and classical antiquity; all love a 'calque' of emotions already impersonated by Bette Davis (p. 25). Livio and Moix do not have sex but rather practice disguise and collage: donning cowboy or Nazi uniforms, sticking photographs of each other's heads on to the perfect bodies featured in muscle magazines (p. 31). Such role-play and fragmentation do not signify inauthenticity or conflicts of identity, however. Rather they represent a celebration of the absence of the beloved and of the precedence of art over nature (pp. 33, 38). From the 'watchtower' of his flat, high up in an ancient *palazzo*, Moix unfurls a giant 'screen' over the city (p. 50). As we shall see, this cinematic perspective will serve both to project and to protect an ostentatious, yet fragile, sense of self.[30]

In this opening sequence, then, Moix embraces the 'paradox and perversity' Jonathan Dollimore associates with Wilde: depth gives way to surface, essence to difference, authenticity to style (*Dissidence*, 15).[31] I shall argue, however, that as in the case of Dollimore's Wilde, Moix's 'perverse dynamic' does not operate outside that heterosexual culture whose norms it tends to subvert, but is rather wholly contained by that dominant culture. In spite of his frequent allusions to an international 'gay sensibility', for Moix homosexual identity is problematic indeed. Like Goytisolo before him, he refuses to admit the existence of a communality of experience based on (homosexual) desire, because he recognizes that that desire is itself culturally constructed (cf. Dollimore, p. 15). Moix's moral master is Pasolini, who preaches the doctrine of a 'full participation in life' achieved through

[30] Compare Moix's early novel *Món mascle* (Barcelona, 1971), Castilian trans., *Mundo macho* (Barcelona, 1990), in which the action is circumscribed by the protagonist's cinematic fantasies.

[31] See also *Dissidence*, 121–30; and Dollimore's original article: 'Different Desires: Subjectivity and Transgression in Wilde and Gide', *TP* 1 (1987), 48–67.

'natural sex' with unspoilt young proletarians (p. 40). But when Pasolini procures him a rent boy, Moix spends the evening analysing the youth's Roman dialect (p. 43). By 'practising [his] languages' Moix demonstrates that literature precedes life; and that the attempt to retrieve a 'popular spirit' through erotics is a sentimental fantasy (p. 40). Pasolini scornfully proclaims that Moix has not a penis, but a 'film archive' between his legs (p. 37). But it is Moix's aim in his memoirs not to repudiate but to vindicate this cinematic identity.

For Moix, then, film comes first. The 'dawn' of the subject takes place amongst the images on the screen; and the vivid colours of cinema eclipse the black and white world of post-war Barcelona. Indeed, the city itself is merely a 'catalogue' of the seedy picture houses in which he spent his childhood (p. 53). Moix claims that he was almost born at Christmas 1941 during a showing of *Gaslight* (the original British version); and was thus already infected in the womb by a taste for melodrama. But unlike Rosa Chacel (who also attests to pre-natal memories) the baby Moix did not wish to be born. Rather, 'life chose him' and he was the result of the city, the street, the historical moment, and the languages that decided 'on [his] behalf' (p. 57). And this cultural construction is also doubling, reflexivity: Moix is born with a caul, a 'second skin' or 'natural clothing'. It is the mark both of exceptionalism (of a unique destiny which transcends an obscure social origin) and of alienation (of an originary screen which intrudes between the subject and his origin). Far from being the space of authentic truth-to-self, childhood is thus for Moix a 'country belonging to others', one to which the adult subject has no unmediated access (p. 61).

Moix's genealogy (again like Goytisolo's) is hybrid. His mother is an exile from that part of Aragon in which Catalan merges into Castilian; his father an authentic Barcelonian, the last in a line that may be traced back to the Middle Ages. Moix, typically, mocks his father's heraldic pretensions (which include, like Goytisolo's father, a coat of arms); and satirizes his patronymic: in Catalan it suggests sadness, stagnant water, and overripe fruit (p. 71). Yet this burlesque etymology masks a serious point. The survival of the Catalan language at a time of oppression is associated by Moix with the continuity of a paternal line that is itself oppressive. It is no accident that he will come, finally, to repudiate his first ('mother') tongue and to write his later novels (and this memoir) in the adopted Castilian. Hollywood movies (much preferred by Moix to inferior domestic product) also represent a wilful alienation from the homeland, a new territory which can be described only by the anglicism 'glamour' (p. 94).

Language is thus the battlefield on which history and identity play out their conflict. And 'Terenci' is the name Moix chose for himself, rejecting the given 'Ramón'. But in post-war Catalunya, everything has two names: the street in which the family lives has both an official, written name and a traditional, oral one; the 'Library of Catalunya' has been blandly baptized by victorious Francoists the 'Central Library'. And as the narrative develops we see that this linguistically constituted division is inflected by class and gender divides which are also historically produced. Thus history and class are concretized in the urban topography: Moix is born 'within the walls' of the Gothic, working-class centre, and pines for the broad avenues of the newer *Ensanche* (literally 'Extension'). The hybridism of genealogy is repeated in the ambiguous location of the family home: halfway between the prostitutes of the Barrio Chino and the respectable bourgeois families of the Diagonal (p. 64). The class position of the Moixs is as perilous as their geographic location: as lower-middle-class merchants (owners of a city dairy and painting business) they lack both the 'authenticating' poverty sought by a Pasolini and the glamorous sophistication longed for by Ramón/Terenci. The city is thus at once a dense palimpsest of historical signs and an enduring symbol of a Catalan identity which transcends the individual as it constitutes itself in time. Later Moix will tell us that each of his 'whims' is determined by his remote ancestors, by the 'traces' left by antiquity in his body (p. 203). The most idiosyncratic spaces of desire are thoroughly colonized by history.

At the age of 6 Moix is taken by his father to a brothel. Here he discovers a new feminine community, curiously similar to those he has met in the dairy and his mother's drawing room (pp. 109, 116). The father tells him that a proper prostitute must be an actress in and out of bed (p. 115). But, characteristically, it is the young Moix who proves himself the better actor. Already skilled at reciting film-star gossip and movie plots to bemused adults, he takes advantage of a more receptive audience in the brothel to replay *Dark Victory*, with his mother in the Bette Davis

role of the blind heroine with a negative prognosis (p. 122). But
the distinction between the child's fantasies and his family's
actual behaviour is blurred: already he understands that the
dramatic attitudes struck by his various relations, however
violent they may appear, are simply functional, an acting-out of
gestures that have no permanent resonance (p. 107). When it is
normal for adults to adopt the masks of social life (when the
father is at once the paterfamilias and the whoremonger) then
Moix's cinematic fantasies seem less affected or bizarre, if no less
idiosyncratic. Still, he fears, the masks will 'invade' him (p. 181).

According to Diana Fuss, one erroneous preconception of constructionism is that nature equals fixity and sociality change (p.
5). And Moix's memoirs, with their frequent repetition and
sometimes garrulous overemphasis, reveal that a stress on the
determining force of history, society, and language is not incompatible with a faith in an essential identity (an identity which is the
effect of essence). For while, on the one hand Moix stresses that
culture precedes nature (that his image of his mother is based on
Lana Turner); on the other his wilfully narcissistic and ingratiating character remains unchanged throughout the book. If experience is 'always already' preceded by fiction then (to cite Fuss
once more) that topos of constructionism itself 'implies essence . . .
hints at an irreducible core' (p. 15). Moix's very stress on contradiction, paradox, and discontinuity is a constant of his narrative
which serves to make it more centred, more homogeneous.

It follows that Moix's engagement with history (other than on
an abstract or deterministic basis) is perilous. Thus of the Jewish
refugees who first tell him tales of the exotic Orient he knows
only from the cinema, Moix writes that 'this is not the time' to
speak of Nazism and its effects in Fascist Spain (p. 76). Or again,
of the anti-Semitic aspects of traditional Easter celebrations, he
writes glibly that 'more Jews were killed [in effigy] in Barcelona
than at Auschwitz' (p. 259). The 'eternal time' of the city cannot
tolerate the singular event of the Holocaust. Nor can Moix
account for the history of the Civil War. Describing his summer
holidays in the little Aragonese town of Nonaspe, he notes that
the castle was called the 'Slaughter House' and children were
terrified of the caves in which prisoners had also been killed
(pp. 238, 251). But in this typically fantastic account, history is
collapsed, with Franco taking his place beside the Roman
triremes (p. 250). Such passages seek the indulgence of the

reader confronted by the innocence and ignorance of a child. But they go unqualified by the adult narrator and seem rather to mark a failure to address political questions which must simply be repudiated, along with the drab Spain of the 1950s. Just as the cemetery in Nonaspe has been destroyed by unidentified bombing in the war, so recent history is obliterated by Moix's indiscriminate indifference to the real.

As Pere Gimferrer notes in his introduction to the volume, *El peso de la paja* is the story of a will or desire ('voluntad')(p. 20). And, like Rosa Chacel, Terenci Moix experiences history as an intolerable constriction on that will. Thus the strikes and demonstrations of 1951 (the first acts of Catalan rebellion against Franco, also described by Goytisolo in his memoirs and novels) serve only to frustrate the child's desire to attend the cinema as usual (p. 149). But Moix's history of his homosexuality suggests that there is no simple opposition between desire and law, that the 'perverse dynamic' is always already in place. Thus Moix claims to have had a gay godfather whom he calls 'Cornelio' after his resemblance to Cornel Wilde. Cornelio and his lover (a respectable doctor) are wholly, if tacitly, integrated into the extended family. Yet that family is virulently homophobic elsewhere: Moix's father says he would rather have a dead son than a queer one ('maricón'). Or again, the strict censorship of the period means that images of female bodies are highly circumspect, while male bodies are openly exhibited in unimpeachably orthodox films, such as those depicting the martydrom of the saints (p. 155). Like the priests who accuse their small charges of committing 'impure acts' of which they were hitherto unaware, such films serve to produce desires all the more intense because they are forbidden. It is instructive here to compare Goytisolo's account of sexual abuse by his grandfather with Moix's version of an unwelcome encounter with a lascivious priest. While Goytisolo is horrified by the injustice of his grandfather's punishment, Moix precociously taunts his teacher before cynically submitting to him when promised handsome rewards (p. 295). It is a sadistic and narcissistic pattern that will be repeated in his relationships with men or boys.

We have seen that Moix (like Chacel) is brought up in a variety of female communities. And he himself associates his homosexuality with a repudiation of his seedy, faithless father and an identification with his glamorous, wronged mother

(p. 106).[32] But the quest for a perfect friend (claimed as a
'natural law') is inspired, as ever, by cinematic fantasies, in
particular the youthful actors Sabu and Dean Stockwell (p. 183).
At his Catholic school, the handsome Blond Boy provokes
identification and envy (p. 174); and the neat Clean Boy an
impossible attempt at imitation (p. 177). But Ricardo, the Rich
Boy, is Moix's first love, one based not on mutuality but on
aggression and the satisfaction of Moix's whims (p. 187). By
scorning Ricardo's lavish gifts and abandoning him in the
cinema Moix discovers that it is only by inflicting pain that he
can feel love (p. 196). Moreover, his desire is sadistic in Leo
Bersani's[33] technical sense: sexual excitement is mimetic and
must be represented (in another body or text) before it can be
experienced (Bersani, pp. 3–4). As the two 12-year-olds enjoy
their first encounter with cinemascope (Henry Koster's *The Robe*
of 1953), Moix exclaims that nothing in life will be more beautiful
than this technological discovery; it is left to the 'grave and
charming' Ricardo to say that their friendship is even more
beautiful (p. 302). For Moix, it is representation that transforms
the world, and this glimpse of reciprocal adult love goes
unrecognized.

But if desire must be projected before it can be felt (and
projected on to the widest possible screen) this does not make it
unreal. On the contrary, for Moix cinematic fantasy is inseparable from historical constitution. Let us look more closely at one
late episode here, an encounter with a star-struck 'ephebe'
amongst the classical ruins of Mérida. Moix has flashed forward
to 1987: after signing copies of his latest novel (which he does
not neglect to inform us had just won a major literary prize) he
is brooding in a bar on the multiple levels of time which tend to
fuse into a consoling eternity: in his imagination the gilded youth
of the 1980s merge into Moix's scandalous generation of the
1960s, and regress back to the 'archetypical ruins' of the classical
city (pp. 203–4).[34] He is approached by a blond 'Viking' who

---

[32] For an account and critique of narcissism and identification with the mother in
the psychoanalytic aetiology of male homosexuality, see Michael Warner, 'Homo-
Narcissism; or Heterosexuality', in Boone and Cadden, eds. (see n. 7 above),
190–206.

[33] 'Representation and its Discontents', *Raritan* 1 (1981), 3–17.

[34] For Moix ruins are the indispensable to the ideal hero of the Catalan novel. See
the opening of *Sadístic, esperpèntic, i àdhuc metafísic* (Barcelona, 1976), 19.

attempts to pick him up. In spite of Moix's indifference, he glimpses the possibility of a 'perfectly literary act of love' amongst the ruins, which would resurrect the child of the Gothic Quarter and the young man of Rome. The youth, of course, has no interest in fantasy and (according to Moix at least) is concerned only with immediate physical demands. But by mythicizing his prospective partner (by projecting him on to the screen of the classical backdrop) Moix has 'nullified' the youth's body. Unable to respond to the urgency of young desire, Moix must return alone to his hotel room, his solitude 'wrapped in the luxury' that is his only consolation (p. 205).

There is more than a touch of the screen goddess here, with Terenci cast as Joan or Bette suffering in mink. But this flagrant self-pity, so typical of Moix, masks a genuine concern for the passing of time and the possibility of encountering the other. He now has not a film archive but 'an archeologist's trowel' between his legs (p. 205). The co-opting of the present by the past and of the libidinal by the cultural suggests a 'history of the present' in which no desire, no identity, can be taken for granted. We shall see, finally, how this 'weak' epistemology relates to adult homosexuality.

As Moix had rejected Ricardo the Rich Boy, so Ricardo disowns him. Returning from holiday in Sitges, the teenage Moix suddenly realizes Ricardo is the 'other self' whom he seeks and confesses his love to him. The latter, however, calls him a 'queer'. It is a word with which Moix cannot identify himself (p. 337). He is stricken with shame, none the less, imagining the mark of the pariah on his forehead (p. 338). At the end of the volume, however, Moix encounters Ricardo once more. This time the scene is Rome in 1969. Again Moix evokes the memory of childhood as an 'archeology' of present suffering and his now glamorous life as a 'collage' or 'screen' of brilliant images (pp. 346–7). And he claims to have wasted his life on the search for the impossible 'companion' who would have his own face, voice, body, and heart. The Boy who was the epitome of all boys is visiting Rome. But Ricardo, at 29, is horribly transformed, his clothes painfully unfashionable and his golden curls replaced by the few 'repugnant' hairs he has left (p. 350). To Moix's surprise, Ricardo narrates the sexual fantasies their friendship had inspired and his subsequent affairs with men. But Moix claims to be as unfamiliar with his own sexuality now as when he was a youth: unlike Ricardo (whom he mentally dismisses as a pathetic 'queen') he has not taken on the burden of homosexual identity:

Ricardo se empeñó en quedarse a dormir en mi apartamento y, mientras subíamos por la tenebrosa escalera particular, apenas iluminada por musculosos brazos de abisinios que sostenían hachones de colores, me iba contando que un cretino le había abandonado y antes abandonó él a otro imbécil, y que, después de muchas aventuras y mucho whisky con soda, se encontraba más solo que la una.

— Tenemos que ser amigos como antes, enanito —murmuraba, con palabras babosas—. El tiempo no ha pasado. Estamos en el 'Fémina'. Va a empezar *La Túnica Sagrada* . . .

Le dejé caer en un sillón. Mientras se entretenía tarareando la sintonía de la 'Fox', empecé a liar el porro de las madrugadas. Con absoluta frialdad, decidí que estaba a punto de abordar la película más sorprendente de mi vida.

Si el destino no me había concedido el genio para parir a Hamlet, ni a Lear . . . la vida me daba, cuanto menos, la oportunidad de fornicar con mi propia memoria.

Veinte años después de nuestro encuentro en el patio de los curas, Ricardito Beauregard se desnudaba sólo para mí. Entonces, la naturaleza volvió a tomarme el pelo. No ha dejado de hacerlo desde que nací, pero en aquella ocasión se pasó de rosca. El prodigioso niño que guió los mejores días de mi infancia, aparecía en su aspecto más patético, completamente borracho y desnudo como una foca. Semblanza por demás exacta, porque al revelarme su cuerpo, pude ver al Ricardito casi treintañero: fofo, barrigudo, con las tetas caídas como un viejo y la piel blancucha y grasienta como la mantequilla. (pp. 353–4)

Ricardo insisted on staying the night in my flat and, as we climbed up the dark private staircase, faintly lit by the muscular arms of Abyssinians bearing coloured torches, he was telling me that one idiot had left him, and before that he left another fool, and that after a great many affairs and a great deal of whisky and soda, he found himself absolutely alone.

'We must be friends like we were before, dwarfy,' he murmured, dribbling. 'Time has stood still. We're back in the Fémina Cinema. *The Robe* is about to begin . . .'

I let him collapse into an armchair. While he was busy humming the Twentieth Century Fox signature tune, I began to roll the joint I used to smoke in the small hours. With complete coldness, I decided I was about to encounter the most surprising film in my life.

If fate had not granted me the genius to produce Hamlet or Lear . . . life was at least giving me the chance to fuck my own memory.

Twenty years after we had met in the school playground, little

Ricardo Beauregard was stripping just for me. Then, Nature pulled my leg again. It hasn't stopped doing so since I was born, but this time it outdid itself. The marvellous boy who inspired the best days of my childhood appeared in his most pathetic guise, completely drunk and as naked as a seal. In fact, the image is almost too accurate, because as his body was revealed to me, I could see little Ricardo at almost 30 years old: spongy, paunchy, his tits drooping like an old man's and his skin as whitish and greasy as butter. (*translation mine*)

As a child Moix's initial identification with femininity leads to a repudiation of it: an extreme close-up of Moira Shearer in *The Red Shoes* produces fantasies of the vagina dentata and the phallic mother (p. 198). Here as an adult we find a similar repudiation of the gay man whose body provokes nausea and disgust. Yet, typically, this repudiation is staged through a parody of Moix's own cinematic sensibility. Thus Ricardo reproduces that collapsing of different levels of time (that atemporality) that Moix loves in cinema.[35] And he invokes that first cinemascope film which was the greatest experience of Moix's childhood. And just as Livio stages the group sex at the beginning of the memoirs, so at the end and in the same apartment, Moix provides the *mise en scène* for the consummate sexual 'scene' that will liberate him from his past, exorcise the image repertory of memory through repetition in the real. But Ricardo's nakedness does not inspire authentic or immediate sensation. Rather, feminized and dehumanized (a soft, breasted beast) he eludes Moix's very studied desire and is diverted into metaphor. As dawn breaks over Rome both are enveloped in their solitude within the 'enormous screen' on which Moix has been projecting his life (p. 356).

Ricardo is alone because he is gay; Moix is alone (or so he tells us) because he is human (p. 357). Having refused to play the homosexual 'role' (having rejected the 'mediocrity' of real sexual relations and concrete physical bodies) Moix is compelled, finally, into the indifferent essentialism of a universal alienation. Ricardo could never understand like Livio that 'no body is worth a fantasy, no city a literature, no love the idea of that love' (p. 358).

But what attracts me in this passage is not its self-indulgent melancholia or overemphatic irony, but rather the redundant detail of the 'Abyssinians' bearing torches on the staircase. Even

---

[35] For temporal fusion in the fiction see José Romera Castillo, 'Anacronismos lingüísticos con clara intencionalidad literaria en *Nuestro Virgen de los Mártires* de Terenci Moix', *EL* 3 (1985–6), 313–20.

here, in what is clearly intended to be the climactic moment of a long and often repetitive memoir, Moix cannot resist the exotic, ornamental detail whose charm lies in its very superfluity. I would suggest, finally, that there is in Moix always a certain remainder which exceeds the sometimes banal 'message'. Often that remainder is itself irritating or ingratiating, as when he specifies the version of *Gaslight* his mother saw when she was pregnant or the name of the literary prize he had been awarded before attending the book fair in Mérida.[36] But it is in the very transparency of this desire to perform for an audience and to gain their love (a desire that has clearly persisted since childhood) that the 'autobiographical pact' between narrator, protagonist, and reader is confirmed. In spite of the promise of the blurb on the back cover, Moix does not 'dive into the depths of his identity . . . into the depths of his tormented sexuality'. Rather he exploits antiquity and cinema as stages for the acting out of defiantly 'flat' images of the subject.

El peso de la paja is the name of a square in Moix's Gothic heart of Barcelona. But it translates not only as 'the weight of straw' but also as 'the burden of masturbation'. There could be no more telling example of the inextricability of public space and private fantasy in Moix's mythical topography. However, that virtuality and hybridism in which Moix takes such pride, that fragmentation and historicization of the subject, gives way to a plurality of essential selves, each of which is self-sufficient. As Fuss suggests: 'Historicism is not always an effective counter to essentialism if it succeeds only in fragmenting the subject into multiple identities, each with its own self-contained, self-referential essence' (p. 20). This serves as a good account of Moix's strategy. For he rejects the seductive mirage of a fixed identity only to replace it with a secondary, molecular narcissism. This prevents his text from addressing historical specificity, from confronting the inescapably political questions posed by homosexual identities. If the limits of the cinema screen are identical with those of the world (if subjectivity is a purely aesthetic category), then there can remain no ground at all on which to take up an ethical position. It is not a problem that seems to worry Moix unduly.

[36] For Moix as irritant, see Pere Gimferrer's introd. to *Mundo macho* (Barcelona, 1990), 6; and Moix's own 'Pròleg per al lector propens a irritar-se', in *Sadístic* (see n. 34 above), 11–14.

5. THE ENDS OF AUTOBIOGRAPHY

Tom Yingling has recently suggested that 'homosexual writers so consistently take as their text the construction of the self that one is tempted to claim there is only one genre of homosexual writing: the autobiographical.'[37] Citing Guy Hocquenghem's claim that 'homosexuality is first of all a criminal category', Yingling asks: 'If he [sic] is only an after-image of others . . . the only question for the homosexual is "Who am I?" or, in its bitchier versions, "How do I look?"' (p. 36). We have seen in this first chapter that identity can be as problematic for feminist women as it is for gay men. And although their answers are very varied, all three writers ask 'How do I look?'. Chacel rejects the photographic image of herself as artificial and inauthentic; Goytisolo scours the family album for evidence of his tainted genealogy; and Moix simulates the fragmentation of the postmodern body in home-made collages. As I suggested in the introduction to this chapter, there is a shift here from depth to surface, from essence to construct. Chacel's 'belief in the real true essence of things, [their] invariable and fixed properties' (Fuss, p. xi) could not be further from Moix's kaleidoscopic videodrome.

These differences recur in the writers' attitudes to their respective names and to the cities they inhabit. Thus Chacel's signature suggests a unique and constant presence-to-self; Goytisolo's 'homonym' a painfully divided subject, longing for integration; and Moix's adopted name a wilfully alienated identity which is the source not of pain but of pleasure. Likewise, while Chacel's Valladolid remains untouched by history, Goytisolo's Paris is integrated into the intellectual and social destiny of Europe, and Moix's Barcelona is at once the historical producer of its citizens' desires and a cinemascopic screen on which those desires can be projected.

Where homosexuality is concerned, Goytisolo's ethics of revelation (in which the difficulty and intimacy of the confession serve to verify its authenticity) could not be further from Moix's casual and gossipy indiscretions, which carry little weight and assume no moral exemplarity. Paradoxically, however, the younger and more careless writer may be the more radical. For while Goytisolo clings (like Gide) to those 'strong' categories of

---

[37] *Hart Crane and the Homosexual Text* (Chicago, 1990).

identity which he hopes to retrieve, Moix decentres or disperses the self (like Wilde) in a continuing gesture of anti-essentialism and anti-humanism (cf. Dollimore, pp. 14, 18). But as Fuss suggests, we should not disparage Goytisolo for his reinscription of essentialism. Indeed it seems likely that his affirmation of a 'deep', deviant desire has more political resonance than Moix's advocacy of fashionably flat simulacra.

One phenomenon shared by all three writers is sado-masochism. Chacel is excited and disturbed by the young girl rolling in the dust and by her mother ripping her fan apart; Goytisolo by Turkish wrestlers and Arab strongmen; Moix by the sufferings he inflicts on his friends and lovers. As Bersani notes, such desires cannot be separated from desire *tout court*. Rather 'the spectacle of pain stimulates a mimetic representation which . . . shatters the subject into sexual excitement' (p. 7). Hence, if homosexuality is for Goytisolo a fixed and irreducible core or 'kernel' of identity, then that core is subject to repeated, pleasurable shattering. Unity gives way once more to fragmentation.

One final concern shared by all three writers is that constellation of related but distinct terms known as disavowal, denial, and foreclosure. For just as Goytisolo and Moix seek, in their different ways, to repudiate the very idea of a homosexual identity, so Chacel rejects that passive and suffering femininity she identifies with her mother. The first moral of these autobiographies, however, is that subjects cannot simply transcend those sex or gender positions in which they have been placed, that they must speak from that position if they are to speak at all. The second moral is that homosexuality is not the absolute Other of popular imagination, but rather the 'proximate': that which is adjacent to the same (of family and society) but is held to be distinct from it (see Dollimore, p. 33).[38] The proximate suggests a sophisticated and disabused understanding of the interpenetration of desire and law that will recur in Goytisolo's trilogy of treason.

[38] For the erotics and politics of proximity, see *Dissidence* 230. For the nearness of the other in Heidegger, see Vattimo, 87; for the other as proximity and exteriority in Levinas, see Alain Finkielkraut, *La Sagesse de l'amour* (Paris, 1984), 67, 70–2.

2

Homosexual Desire in Goytisolo's Trilogy of Treason

I. THE HOMOSEXUAL QUESTION

Critics have often written on the theme of sexuality in Goytisolo's trilogy, but have rarely raised the question of homosexual desire in its specificity.[1] My aim in this chapter is to raise that question without either reducing homosexuality to a stable 'theme' or 'content' or isolating it from those other questions (of gender and 'race') by which it is constantly inflected. I shall not be concerned with the relation between the empirical author and the fiction he has produced; nor shall I attempt an 'allegorical' reading. This is because both the author-function and the appeal to a 'latent' meaning deep within the text are often complicit with medicalizing views of homosexuality as the hidden secret that must constantly be brought to the surface, repeatedly exposed to the light of examination.

I treat homosexual desire, then, not as literary theme or psychological trait, but as question, and one posed within language and history. As question, homosexuality poses a chal-

[1] In this ch. I cite the following texts: *Señas de identidad* (Barcelona, 1976) (first pub. 1966); *Reivindicación del conde don Julián* (Barcelona, 1982) (first pub. 1970); *Juan sin tierra* (Barcelona, 1977) (first pub. 1975). I have also referred to Linda Gould Levine's annotated edn. of *Reivindicación del conde don Julián* (Madrid, 1985). Eng. trans. *Marks of Identity*, trans. Gregory Rabassa (London, 1988); *Count Julian*, trans. Helen R. Lane (London, 1989); *Juan the Landless*, trans. Helen R. Lane (London, 1990). For homosexuality in Goytisolo, mostly with references to anality, see Abigail Lee Six, *Juan Goytisolo: The Case for Chaos* (New Haven, Conn., 1990), 47–8, 114. One critic who assumes that Goytisolo wishes to remain faithful to a homosexual 'identity' (albeit an identity displaced into mysticism) is Linda Gould Levine: 'El papel paradójico del Sida en *Las virtudes del pájaro solitario*', in *Escritos sobre Juan Goytisolo: II Seminario Internacional sobre la obra de Juan Goytisolo* (Almería, 1990), 225–36 (p. 233). I argue in this ch. that Goytisolo offers a critique of 'identity' in all its forms. Bradley S. Epps is one of the very few Hispanists familiar with recent gay theory; see 'The Violence of the Letter: Oppression and Resistance in Three Texts by Juan Goytisolo', unpub. Ph.D. diss. (Harvard University, 1990); 'The Ecstasy of Disease: Goytisolo, AIDS, and Hispanism', unpub. paper read at Questions of Homosexuality conference, IRS London (June 1991).

lenge in a number of spheres: the subjective (the construction of identity), the literary (the conventions of realism), and the sociopolitical (the institutions of the dominant order). My thesis is that homosexual desire creates the possibility of an integrated critique of these three levels as they appear in Goytisolo's fiction; respectively, in his polemic against the literary character, his advocacy of formal experiment, and his proposition of strategies for resisting power. In the last epigraph to *Don Julián* Goytisolo cites Sade's quest for a crime which would have a 'perpetual effect' and produce 'a general corruption or disordering'. I would suggest that one example of this interminable disturbance, which (as Sade says) is operative even when the person who causes it is asleep or dead, is homosexual desire.

In this chapter I take my understanding of homosexual desire mainly from the work of Guy Hocquenghem and from critiques of his work by Jeffrey Weeks and Gilles Deleuze.[2] Weeks's excellent preface to Hocquenghem's major work (the only one to be translated into English) is a good introduction to the field. Paraphrasing Hocquenghem, Weeks claims that homosexual identification serves as a 'challenge to the bourgeois ideology of familial and reproductive sexuality and male dominance' (p. 9), and suggests that the aim of a theoretically informed lesbian and gay studies would be to analyse 'how the "homosexual" as a social being is constructed in a capitalist society' (p. 10). Weeks makes out three stages in Hocquenghem's argument: first, the analysis of paranoid hostility to homosexuality; second, the relation of that hostility to the Oedipal family and reproductive sexuality; third, the attempt to resist familial sexuality through anti-capitalist and anti-Oedipal struggles. For Hocquenghem, such a programme requires the rejection of the implicitly trans-historical model of the Oedipus found in Freud and Lacan and a re-examination of the role of psychoanalysis within history of the kind carried out by Deleuze and Guattari (pp. 16–17). However, unlike Anglo-American anti-psychiatry of the same period,

---

[2] I cite the folowing texts: *Homosexual Desire* (London, 1978) (orig. pub. in French, 1972), introd. by Jeffrey Weeks; *L'Après-mai des faunes: Volutions* (Paris, 1974), introd. by Gilles Deleuze; *La Dérive homosexuelle* (Paris, 1977); *La Beauté du métis* (Paris, 1979). Hocquenghem was a founder member of the French gay liberation movement (FHAR) and a regular columnist for *Le Gai Pied*. Although Goytisolo was resident in Paris during this period and was aware of Hocquenghem's role as an activist, he did not meet him (private conversation with author).

Deleuze and Guattari (and Hocquenghem) are anti-humanist: rather than seeking the liberation of the self from sexual repression, they suggest we abandon the very concept of 'self' and replace it by 'desiring machines'. The fundamental premiss is as follows: confronted by a loss of shared social meaning (or 'code') capitalism reinvents the family (and consequently the self) as the locus of social control. As Weeks puts it:

As society becomes more 'civilized' (capitalist), the level of code in the desiring machines decreases; society struggles against the progressive loss of shared meaning as it would be destroyed by total decoding (schizophrenia). The family is therefore constituted as an artificially 're-territorialized' unity where social control has been relocated and in which forms of social organization can be reproduced ... thus the privatized 'individual' that psychoanalysis studies within the Oedipal family unit is an artificial construct, whose social function is to trap and control the disorder that haunts social life under capitalism. (p. 18)

The important term here is 'territorialization'; that is, the investment of libidinal energy within fixed parameters.[3]

This radical attack on the coherence of the 'molar' (or unified) self suggests that the *naïvetés* of a certain 'homosexual history' (which speculates as to whether a person was 'really' gay or not) are no longer possible. Rather we should examine the 'conditions of emergence' of definitions of the homosexual, the ways in which 'the principal ideological means of thinking about homosexuality ... are intimately, though not mechanically, connected with the advance of Western capitalism' (p. 21). As an example of 'perverse reterritorialization', homosexuality is manufactured in a double movement: first, through the creation of a scapegoated minority; second, through 'the transformation of repressed homosexual elements of desire into the desire [by "heterosexuals"] to repress ["homosexuals"]'. Sublimated homosexuality is thus the basis of the paranoia and panic about homosexuality 'which pervades social behaviour' (p. 22).

This paranoid society is dominated by the phallus. And, as an antidote to the hierarchic mode of phallic competition, Hocquenghem proposes a re-evaluation of the anal function. As Weeks points out, Hocquenghem is not to be taken literally at this point: there was no evidence even in the Sixties that anal inter-

---

[3] Cf. Severo Sarduy, 'La desterritorialización', in *Juan Goytisolo*, ed. Gonzalo Sobejano (Madrid, 1975).

course played a unique or exclusive role in sex between men (p. 24).[4] Rather Hocquenghem is attempting to 'suggest the symbolic consequences of the dominance of the phallus' (p. 25), by proposing a new kind of social organization. The recovery of anal desire (hitherto dismissed or sublimated) would pose a challenge to the division between public and private on which society is based: to lose control of the anus is to risk the loss of individual identity because that control stakes out the boundary between self and other (child and faeces, inside and outside). Hocquenghem's suggestion that the anus be 'grouped' (that is admitted to communal representation) is thus not—or not merely—a rationalization of a certain gay sexual activity (polymorphous 'scattering') (p. 26); it is also a rejection of homosexuality as an individual 'problem' in favour of homosexuality as a communal relation. The ontological definition is replaced by a libidinal position.

Weeks is not uncritical of Hocquenghem's project. He raises three specific questions which, he claims cannot be accounted for by *Homosexual Desire*. First, if anti-homosexual paranoia is a product of capitalism, how can we explain the fact that attitudes have indeed changed in the twentieth century and taboos have not remained fixed? Second, if reterritorialization is a global phenomenon, why is it that certain people become 'manufactured' as 'homosexuals' and others do not? Third, if the anal is to be promoted as the antidote to phallic supremacy, what significance does this have for lesbian desire (p. 23)? As we shall see later in the chapter, these three questions (of historical change, subject position, and gender difference)[5] may also be

---

[4] In spite of superficial appearances, Hocquenghem does not, naïvely, take the anal as a necessarily subversive space; nor does he collapse homosexuality into anality and vice versa. For anal intercourse in D. H. Lawrence as the 'perverse' reinscription of heterosexuality in alterity, see Dollimore, *Dissidence*, 274–5.

[5] I shall argue that neither Hocquenghem nor Goytisolo accounts for gender difference in their privileging of anality. For a very different reading of anality in the era of AIDS (which shows how receptive anal sex is gendered as 'feminine' in heterosexist fantasy), see Leo Bersani, 'Is the Rectum a Grave?' *October* 43 (1987), 197–222. The plurality and liminality of the anal in Hocquenghem might be seen as anticipating later feminist psychoanalytic accounts of the woman's body. See the title essay of Luce Irigaray's *Ce sexe qui n'en est pas un* (Paris, 1977), 23–32; and my *The Body Hispanic*, 20–1, for an account of this text. But note also Margaret Whitford's warning on Irigaray's supposed 'celebration' of femininity: 'When Irigaray describes the female imaginary in *This Sex* as plural, non-identical, multiple . . . this is not a recommendation that relationships between women in the real world should be of [this] kind.' *Luce Irigaray: Philosophy in the Feminine* (London, 1991), 81.

asked with profit of Goytisolo. But Weeks also raises a more general point, which is even more urgent in Goytisolo's case:

> In rejecting the myth of the 'normal' . . . and in emphasizing the need for conscious struggle against it, Hocquenghem, like Deleuze and Guattari, is in danger of creating a new myth: the revolutionary potential of the marginal, a myth which ignores the real problems of power in modern capitalism. (p. 27)

By aestheticizing marginal subjects (Arabs, 'homosexuals') Goytisolo also risks setting up a reverse hierarchy which distracts attention from the power structures which effect that original marginalization.[6] I shall suggest myself, however, that just as Hocquenghem and Deleuze avoid utopianism through a painstaking critique of Marx and Freud, so Goytisolo avoids romantic idealism through a far-reaching analysis of Eurocentrism and reproductive sexuality.

Juan Goytisolo's trilogy of treason is made up of *Señas de identidad* (1966), *Reivindicación del conde don Julián* (1970), and *Juan sin tierra* (1975). In the pages that follow I examine the varied configurations of homosexual desire in each of these books. In *Señas*, homosexual desire is marginalized and Oedipalized; in *Don Julián*, it is internalized and traced back to infantile fantasy; and in *Juan sin tierra* it is 'grouped' or 'scattered', presented not as a character trait, but as a 'desiring machine'. I also focus on one passage from each novel, passages which stress the connection between ethnicity and homosexuality.

Some critics have pointed to a development in the trilogy, stressing those points at which Alvaro Mendiola, indisputably the protagonist of *Señas*, coincides with the nameless narrator of *Don Julián* and the multiple voices of *Juan sin tierra*. And a sense of a teleological, even dialectical, movement is reinforced by the covers of the Seix Barral editions I have used. Thus *Señas* superimposes a multiple portrait of a white man on a map of Spain, suggesting the interconnection of personal and national identity; *Don Julián* sports a hazy crucifixion overseen by a ghostly King Kong, suggesting the irruption of Africa into the

---

[6] In his generally positive account of Hocquenghem's co-option of psychoanalysis for homosexual politics (*Dissidence*, 206–9), Dollimore argues that, in spite of the joyful anarchy of his anti-humanism, Hocquenghem still appeals to a disguised essentialism of desire (p. 212). Dollimore is, however, unfamiliar with Hocquenghem's French texts on activist politics and 'race'.

European imaginary; and finally, *Juan sin tierra* offers a pair of rounded objects (breasts, buttocks, or tombstones?) looming out of the darkness into a blue heaven: cultural difference is sublated into the elemental forces of nature. The specific conflict between European and African is thus apparently resolved on a higher level of synthesis. According to Hocquenghem, however, homosexual desire challenges this kind of dialectical reasoning by proposing a new mode of argument that is not linear but annular. The icon of the annular is not the pyramid of phallic hierarchy, but the contingent or concentric rings on the surface of water.

The cover to Linda Gould Levine's annotated edition of *Don Julián* poses the question of cultural difference once more. The photograph shows four men (Arabs?) clothed ceremoniously in white robes. Two of them clutch swords, and one is engaged in animated conversation with another. While a credit is given for the photographer, no indication of the names or identities of the subjects themselves appears. The men are aestheticized in their otherness: abstracted from history and geography and rendered all the same. Their frozen gestures suggest an oral community centred on phallic competition between men (the vertical swords). However, the fact that they form a group (anonymous, acephalous) may be significant. Their identity is not to be understood as an individual 'condition'. And on closer inspection we notice differences between them: the man on the right has paler skin and more 'Semitic' features than his companions. He also sports a pair of yellow slippers. Difference is thus reinscribed within the same. In rather a similar way the homosexual is (for Deleuze) not 'he [sic] who remains with the same sex, but he who discovers innumerable sexes of which we have no idea' (*L'Après-mai*, 9). Like the men in the picture, 'he' escapes territorialization, can no longer be frozen into the image of exotic other. The question is raised by Goytisolo's treatment of homosexual desire, then, is whether it is possible to avoid the deadly fixity of the imaginary without succumbing to the alienation of the symbolic; whether there is a space, however perilous and provisional, between the twin territories of madness and Oedipalization.

2. *SEÑAS DE IDENTIDAD*: REPRODUCING THE OEDIPUS

Señas de identidad juxtaposes a narrative in the present of Alvaro Mendiola's return to Spain from Paris with a narrative in the past of his experiences at home and abroad. Goytisolo presents a sequence of scenes in a broadly naturalistic mode of Alvaro's bourgeois childhood in the Civil War; of his post-war education in Barcelona; of his friend Antonio's internal exile in the south of Spain; and finally of Alvaro's experience of the immigrant community in Paris and his affair with fellow exile Dolores. Translated into English as *Signs of Identity*, the French *Pièces d'identité* suggests more subtly both bureaucracy and fragmentation: the disrupted exposition of the novel will confirm that the 'identifying marks' of the title at once constitute and alienate a sense of self.

In the first chapter Alvaro returns to the family home, the 'mythical' setting of his childhood (pp. 12, 14). In the photo album, with its images of successive generations (including a slave-owning Cuban great-grandfather), Alvaro seeks the 'lost key' to his youth (p.16). However, the family is a 'degenerate race', which is fading away (pp. 17–19); the various aunts and uncles have died childless and the family tree is now 'sterile' (p. 49). Alvaro remembers a scene emblematic of this gulf between the generations, when his senile grandmother failed to recognize him. In spite of his search for soulmates amongst his ancestors, Alvaro's life will be one of rupture and dispossession (pp. 54–5).

From the very beginning, then, *Señas* re-enacts the Oedipal drama. It stages a return to the protagonist's origin and to the scene of his father's death (p. 108), and it sets his quest for identity in the context of that origin and that death. The narrator frequently comes back to images of dissolution and dispersal: just as the father rots in a common grave, so memory of the past is lost for ever (p. 110). However, far from welcoming this dissolution as one might have expected, the rebellious Alvaro is nostalgic for the integration of experience and identity: after so many years of exile, the 'lost unity' of self and nation prevents him from achieving a 'reconstitution' or 'synthesis' of his personal history (p. 159).[7] The quest for the father, killed by Republicans in the war, will be fruitless: Alvaro is 'unable to

---

[7] For a Lyotardian reading of history in the trilogy, see Abigail Lee Six, 'Breaking Rules, Making History: A Postmodern Reading of Historiography in Juan Goytisolo's Fiction', in *History and Post-War Writing* (Amsterdam, 1990), 33–60; for a Bakhtinian reading, see Ariel del Barrio, *Dialogismo y novela: el principio dialógico en las novelas de Juan Goytisolo* (Santiago, 1990).

know' his father (p. 154). And this interruption of the generative process is experienced as loss, not liberation.

The residual nostalgia for reproduction (of the family and of its history) is supplemented by a compulsory heterosexuality which legitimates casual misogyny and homophobia. In his sentimental education Alvaro's conquests of women are inseparable from his social and political progress: thus his casual initiation into heterosexual intercourse with a Barcelona prostitute (p. 78) mirrors his introduction to the mysterious geography of the Catalan capital. Much later, Alvaro's encounter with Europe is compared to his deepening love for Dolores (p. 317), who comes to embody his past in exile (p. 336). There is thus little reciprocity in heterosexual relations as depicted within the novel: the woman is generally the vehicle through whom man explores his territory and in whom he invests his experience. A free spirit, Dolores is initially presented as the woman who longs to swim naked and pick up men in the street (p. 49). And when they first meet, Alvaro is captivated by her short, masculine hair and 'ambiguous' appearance (p. 325). But Dolores is only too willing to sleep with Alvaro's friend Antonio if he so wishes; and in the present-day narrative serves mainly to freshen Alvaro's glass and nag him to stop drinking (p. 135). Alvaro satirizes his fellow exiles for the way in which their attitude to France is determined by the treatment they receive at the hands of French women: at first they are fascinated by Gallic language and culture; but after the first disappointment their 'manhood' seeks solace with a more conciliatory Spanish spouse (p. 251). Ironically, however, Alvaro's relationship with Dolores is not so very different in kind. And if he does not express the brutality and contempt for women that his friend Antonio shows for prostitutes (pp. 208, 222), Alvaro's use of women is also acquisitive and instrumental. He has indeed 'penetrated Dolores with his desire' (p. 181).

In the Oedipal fantasy of (male) return to origin, women also have a role to play: through cunnilingus Alvaro seeks to return to the womb which he wishes he had never left (pp. 120, 158). If Alvaro seeks to preserve the (male) past of political action from oblivion, here he also aspires to a (female) space of atemporality, outside phallic competition. As the representative of a displaced post-war 'generation' (p. 155) Alvaro can neither shoulder the masculine burden of paternity nor trust to the feminine function of reproduction: the only women in the novel who bear children are those whose anonymous biographies form the material for a documentary that Alvaro never completes (p. 382). Amongst the new 'freedoms' of Spain in the Sixties is the 'freedom to procreate absurd children' (p. 231). Filiation is re-established only in a grotesque form.

But if (physical) reproduction is disrupted or ridiculed in *Señas*, Goytisolo continues to reproduce misogynistic and homophobic images in the novel. Thus a dissolute college friend of Alvaro remarks that the only interesting people in Barcelona are 'whores and queers'; and Alvaro himself pours scorn on 'frigid' women (pp. 75, 145). Amongst the male friends who help Alvaro in his project of self-discovery is Paco, affectionately called 'maricón' by the others (p. 235), as are at least three other characters in twenty pages (pp. 279, 286, 298). Here Goytisolo is satirizing youthful exiles in Paris, whose lack of success with Parisiennes makes them eager to insult prospective rivals. But it is not enough to say that such language was (and is) part of everyday (heterosexual) speech. For the narrator himself is the vehicle for a more insidious homophobia: thus amongst prisoners held by police in Barcelona is a callow youth ('jovencito') recognized by a rouged and buttonholed queen; one drunken evening in Paris, Alvaro finds himself in a 'curious' literary salon full of pale 'jovencitos' with gazelle-like eyes; and men in a Venetian bar are said to have dyed hair and sport 'little gold chains' ('cadenitas')(pp. 264, 265, 360). The repetition of the dismissive diminutive ending is significant here. For it reinforces stereotypes of homosexuality as criminal, effeminate, and effete. More importantly, however, homosexuality appears to be ubiquitous, even as it is exiled from the central space of the narrative, attributed to secondary and marginal characters. As Hocquenghem says (*Desire*, 59), there is clearly a desiring relation between disciplinary forces and the homosexual subjects they pursue: the policeman mimes anal penetration behind the *jovencito*'s back. The will to knowledge of government authorities, expressed in the police files cited at length in chapter 4, extends deep into the sexual arena. But homosexuality is also presented as one of the factors which disrupt reproduction and the smooth succession of generations: the scandal faced by even the best families include 'a queer heir' and juvenile leftist agitators (p. 286–7). Here homosexuality and political resistance are juxtaposed but not related to each other: Goytisolo chooses not to make the connection.

Elsewhere, however, there is a clear connection between political repression and sublimated homosexual desire. This is concretized in the leitmotif of the (male) hand placed on the (male) shoulder. Thus Alvaro's fascist uncle Eulogio of the 'brilliant black eyes' lays his hand on his young nephew's shoulder; the Falangist doctor does the same to leftist militant Antonio, just as (chillingly) the torturer had done in prison (pp. 134, 203, 170). The twists and turns of Goytisolo's homoeroticism here correspond to Hocquenghem's account of 'anti-homosexual paranoia'. For Hocquenghem, the problem is not homosexual desire, but fear of homosexuality. Through an unholy alliance of clinical and criminal institutions, capitalist society has manufactured homosexuals as a category marginal to society, yet central to society's disciplinary practices (*Homosexual Desire*, 35–7). It follows that homosexuality is inseparable from those dominant forces which have called it into being: as Hocquenghem puts it, 'the very mode of existence [of homosexual desire] calls into question again and again the certainty of its existence' (p. 39).

Rejecting Freud's definition of homosexuality as 'persecutory mania', Hocquenghem shifts attention to the (heterosexual) paranoia that seeks to persecute. In such libidinally charged sites as the law courts the 'presence of desire in the social machine' is revealed in a nakedly direct manner (pp. 42, 47, 58). The sublimation of homosexuality effected by the legal and medical establishments is thus 'the basis for the functioning of the great social machines'. It masks the triumph of the molar self (monolithic, inflexible, homogeneous) over the molecular subject (multiple, mobile, heterogeneous). Moreover, this external repression is internalized by means of Oedipal triangulation. Having discovered that the libido is the basis of affective life, Freud abandons his original belief that it was autonomous and polymorphous, and confines the libido within the boundaries of the 'privatized family' (pp. 59, 63). Homosexuality can then be safely defined as lack (the hatred of women) and desire as production replaced by sexuality as reproduction. The (newly privatized) homosexual is said to be narcissistic: 'by making his [sic] anaclitic choice on a narcissistic basis the homosexual is ... deprived of an object' (p. 66). Although it is defined in negative terms (loss, absence), this homosexuality becomes curiously substantial, indeed determining for the subject: 'homosexuality is no longer a relation of desire but an ontological standpoint' (p. 74). From a relative position it becomes an essential identity.

We have seen that *Señas* bears out Hocquenghem's first rule of anti-homosexual paranoia: that the legal system exists to discipline and punish perverse subjects rendered both marginal and ubiquitous by those same authorities. The punishment of scapegoats such as the *jovencito* prevents the generalized and sublimated homosexuality of male institutions (of prisons and political parties) from coming to light. However, elsewhere in the novel Goytisolo also reconfirms the second stage of Hocquenghem's argument: the existence of a privatized, internalized homosexuality fostered by psychoanalysis, which is not a criminal but an ontological category. In the first chapter the child Alvaro comes across the Andalusian migrant worker Jerónimo on the family estate. Jerónimo is said to have black eyebrows and a copper-coloured face (pp. 42, 44). Alvaro spends (apparently chaste) nights with him in the barn, even though he knows him to have a gun. When Jerónimo disappears he is revealed to have been a resistance fighter; and his loss, we are told, prefigures the suffering Dolores will later cause the adult Alvaro (p. 48).

This childhood episode goes unmentioned for some three hundred pages, only to return unexpectedly in the midst of Alvaro's account of his affair with Dolores. Alvaro confesses that there are things of which he cannot speak, 'holes' in his biography (p. 338). He goes on to recount a scene in which he picks up an Arab in a Parisian street:

Una escena familiar te ronda la memoria: estás en el París industrioso del canal Saint Martin y un sol invernal, rezagado, brilla sobre las aguas.

Paseas despacio. El árabe ha abandonado la contemplación del panorama de las grúas y suelta a andar a su vez, cauto y receloso, con las manos hundidas en los bolsillos. A una veintena de metros de él puedes observar a tus anchas sus botas de goma, los pantalones de burdo azul machón, la zamarra de cuero con las solapas forradas de piel, el pasamontañas de lana ceñido a la cabeza. Su presencia discreta gobierna la calle. Al llegar a los jardincillos desnudos del square tuerce en dirección al bulevar, aguarda sin volverse el semáforo verde, atraviesa la calzada y, tal como has previsto tú, continúa su marcha hacia La Chapelle bajo el techo del aéreo. Le imitas.

. . . El metro pasa zumbando encima de vosotros y su sacudida estremece brutalmente el suelo. Sustraído de pronto al tiempo y al espacio recuerdas que un día, en un hotelucho cercano, hiciste el amor (¿con quien?) aprisa y corriendo (era tarde, tenías una cita en la France Presse) y tu eyaculación había coincidido exactamente con el temblor provocado por el tránsito de los vagones. (¿Consecuencia lógica del ruido o casualidad pura?) Desde entonces, piensas con nostalgia, no has vuelto a probar jamás.

. . . (Como necesario horizonte para ti, el rostro de Jerónimo, de las sucesivas reincarnaciones de Jerónimo en algun rostro delicado e imperioso, soñador y violento había velado en filigrana los altibajos de tu pasión por Dolores con la fuerza magnética y brusca con que te fulminara la primera vez. Cuando os separasteis se fue sin darte su dirección ni pedirte la tuya. Tenía dos mujeres, seis hijos y nunca supiste como se llamaba.)(pp. 339–40)

A familiar scene goes round and round in your memory: you are in that busy part of Paris near the Saint Martin canal, and a late winter sun is shining on the water.

You are walking slowly. The Arab has abandoned his contemplation of the hoists and starts walking, careful and suspicious, with his hands in his pockets. Sixty feet away from you, you can easily observe his rubber boots, his coarse blue denim pants, his leather jacket with fleece lapels, the wool cap tight on his head. His discreet presence governs the street. When he reaches the small, naked gardens of the square, he turns in the direction of the boulevard, waits for the green signal without turning, crosses the street, and, just as you figured, continues walking toward La Chapelle under the rusty roof of the elevated. You imitate him.

. . . The train hums past above and its roar brutally shakes the ground. Suddenly removed from space and time, you remember that one day, in a shabby hotel nearby, you had made love (with whom?) on the run (it was late, you had an appointment at France Presse), and your ejaculation had coincided exactly with the trembling brought on by the passing of the train. (The logical consequence of the noise or pure chance?) Since then, you think nostalgically, you haven't ever tried it again.

. . . (As a necessary horizon for you, the face of Jerónimo, of the successive reincarnations of Jerónimo in some delicate and masterful face, dreaming and violent, had watched like a hallmark over the ups and downs of your passion for Dolores with the magnetic and brusque force with which it had struck you the first time. When you separated, he left without giving you his address or asking for yours. He had two women,[8] six children, and you never did find out his name.)(pp. 282–3)

The scene is 'familiar' (it has happened often) and the partner is lent a definite article ('*the* Arab', suggesting a number of nameless others). The narrator lingers fetishistically on the pick-up's clothing. And in the midst of this encounter he is taken back by involuntary memory to a previous occasion, in which the moment of orgasm and the rumbling of a metro train fortuitously coincide. The present sexual act is not described, is subject to an ellipse. Rather it is explained (parenthetically) as the compulsive repetition of a primal experience, the passion for Jerónimo. Homosexual desire is thus interwoven with the varied course of Alvaro's heterosexual relation with Dolores: it is caught up in the delicate tracery ('filigrana') of the libidinal text.

Here, then, homosexuality is presented in Oedipal form as a compulsion to repeat the past, an internalization of the external, an individual 'case history'. But it is also (and more positively) presented as a multiple, anonymous relation of desire, which is ignorant of origins and identity, and exists only in an eternal present. This new homosexual desire is directed not to the inside (the same of personal identity) but to the outside (the other man from the south: Andalusia or North Africa).

This eroticization of the other male (of the male as other) will be much developed in the later novels. But what is specific to *Señas* is the problematic status of a bisexual protagonist in a work which offers itself as an allegorical history of the nation. We have seen that Goytisolo relies heavily on heterosexual (indeed heterosexist) narrative structures: women serve as the medium through which male desire achieves transcendence and sublimated homosexuality dare not be acknowledged. But Alvaro's official *Bildungsroman*, in which he appropriates a named woman and a clearly defined north European territory, is interrupted and thus subverted by an unofficial and fragmentary narrative of anonymous homosexual encounters, which permits no development in time or space. This second narrative (which resists allegorization, which speaks only of itself) undermines the totalizing claims of the first. Exiled from history, from the orderly succession of generations, homosexual desire cannot be assimilated to the narrative of national identity. Alvaro's intermittent

---

[8] Probably better translated as 'wives'.

acknowledgement of his 'instinctive' search for love amongst Arabs and blacks (p. 366) betrays the uncomfortable fact that 'alongside . . . conscious political investments there is a system of unconscious libidinal investments . . . [that is] repressed' (*Desire*, 122). Although Goytisolo does not make the point himself, Alvaro's alienation from the working class and from traditional class-based politics suggests that the latter 'do not tolerate the interference of the private . . . in the sphere of official relations between the classes' (p. 123). Once more, homosexual desire is a disruptive anomaly. Moreover, the implication that sexual-object choice is arbitrary and impersonal (Goytisolo compares it here to magnetism and lightning) is incompatible with the naturalist idea of a literary character whose plausibility must depend on integration and consistency. In the traditional form to which Goytisolo clings here, a bisexual hero is simply too idiosyncratic to be representative of the national destiny, too anomalous to 'typify' his generation. Indeed, he tends to call into question the legitimacy of the term 'generation' as a way of approaching history.

Ironically, however, there is indeed a connection (unstressed by the narrator) between homosexual activity and political struggle. There are in the novel a number of scenes where resistance to power takes forms as multiple, fortuitous, and acephalous as Hocquenghem's 'pick-up machine' (p. 116). For example, charcoal-makers spontaneously rebel against the pre-war cacique; and Alvaro's fellow students stage a post-war demonstration in the streets of Barcelona in which participants are mobile, multiple, and anonymous (pp. 136, 245). Both these rebellions are doomed to failure. But (like the scene with the Arab) they point the way forward to new structures of politics and desire. If *Señas* tends, still, to reconfirm the belief in a (lost) plenitude of experience to which the individual seeks renewed access, it also suggests in spite of itself, the possibility of bypassing the Oedipus and hence the very idea of individual (sexual) identity.

3. *REIVINDICACIÓN DEL CONDE DON JULIÁN*: BARING THE PHALLUS

Deleuze defines homosexuality not as a (Freudian) regressive interiority, but as a 'relation with the outside', typified by 'the exchangeability and mobility of roles, [and] a certain treachery' (*L'Après-mai*, 9–10). The title of *Don Julián* alludes to one of the most notorious traitors in Spanish history: the legendary Christian knight who facilitated the Moorish invasion of the Iberian peninsula. My purpose here is to chart the sometimes surprising relation between sexual and political betrayal in the novel, a treason which focuses (like the competing definitions of homosexuality cited above) on the alternation between interiority and exteriority, the body and the state.

Like *Señas de identidad*, *Don Julián* juxtaposes a present time of writing with a past of recollection. And like *Señas de identidad*, again, it explores the complex intersection of a personal and a national history. The anonymous narrator (who is identified on at least one occasion with the Alvaro Mendiola of *Señas* (p. 58)), wanders through the city of Tangier, visiting a pharmacy for anti-syphilitic treatment, a decrepit Spanish-language library; the Arab steam baths or hammam. But this aleatory narrative, determined by the 'perverse geometry' of the city streets and extending over the span of just one day, is interspersed with multiple versions of a single childhood trauma (sometimes told in the guise of a rewritten fairy-tale) and anachronistic parodies of Spanish history (in which Seneca, Franco, and Isabel la Católica rub shoulders). As we shall see, 'perverse' (non-reproductive) sexuality has a much greater incidence in this novel than in the previous one, as does that other deterritorializing theme, the challenge of ethnic alterity.

The first section of *Don Julián* sets up a series of motifs which will be elaborated throughout the novel. First there is the Arab city, represented as heterogeneous, incommensurable, and atomistic (p. 21). Second, there are the pleasures and pains of phallic penetration, initially presented in the form of the pharmacist's syringe (p. 30). Finally, there is the history of the Spanish nation and its literature, whose 'natural' development is parodied in a mock-heroic paean to the 'river' of Castilian poetry, which flows inevitably from humble source to majestic torrent (from Lope to Lorca) (p.33).[9] The view of history as filiation or teleology (the succession of generations, the achievement of maturity) is associated with the praise of an idealized Castilian topography to be

---

[9] For intertextuality in the novel, see Alicia Ramos, 'Texto y contexto en *Reivindicación del conde don Julián* de Juan Goytisolo', *LD* 19 (1989), 171–5.

found in writers such as Antonio Machado. But for Goytisolo
the nation-landscape is a body: the 'bony' plains and 'fleshless'
boulders of Castile give way to a fantastic vision of a country
'oozing pus and greatness through the cracked fissures of its
scars' (p. 34). The idealizing abstractions of national myth are
here displaced by the all too material effusions of the body:
libidinal flux disrupts the stable territory of high culture. Even
'perverse' desire has been safely trapped within recognized
boundaries: Lope's *El castigo sin venganza* (an Oedipal romance of
incest and adultery) is quite literally 'bound' in a yellowing
volume of Spanish classics (p. 37). The narrator's crushing of
insects within the pages of such volumes is thus not merely an
adolescent gesture of rebellion against the fatherland and its
heritage ('patria', 'patrimonio'). It is also an attempt to establish
a new and aleatory topography, a corporeal territory: the splat-
tered insects produce 'capricious geographical forms, islands,
archipelagos' (p.37).

Central to this project of deterritorialization (of laying bare
the movement of desire in the social machine) is the division
between inside and outside. The squashed insects spill out their
viscera. But the first section of the novel is also full of internal
spaces which jealously preserve their privacy. Thus a young
Spaniard's body is a 'crypt' in which her country's civilization is
stored (p. 28); the toilet in which the narrator first urinates on
an unseen figure (a recurrent motif of the novel) is a 'grotto' or
'cave' (p. 58); the hammam is a Virgilian underworld, a (male)
enclave which lends itself to reverie (pp. 84–5). And the second
section of the novel opens with a call to move 'towards the
inside': 'hacia dentro' (p. 89). But here interiority is explicitly
gendered as feminine: a childhood fantasy is of the monstrous
flower-seller who inserts the infant into her 'cavern' (p.100);
dwarfish figures urinate into the 'cavern' of a grotesque American tourist, who has been (momentarily) killed by the snake-
charmer's beast (p.107). This vaginal space is coded as negative,
the locus of religion and nationalism, reserve and repression: the
narrator is forced to prostrate himself before the 'little chamber'
of the Virgin (p. 108); the Spirit of Castile lodges in the 'marrow'
of the body, its innermost sanctum (p. 111). And in the third
section of the novel, this 'feminine' territory is invaded, its inner
space violated. Thus in a scene reminiscent of the visit to the
Underworld-hammam, voracious groups of tourists explore

Isabel la Católica's vagina-grotto (p. 164); and the Spanish nation violated by Arab leader Tariq and his men is compared to a vagina ('coño') subjected to multiple rape (p. 172). In such scenes Goytisolo's desecration of the myths of Fascist historiography is wholly compromised by misogynist stereotypes: to exchange Isabel the saintly wife and mother for Isabel the lascivious striptease artist and self-flagellator is to remain trapped within the binary logic of Madonna and whore, active and passive, masculine and feminine. Such hierarchies require not inversion, but displacement.

But if Goytisolo leaves no space for female desire (the vagina is a receptacle not an agent), then male desire looms ever larger. *Don Julián* is a novel of phallic competition. The narrator humorously addresses his 'harmless and flaccid' penis as he urinates (p. 59); and the 'little lettuce' of the Spanish penis is often contrasted with the great snake of the Arab, the erect viper which will serve as a sceptre after the second Moorish invasion (pp. 126, 135). Goytisolo seems here to be reconfirming, rather than challenging, Hocquenghem's proposal that (patriarchal) society is based on competitive phalli. For Hocquenghem, the phallus is 'the One' (*Desire*, 81), the dominant signifier in our culture. It is the possession of a phallus which 'guarantees every man a social role' (p. 83). Subject to relentless symbolization, the phallus is the overt basis of social life, the object which reflects a man's image back to himself and to others. The phallus thus serves as a means of closure, of policing the social and libidinal territory: 'to centre on the penis eliminates . . . the other desiring machines, by means of the creation of a closed and univocal object-person' (p. 106). Contrary to popular conception, phallic competition is thus not characteristic of gay men, but rather of phallomorphic society: 'only repressed and imaginary homosexuality is competition of phalli' (p. 92). By identifying the Arab man with the phallus and by associating him with an idealized male friendship (the narrator and Tariq, his companion in arms) Goytisolo thus seems to be reproducing the structures of patriarchy and its stereotypes of homosexual desire.[10]

---

[10] For another attempt to 'subvert' the phallus through mimicry which succeeds only in reinforcing its privilege, see Lee Edelman, 'Redeeming the Phallus: Wallace Stevens, Frank Lentricchia, and the Politics of (Hetero)Sexuality', in *Engendering Men*, ed. Joseph A. Boone and Michael Cadden (New York, 1990), 36–52.

However, as Hocquenghem suggests elsewhere (*Après-mai*, 165) phallic penetration amongst men should not be assimilated to heterosexual intercourse. Freed as they are from the burden of social utility, homosexual roles are unstable and reversible at any moment (p. 162). Gay sex thus may 'mime' the straight version, but cannot be reduced to it. And elsewhere in the novel phallic penetration is no longer heterosexual rape, but is clearly open to reversibility. The phallic icons of scorpion, spider, or snake pierce their victims irrespective of gender: the boy-child is fascinated when the scorpion kills a grasshopper (p. 91); the man infected with rabies by a dog bite will infect the bloodstream of the healthy Spanish nation in turn (pp. 132–3); in the new version of Little Red Riding Hood to which I return in a moment, the adult will penetrate the child, but the identity of each remains unfixed, mobile. More generally, as the novel proceeds, the motif of phallic competition (of the great One) gives way to a proliferation of sado-masochistic perversions, the most recurrent being the act of urinating on a child: an Arab is said to have peed on a baby and the narrator does the same to an 'idiot child' (97–8). The final confrontation of wolf-man and child-victim also involves ritual urination (p. 223).

In an earlier sequence the narrator reads the graffiti on a toilet wall. They are 'polyglot glosses' addressed to the unknown God cited by Paul in Athens (p. 59), a God who clearly does not satisfy his votaries as they keep repeating the messages over and over again. One man seeks a woman 'for ten times a night', a policeman seeks a discrete man with his own room, one praises women 'from seven to seventy five', another hymns the virtues of 'disciplining' children (p. 59). Here the narrator (and reader) are quite literally confronted with the multiplicity of desire, which (as Hocquenghem says) cannot be neatly divided into the binary of homosexual and heterosexual (p. 35). As an 'arbitrarily frozen frame' (p. 36), each inscription bears witness to the irreducible plurality of the perverse. Hocquenghem claims that even in the singular the French 'pervers' (written invariably with an 's') is 'intrinsically plural' (*La Dérive*, 101). 'As opposed to the unicity of the normal', he continues 'perverse multiplicity contains incommensurable distances within itself . . . We are displaced along a vanishing point from the horizon instead of building a centred hierarchy' (p. 102). For Hocquenghem there can therefore be no 'type' or 'individual' who embodies non-reproductive sexuality: 'it is less a question of describing a perverse type, of identifying him or her, than of tracing with the finger lines of conjunction, encounters, in which individuality is abolished to give way to the display ["évidence"] of the most unexpected relationships ["mises-en-rapport"]' (p. 102).

This is precisely the result of Goytisolo's challenge to reproductive sexuality, at its most effective: rather than erecting a single or 'molar' oppositional term (such as a clearly identified homosexuality) he sets in motion a multiple 'molecular' machine, which carries difference within itself. He thus avoids the trap of a 'reverse hierarchy' whereby a stable homosexual identity would simply replace its heterosexual equivalent. The pyramid is substituted by the horizon (the *cas-limite* of subjectivity) and the individual by the subject position (sexuality as *mise-en-rapport*, not essential identity).

If we look more closely at Goytisolo's accounts of inside and outside (essence and accident) we shall find that they are subject to a rhythmic disturbance that has sometimes gone unnoticed. Thus Goytisolo seems at first to distinguish between mask and face, shell and fruit. In the satire on 'Spanish philospher-king' Seneca, the goody-goody son Alvarito exchanges his face for a 'granitic' mask, which becomes a fixed point of reference for the people (p. 116). He metamorphosizes into 'El Figurón' or 'figurehead'. But when (the same?) Don Alvaro is attacked by insects in the library, the collapse of his mask leads to dissolution and finally annihilation. Mask and face are here inseparable. Or again, in the fantasia on the history of Spanish literature, the narrator deplores the decadence of the Castilian language: the flesh ('pulpa') has dried out leaving only the shell ('cáscara') behind (p. 157). But as Goytisolo's own pleasure in parodying academic rhetoric suggests, there can be no simple division between ornamental and natural language. Such an attempt would be as absurd as the 'purification' of Arabic-derived terms from Castilian satirized at the end of the chapter (p. 197).[11] Once the old myths of cultural exclusiveness are lost (once 'olé' stands revealed as a loan-word from Arabic) the 'puppet' of

[11] As is well known, Goytisolo's account of the Spanish debt to Arab culture owes much to Américo Castro. See Marina Martín, 'Juan Goytisolo en deuda con Américo Castro: *Reivindicación del conde don Julián*', *LP* (1989), 211–23.

nationalism gesticulates in the void, its strings severed (p. 200).[12] But, ironically, Spain has already been conquered by global consumerism, reduced to a 'mask' or 'role' (p. 137). And this is a more insidious transformation which Goytisolo's new Moorish invasion cannot reverse.

Hocquenghem suggests at one point that we should 'faire l'homosexuel', play homosexuality as a role (*La Dérive*, 15). And I would suggest that it is as representation (as playing out or working through) rather than as experience (as identity or ontology) that we should read the final narrative of homosexual desire in *Don Julián*, the new version or versions of Little Red Riding Hood. I have noted how the various stages of this narrative are played out in different guises through the book before being given definitive expression at the end. And it is tempting to see this incident as both origin and end of the novel: the primal scene which explains the narrator's subsequent actions, the narrative climax towards which the disparate desires have been leading. In the opening pages the narrator promises 'a new psychoanalytic version of the fairy tale with mutilations, fetishism, blood' (p. 13). The second chapter introduces the motif of sadistic urination on a child (p. 95) and echoes the common place that a single scene of corruption may be the cause of a child's ruin (p. 102). And the final chapter begins with the child Alvarito raped by his 'grandmother' Julián's 'big cock' and thrown into a well (p. 209–10). The murder is at once repeated: Alvarito the bird is killed by a snake; Alvarito the insect is ingested by a carnivorous plant (p. 211). Finally the story is told in its definitive, extended form. The child receives his erotic education at the hands of the fascinating and terrifying Arab man 'Bulián', who initially professes love for him (p. 221). The boy's buttocks are sand dunes crowned by the palm tree of the Arab's phallus (p. 222). But soon he is subjected to urination and flagellation, and forced to betray his mother (p. 225). The child's innocent appearance at school and church is confounded by covert worship of the 'snake', and his body is eaten away by

---

[12] In *España en tres novelas de Juan Goytisolo* (Madrid, 1988), Gloria Doblado warns that Goytisolo's advocacy of 'anarchy' can lead only to the 'total destruction of Spain' (p. 166). She is apparently unaware that, on a textual level at least, this is precisely what the trilogy is attempting to achieve.

the (syphylitic) signs of secret vice (p. 226). Finally, he is forced by Bulián to commit suicide (p. 230).

Let us examine this final scene more closely:

el niño quisiera arrepentirse de sus crímenes, pero no se siente con fuerza para ello : sus sentimientos y facultades se han embotado y le falta la fe : el eterno castigo le deja totalmente indiferente y espera como tú la guillotina : la cortante caída del telón : con sus dedos deformes escribirá la cínica y atroz despedida que encopetados pajarracos nocturnos recitarán después ex cathedra para escarmiento y lección de futuras, carpetovetónicas y siempre mal generadas generaciones : como un sonámbulo cogerá la cuerda que tú le tiendes y la sujetará al techo : tus ojos feroces espían sus movimientos de autómata y tu fuerte compañera, la culebra, sale de su vellosa guarida y le observa también : radicalmente enhiesta y con la capucha tendida hacia adelante : oscilando al burilado son de la música que insinuas tú : mientras, encaramado en una silla, el niño se anuda cuidadosamente la soga en torno del cuello : desmedida y voraz : y se deja caer : contenido fervor que estalla como un fastuoso cohete : balanceándose : y así como en la mente del que agoniza desfila entera la vida en unos cortos instantes, así su primitivo candor fugitivamente aparece : delgado y frágil : vastos ojos, piel blanca : el bozo no asombra aún, ni profana, la mórbida calidad de las mejillas : y tal halcón al acecho, apuras la brevedad del milagro : abrazándote a él : serpiente troglodita, flagelador hircino : en simbiosis fulminea : impugnando la muerte que os cierne : monstruo no, ni bifronte, ni Jano : tú mismo al fin, único, en el fondo de tu animalidad herida (p. 230)

the child would like to repent of his crimes, but he no longer has the strength to: his feelings and his faculties have been dulled, he has lost his faith: eternal punishment leaves him totally indifferent, and like you he awaits the guillotine: the curtain falling as swiftly as a deadly blade: his hand with the deformed fingers will pen the cynical and painful farewell that coxcombic night birds will later recite *ex cathedra* to serve as an example and a lesson to future generations of quintessentially little Hispano bastards: like a sleepwalker, he will seize the rope you hold out to him and attach it to the ceiling: your piercing gaze follows his every robot-like movement, and your stout companion, the snake, emerges from its hairy retreat and also watches him, rising up the full length of its body, its hood thrust forward: weaving back and forth to the haunting, piercing, hypnotic melody that you are playing: as the child, standing on a chair, carefully knots the disproportionately long, voracious length of rope around his neck: and lets himself fall: pent-up fervor that explodes like a splendid fireworks display: swaying back and forth: and as the entire life of a dying man flashes past his eyes in the space of a few seconds, so the child's original innocence fleetingly reappears: thin and frail, huge eyes, pale white skin: not the slightest trace of a beard profaning his softly rounded cheeks: and like the falcon diving on its prey, you will hasten the miracle: pressing him to your bosom: a troglodytic reptile, a hircine flagellator: in a fulgurating symbiosis: impugning death threateningly hovering overhead: not a monster or a two-faced creature, or a Janus: you yourself at last, become one and indivisible, in the very depths of your tortured animality. (p. 195)

In Hocquenghem's terms (borrowed, of course, from Deleuze and Guattari) the passage seems at first sight to be an example of the 'perverse reterritorialization' of homosexuality (*Desire*, 79). When the 'codes' fail (when the alienation produced by capitalism destroys any sense of shared social meaning) then the homosexual will be set up as a 'case history', to serve as both scapegoat and licensed deviant. Thus in *Don Julián* the chaotic atomism of modern society after the dissolution of the national myths gives way to what appears to be a personal biography. And this case-history serves to unify and legitimate the disparate fragments of which the novel has so far been composed. The binaries, it would appear, are finally back in place: 'you' (Julián/ Bulián) endowed with the potent snake, watching his prey like a falcon; and 'the child', innocent and passive as ever, his lost purity reappearing at the moment of death. Goytisolo would thus seem to be reconfirming phallic closure and the rigid role-playing of (heterosexual) intercourse.

Yet it is significant that the victim here (whom critics have taken to be both a representation of the narrator in his youth and a symbol of traditional Spain) should be a child. As Hocquenghem notes of paedophilia: 'When one touches on desiring relations between minors and adults, one confronts the whole system of repartition which cuts off the child from the adult in each of us, and which separates them in the social body' (*La Dérive*, 109). The division between infant and adult is thus one of the bases for the psychic and social structures on which our culture is based. Rather than depicting a benignly egalitarian and reciprocal gay relationship, Goytisolo chooses a spectacularly violent and unbalanced homosexual liaison as end and origin of his novel. Like Hocquenghem, he refuses to be confined to a 'vanilla' homosexuality ('une homosexualité "blanche"' (*La Dérive*, 123)), one which is readily recuperated by a benevolent bourgeoisie.

And if Goytisolo seems here to trace homosexuality back to infantile trauma, which must endlessly repeat itself in different forms, then the texture of his writing in *Don Julián* (unlike in *Señas de identidad*) does not allow the reader to take this final passage 'straight', to read it as the representation of the unprob-lematically real. Indeed the scene of erotic performance is flagrantly theatrical: curtains fall, rockets explode, and the hooded serpent sways to the music of its master. And the two 'characters' represent roles or positions rather than stable ident-ities. At the beginning of the seduction narrative we read '"the" child: which child?: yourself a quarter century ago' (p. 214). But Julián is also addressed as 'you' and his name is constantly changing. The final union of the partners ('you yourself in the end') suggests not so much the symbiosis of past and present in an individual identity as the fragility of all sense of self. For the 'depths' of the narrator's being are called into question by the very language that serves to invoke them, based as it is on fantasy and parody.

In his introduction to *Homosexual Desire*, Jeffrey Weeks suggests (after Deleuze) that subjects can take up three attitudes to the Oedipus: acceptance, which will result in neurosis; rejection, which leads inevitably to madness; or critique, which Deleuze christens 'schizoanalysis' (p. 19). I would suggest that in *Don Julián* Goytisolo, finally, follows this last course: decoding the movement of desire in the social machines, revealing phallic competition as the theatrical performance it really is. To those angered by Goytisolo's phallocentrism, then, I would suggest that his texts at their best lay bare the role of the phallus as transcendent signifier, strip it of its symbolic veil, and wrap it in the curtain of representation. Just as polymorphous desire cannot be anchored to the single goal of the phallus, so Goytisolo's transparently intertextual writing refuses to be assigned to a single centred origin, be it character, narrator, or author.

The insistence of instability and reversibility even in the realm of the phallus is stressed in the last pages of *Don Julián*. The murdered child, now a 'celluloid dummy', is paraded through the market place and is suddenly reborn (pp. 238–9). The private space of sexual encounter and psychological investigation thus cedes to the public sphere of the Arab city and its multiple, acephalous groupings. Like the doomed uprisings in *Señas de identidad*, the 'human river' of the souk (p. 238) suggests that dispersal of identity, that critique of the privatized individual, which takes homosexual desire as its primary model.

4. *JUAN SIN TIERRA*: GROUPING THE ANUS

As its title suggests, *Juan sin tierra* (even more perhaps than *Don Julián*) is a novel of deterritorialization. The action flits from Cuban sugar plantations to Moroccan marketplaces, via the sewers of Manhattan and the fantastic landscapes of Spanish literary history. And the narrative abandons almost all reference to personal history: the reader is led back not to the primal trauma of infantile fantasy but to the scene of writing itself, in which the narrator confronts the virginal, white page with his phallic pen. In its satire on Castro's Cuba *Juan sin tierra* offers the most explicit critique of leftist politics in the trilogy, and in its parody of the modes of realism it carries out the most acerbic attack on traditional literary values. Moreover, in its frequent and explicit references to homosexuality, *Juan sin tierra* presents perhaps the best opportunity to trace the connections between the separate yet mutually determining spheres of the political, the literary, and the libidinal.

The first of the novel's seven unnamed sections opens with a voluptuous description of the photograph of a black woman singer on a record sleeve: her breasts heave like the waves of the Caribbean. The sensual promise of this 'queen of rhythm' (p. 13) has however been betrayed by the deadly repression of a monolithic government which is 'siempre Fidel' ('always faithful/ always Fidel')(p. 14). The Cuban plantation (now transported back in time) is the narrator's 'original sin' (p. 15): it is the property of the great-grandfather we met in *Señas de identidad*.

However it is also quite explicitly a 'stage set', a fictional space reminiscent of the nineteenth-century *costumbrista* novel (p. 16). And the actual slave-owners of the period are fused, anachronistically, with a number of parallel families: those of European royalty, Castrist oligarchy, and the celestial inhabitants of a Caribbean heaven.[13] These families represent the three discourses of economics, politics, and religion each of which is

---

[13] For politics and role-play, see Joan M. de La Cova, 'What Kind of Games are These Anyway? The Metafictional Play and Politics of *Cobra* and *Juan sin tierra*', *RHM* 43 (1990), 206–17. For spatiality and temporality, see Abigail Lee Six, 'Sterne's Legacy to Juan Goytisolo: A Shandyian Reading of *Juan sin tierra*', *MLR* 84 (1989), 846–59.

founded on the sublimation of the anal. Thus the slave-owners' 'throne', a toilet recently arrived from Britain, is contrasted with the slaves' communal ditch (p. 16). In the former, faeces are deposited in discrete privacy, as in a bank (p. 19). In the latter they are humiliatingly exposed to public view.[14] By enforcing a rigorous separation between human beings and bodily functions, between master and slave, the WC is a 'sublimatory' device (p. 20) which transforms the libidinal into the cultural. Thus the chaplain (the ubiquitous 'Vosk') lectures the slaves on Christian virtues: the Virgin did not defecate, for the diabolical 'eye' is a source of evil and degradation (p. 21); and he claims that, being more anal than whites, blacks are more easily tempted by sodomy (p. 23). However, in Goytisolo's parodic formulation there is plainly a desiring relation between the agent of repression and the objects of his surveillance: Vosk enumerates the multiple sexual practices he attributes to the slaves (p. 26) and recites an exhaustive catalogue of their supposed perversions, couched in the decent obscurity of Latin (p. 32). Vosk claims that the slaves' bodies may be in shackles, but their souls are free (p. 35). However, Christian ideology, stressing here that the black soul should be purified ('like sugar', p. 37) would imply the opposite: the soul is the prison of the body: for the supposed spiritual delinquency of the slaves is used as a rationale to justify their physical exploitation.

The anal 'grouping' of the slaves (enforced communal defecation) exemplifies their degradation. But it also points the way to a process of desublimation which will unravel the tangled braid of political, economic, and religious discourses. In 'Capitalism, the family, and the anus' (the fourth chapter of *Homosexual Desire*) Hocquenghem draws a connection between Freud's view of the anal stage as that which lays the foundations of personal identity and Marx's analysis of private property and the circulation of money (pp. 82–3). Before achieving anal cleanliness, the child is not a responsible person. *Propreté* and *propriété* are intimately connected: 'Control of the anus is the precondition of taking responsibility for property. The ability to "hold back" or to evacuate faeces is the necessary moment of the constitution of

---

[14] For the anal function in *Juan sin tierra* with particular reference to Francisco de Quevedo, see Héctor R. Romero, 'Sexo y escatología en las novelas más recientes de Juan Goytisolo', *Iris* 1 (1989), 177–86.

the self' (p. 85). Conversely 'to "forget onself" is to risk joining up, through the flux of excrement, with the non-differentiation of desire.' It is no accident, then, that when Goytisolo depicts the eventual humiliation of his slave-owning family it is through their involuntary emission of bodily fluids: struck down by the slaves' black magic, they exude saliva and phlegm over their white clothes; and menstrual blood soaks through the young girls' dresses (p. 449). When the masters finally lose control of their bowels, it is a signal for the slaves to abandon the plantation (p. 46). Goytisolo's 'excremental obsession' is thus not merely a gratuitous shock tactic. It is also a pointer to the interdependence of capitalism and reproductive sexuality, both of which sublimate the anal. I shall argue later that it also suggests a new model of homosexual desire which (unlike in *Don Julián*) is no longer dependent on phallic competition.

The second section of *Juan sin tierra* juxtaposes homosexual and heterosexual practice. The former is staged as a perverse spectacle for tourists. The narrator seeks out the most abject partner he can find in the souk: filthy, blind, syphilitic (p. 64). Sex with this 'fraternal and illegal body' is compared to birds of prey slashing at each other with their claws. European voyeurs, fascinated and disgusted, offer a polyglot commentary. One presents himself as sociologist, asking 'At what age did you first realize . . . ?' (p. 66). Here Goytisolo parodies the medicalization of homosexuality which, when challenged by the immediacy of present desire, can respond only by tracing it safely back to a point in the past. Another voice is heard saying that the lovers should be shot. And this anti-homosexual paranoia also takes the form of an anxious defence of reproductive sexuality: after watching the two men come, one (heterosexual) couple hurry off to their room to 'make a nice, blond baby' (p. 67).

But if the repression of anal and homosexual desire provides the basis for the great social machines, then the propagation of genital heterosexuality ensures that those machines continue to function. The coarse coupling in the souk gives way to the 'nuptial bed' of 'your enemy': the Reproductive Couple (p. 67). The myth of the latter is propagated by all nations in all the media, obsessively repeated by cinema, newspapers, and television (p. 67). Heterosexuality is thus inextricable from consumerism and the universal expansion of capital: the Third World provides a picturesque back drop for the exploits of the Couple in commercials for drinks, cars, or holidays (p. 68). And far from confronting the 'other' sex, heterosexual acts stimulate a delirious reproduction of the same: the two bodies are 'symmetrically disposed' and the Couple (which can neither age nor fall ill) are self-perpetuating, lost in admiration for themselves (p. 69). Tastefully displayed in the window of a department store for a respectful audience of shoppers, the Couple (their two hearts one (p. 71)) prepare for conjugal union by studying an illustrated manual of sexual positions permitted by the Church, those which 'without neglecting the generative aim provide the future parent with a gentle, moderate satisfaction' (p. 71). However, having decided to attempt intercourse with 'methodical precision' (p. 72) the Couple are disappointed when the expected erection fails to materialize. Punning on linguistic and libidinal 'conjugation', Goytisolo expresses their disfunction in conditionals and subjectives: 'if I had . . . you would have; if you had . . . I would have' (p. 73). However the 'word' (phallus) does not rise. The true narcissism, then, is not the homosexual seeking a fraternal body in the souk, but the heterosexual attempting to express a desire so ubiquitous as to be indistinguishable from the society that so tirelessly attempts to promote it. The acedia or aboulia of reproductive sexuality is the nausea of consumerism: no space is uncolonized by the same, no relation free of commodification.

Goytisolo next introduces a series of non-reproductive figures which erase the memory of the Couple: King Kong engages in cunnilingus with a willing female partner (p. 75); the writer enjoys his solitary, barren pleasure, akin to masturbation (p. 77); and from the sewers of Manhattan, reptiles invade city apartments through the lavatories (pp. 78–9). In such urban myths oral, genital, and anal mingle and fuse. But Goytisolo praises another antidote to reproduction: the drag queen (Spanish 'loca'). Descending to a 'crypt' in search of the sacred snake, the narrator comes across a flurry of fellow worshippers: fanning themselves or turning up their fur collars; gossiping hysterically or powdering their faces (pp. 83–4). This agitation is a response to the repression of the 'tribe' to which they belong: since the time of Isabel la Católica and the *auto da fé* they have been impelled by 'ancient atavism' to embrace theatrical emphasis and hyperbole. The 'fantastic soliloquy of the queens' is said to avenge the memory of their king, here depicted as an elegant 'flamingo' (p. 85). The reference is to Enrique IV, the effeminate brother of Isabel reviled by Catholic historians.[15]

In Goytisolo's eyes queens seem trapped: their behaviour is primarily reactive, a response to a history of repression. But they are redeemed by their theatricality. Hocquenghem also praises the artificiality of queenly behaviour: the grain of madness typical of queens (French 'folles') is preferable to the 'bright agora of sexual identity' proclaimed by some 'liberated' homosexuals (*La Dérive* 18). The 'queen machine' ('machine folle') is irreducible to sexual 'reality' or psychological 'truth' (p. 141). Unlike successful transvestites who faithfully reproduce a feminine reality, queens are 'fictional beings' without psychology, more 'events' than individuals (p. 143). Hocquenghem goes so far as to distinguish the 'Latin queens' he has seen in Barcelona from the dull Anglo-Saxon gays who speak of 'responsibility' and 'emancipation' (p. 145). I would suggest then, that Goytisolo's praise of the queen can be linked to his critique of sexual identity and of psychological integrity. Like Goytisolo's fictional characters, queens have no fixed names or stable psyches; and both revel in parody and citation.[16]

In Goytisolo's new version of Spanish history the expulsion or annihilation of homosexuality is a constant, of which the mysterious death of Enrique IV is but one example. During the Reconquest Christian kings forced the closure of the Moorish communal baths, which were held to sap the strength of soldiers and incite them to sodomy (pp. 169–70); the *autos da fé* of the Inquisition—here described parodically in terms of a bullfight (p. 173)—drew some of their victims from amongst those who committed the 'nefarious sin' (p. 175); in the hierarchy of Spanish classes, the foulest-smelling and lowest person is the one most frequently given to sodomy (p. 196).

By way of contrast, Goytisolo offers the exemplary story of a child whose name is familiar from *Señas de identidad* and *Don Julián*: Alvarito. Disgusted by his bodily functions, the saintly child decides to stop defecating. Although the serpent tempts him to 'let himself go' (p. 205) Alvarito does not do so; and his

---

[15] See Dollimore, *Dissidence*, 312–13, for the link between the elusive 'homosexual sensibility' (much in evidence in this passage) and theorizations of colonial subjects and women also relevant for Goytisolo.

[16] See Dollimore, *Dissidence*, 297–9 for the 'containment' of transvestism in which closure eradicates its challenge to the dominant order.

self-control is rewarded when his faeces are miraculously voided through the skin as an aromatic exhalation (p. 206). Alvarito is emblematic of a constipated Spain which strains to produce undigested and compact literary works but sometimes gives off oliferous pearls (p. 210).

Rejecting this old empire of sublimation and the newer Communist 'utopia without an arse . . . where they neither fuck nor shit' (p. 217), Goytisolo proposes a burlesque grouping of anality: party officials will sit on their 'thrones' in front of the people (p. 221); posters of the leader's arse will be displayed throughout the nation (p. 223); there will be no flag or national anthem, but a radical democratization through communal defecation (p. 226). In further protest against the Reproductive Couple, a 'sex machine' like a Calder mobile will be set up, facilitating endless, anonymous couplings without distinction of gender, race, or age (p. 228).[17]

The use of 'structure' and 'construction' in this passage suggests the 'desiring machine' of Deleuze and Guattari, in which an infinite number of combinations are plugged into one another. This is what Hocquenghem calls the annular (anular) mode:

The anus's group mode is an annular one, a circle which is open to an infinity of directions and possibilities for plugging in, with no set places. The group annular mode . . . causes the social of the phallic hierarchy to collapse. (*Desire*, 97).

Goytisolo's destabilizing anal utopia dramatizes both the infinity of desiring relations and the collapse of the phallic hierarchy. Grouping the anus thus abolishes the difference between public and private (phallic and anal) on which social life depends:

Every man possesses a phallus which guarantees him a social role. Every man has an anus which is truly his own, in the most secret depths of his person. The anus does not exist in a social relation, since it forms precisely the individual and therefore enables the division between society and the individual to be made. (p. 83)

Goytisolo's advocacy of the anal thus provides a link between his critique of the repressions perpetrated in the name of revolution-

---

[17] Cf. the 'sexual pinball machine' of gay Valencian novelist of the 1970s, Lluís Fernández. I am grateful to Josep-Anton Fernández for bringing this coincidence to my attention. See his 'Death and the Angel in Lluís Fernàndez's *The Naked Anarchist*', unpub. paper read at Questions of Homosexuality conference, IRS London (June 1991).

ary politics and his attack on the 'normalization' enforced by the conventions of literary realism: both depend on a hierarchy of discourses and a stable conception of human identity and agency. In the holy texts of realism Saint Luke—alias Lukács (p. 249)—preaches that the novel is 'the objective reflection of socio-historical reality' (p. 254). Goytisolo makes a vital connection here between the realist novel and reproductive sexuality: both share the common aim of engendering 'live people' (p. 263). By quite literally killing off one of the few named characters in his novel (the execrable Vosk) Goytisolo thus proclaims to his readers the autonomy of a literature which (he claims) need not confine itself to reproducing the world (p. 284).

In the final *ars poetica* of *Juan sin tierra* Goytisolo inveighs once more against utilitarian models of literature and argues for a fiction based not on the progression of a classic plot but on the random grouping of textual elements: 'agrupaciones textuales' (p. 159). However, this need not lead to a sterile aestheticism. We seen that while refusing to reproduce 'reality', Goytisolo forces the reader to reflect on very material questions of 'race', gender, and sexuality. Indeed, one aim of Goytisolo's 'unproductive' writing is to counter the kind of utilitarian, procreative writing that 'changes the *crimine pessimo* into an existential metaphor' (p. 297). For Goytisolo (as for Hocquenghem) homosexuality is a desiring relation not an ontological truth: it resists symbolization.

Let us look, finally, at a passage in which 'race' and sexuality come together once more in a scene of delirious and anonymous lovemaking:

y el amor que hallarás junto a ellos será ardiente y estéril como las planicies del desierto : lejos de las grutas fungosas y húmedas que abrigan la nocturna actividad del agua soterrada : todo límpido acá : cuerpos nudosos, flexibles, cuya sinuosa trabazón evoca a distancia la escueta convexidad de las dunas : cuando la calina emborrona sus formas obtusas y el soplo abrasador del simún remata la labor de esfumino invistiendo al leonado paisaje de brusca palpitación animal : curvas y más curvas imbricadas en recio oleaje, comunidad promiscua que elasticamente se acopla sin deformarse, simultaneidad de tensiones y abrazos en la cálida y maleable textura : irradiaciones serpentinas que corren sobre la piel vibrátil y esculpen delicadamente sus líneas con sobriedad magistral . . . sólo músculo y piedra : deshecha, corroída, erosionada por la acción sostenida del viento : sin lluvia seminal que la fecunde : ¡seca, seca! : la verdura es esfuerzo y premio : el tronco solitario de la palmera indica la presencia invisible del pozo, pero no beberás en él : la saciedad común a los simples te asquea : el brote robusto del árbol desbarata sus leyes caducas, con orgullo bastardo apaciguarás lentamente tu sed : su savia amarga te basta . . . el desierto te invita de nuevo, vasto y tenaz como tu deseo, y te internarás en la maciza configuración de su implacable pecho cobrizo : brazos montuosos amurallarán la línea del horizonte, aislándote misericordiosamente del mundo fértil y hostil : paso a paso, sobre el escudo de su abdomen liso, alcanzarás el oasis más próximo gracias al fino instinto de los meharís (pp. 86-7)

and the love that you will find in their company will be as burning and as sterile as the desert plains: far from moist, moss-covered caverns that shelter the nocturnal activity of the underground water: everything is clean here: supple, muscular bodies, whose sinuous articulations are mindful of the smooth convexity of the distant sand dunes: when haze blurs their rounded forms and the searing breath of the simoom finishes its work of shading, imparting a sudden animal palpitation to the tawny landscape: curves and more curves superimposed in surging waves, a promiscuous community that resiliently couples without becoming shapeless, simultaneous tensions and embraces in the warm and supple texture: serpentine irradiations that run over the undulating skin and delicately sculpt its contours with masterful sobriety . . . nothing but muscles and stone: wasted away, corroded, eroded by the continual action of the wind: with no seminal rain to fecundate it: dry, so dry!: greenery is a sign of great effort and a reward: the solitary trunk of the palm tree indicates the invisible presence of the well, but you will not drink from it: the satiety common to the simple in heart fills you with loathing: the vigorous growth of the tree subverts its superannuated laws and with illegitimate pride you will slowly quench your thirst: its bitter sap is enough for you . . . the desert beckons to you once again, as vast and stubborn as your desire, and you will penetrate the dense configuration of its implacable copper-coloured breast: mountainous arms will wall off the line of the horizon, mercifully isolating you from the fertile and hostile world: striding step by step across the sheath of its smooth abdomen, you will reach the next oasis thanks to the subtle instinct of the Meharis. (pp. 71-2)

This passage follows the one we discussed earlier on the subterranean realm of Enrique IV and his court of queens. The narrator rhapsodizes on his love for Arab men; and the scene moves from the privatized internal space of the phantom court to the public external space of the desert. Even the bodies of the love objects seem to lack interiority here. Like the dry 'surface' of the desert, they conceal no inner space or secret liquid. The libidinal skin of the foreign body is fused metonymically with the landscape with which it is associated: the sand dunes which, caressed by the wind, are invested with animal mobility. The nature of the desert is endless flux, multiple imbrication; like ocean waves, the sand dunes register the successive pulses of (libidinal) energy without being destroyed by them. As in *Don Julián*, the phallic form of the palm rises once more over the desert. But the narrator refuses the consolation of hidden riches: desire is insatiable and interminable when confronted by the unbounded (deterritorialized) space of the desert. Like Father Foucauld and Lawrence of Arabia, the narrator seeks to merge with the other which is the object of his fascination: we are told that they become 'his' people.

Hocquenghem argues that there are two directions for homosexual desire: either the (Gidian) 'ascent towards sublimation, the superego, and social anxiety' or 'a descent towards the abyss of non-personalized and uncoded desire' (*Desire*, 81). In this passage at least, Goytisolo defiantly chooses the latter course: the anonymous, anti-social grouping or scattering of libidinal pulse. And paradoxically this 'abyss' is to be found on the surface (of the body, of the desert) and refuses the reassuring consolations of psychic depth (the pit or well). Homosexual desire thus implies the loss of identity for both subject and object: the second person addressee is both the narrator and those historical figures (Foucauld, Lawrence) who in Goytisolo's text seek abjection at Arab hands.

Goytisolo's aestheticization of the Arab body coincides with Hocquenghem's in *La Beauté du métis*. In a section called 'Passion de l'étranger', the latter proclaims: 'Perhaps I am only "homosexual", as people stupidly say, as a way of being for the foreigner/being abroad ["être à l'étranger"] . . . a way of belonging to him and being in his house' (p. 10). Once more the foreigner's body is a territory, as revealed by the pun on the twin meanings of 'l'étranger'. And once more homosexual 'object choice' is preceded by cultural difference, the same reinscribed within the other. In *Juan sin tierra*, as in *Señas de identidad* and *Don Julián*, 'race' is once more inextricable from sexual preference.[18]

---

[18] For 'race' and male homosexuality, see Kobena Mercer and Isaac Julien, 'Race, Sexual Politics, and Black Masculinity: A Dossier', in *Male Order: Unwrapping Masculinity*, ed. Rowena Chapman and Jonathan Rutherford (London, 1988), 97–164.

4. THE HOMOSEXUAL DRIFT

In the opening pages of *Homosexual Desire* Hocquenghem argues that the very phrase 'homosexual desire' is meaningless: desire emerges in mutiple form and any attempt to fix this movement will be 'an arbitrarily frozen frame . . . a fallacy of the imaginary' (p. 36). My reading of Goytisolo's trilogy of treason would tend to bear out this hypothesis: Goytisolo never considers homosexuality as a discrete theme or stable content, but always in relation to other terms: transvestism in *Juan sin tierra*; pedophilia and sadomasochism in *Don Julián*; heterosexuality in the bisexual protagonist of *Señas de identidad*. Amongst the catalogue of sexual variations he offers us, the one combination Goytisolo refuses to represent is the long-term homosexual relationship, the gay equivalent of the heterosexual Couple ridiculed in *Juan sin tierra*. Like Hocquenghem he seems to be nervous of a 'white', normalized homosexuality, one easily co-opted by consumerism and eagerly accepted by 'tolerant' heterosexuals. The logic of Goytisolo's argument would seem to coincide with Hocquenghem's: rather than be integrated into a capitalism which will cheerfully colonize all forms of desire, we should 'untie' or 'undo ourselves' from homosexuality ('se déprendre', 'se défaire' (*La Dérive*, 16, 158)). This is what Hocquenghem means by the 'homosexual drift'.

Goytisolo thus refuses to isolate homosexuality from both the reproductive sexuality which has produced it as its other and the infinite band of perverse (non-reproductive) desires with which it is fatally associated. And he constantly inflects it with historical and geographical determinants: homosexuality is consistently different from itself as well as from its rival 'frames' of desire. In the novels Goytisolo moves from a privatized, Oedipalized homosexuality of the old school (reproduced in *Señas de identidad*, parodied in *Don Julián*) to a more modern grouped, externalized homosexuality in *Juan sin tierra*. And his focus on the Arab pick-up in all three novels reinforces a vision of homosexuality as that present encounter which refuses to be traced back to psychic origin or infantile trauma. However, his abstraction and aestheticization of the Arab body (which always remains the same, which cannot be distinguished from the desert it inhabits) makes it impossible for Goytisolo to offer a historical account of Arab or Moslem cultures comparable to the one he makes for Spain.

One would hardly suspect from the novels that many of the countries he describes remain subject to dictatorships as bloody and repressive as the regimes of Franco and Castro so mercilessly parodied in the trilogy; or that in at least one of them homosexuality is punishable by death.[19] To acknowledge the specificity of Arab and Moslem histories would be to effect the radical change that is promised but not realized when the last lines of *Juan sin tierra* stutter into arabic transcription and (finally) script.

On the other hand, Goytisolo's idiosyncratic treatment of European history (his juxtaposition of Seneca, Isabel, and Franco) is no casual anachronism. Rather it suggests the rejection of (Western) history as an orderly succession of generations, a rejection which Hocquenghem ascribes to the disordering effect of homosexual desire. And if Goytisolo (like Hocquenghem) does not show us why certain individuals become 'homosexuals' and others do not, it is because (like Hocquenghem, again) he comes to reject the very notion of 'individuality', of a medicalizing case-history. Of Jeffrey Weeks's three objections to Hocquenghem, then, (historical specificity, individual particularity, gender difference) Goytisolo can only be found guilty on the last charge. The casual sexism of *Señas de identidad* and the fantastic violation of the woman's body in *Don Julián* reveal an unwillingness to consider the subversive possibilities that a specifically feminine sexuality holds for patriarchy and Eurocentrism. The all-male utopia of *Juan sin tierra* poses a challenge to reproductive norms, but the acknowledgement of lesbian desire would inscribe an additional difference, a continuing disturbance into that landscape.

In his critique of history, Goytisolo shifts attention from time to space, from generation to territory. His paeans to the delirious geometry of the Arab city suggest social structures based not on (Freudian) filiation or vertical hierarchy, but on horizontal contingency or grouping. The city is like the pick-up (French 'drague', Spanish 'ligue'): apparently chaotic, it is subject to a decentred, aleatory choreography in which each subject plays his or her accepted role. In Deleuze's terms, it is a 'desiring

---

[19] Since the Gulf War of 1991, Goytisolo's criticism of political (but not sexual) repression in Arab countries has been outspoken. See 'Juan Goytisolo: La mirada del Islam', interview with Elvira Huelves, *El Mundo* (7 Oct. 1990), 10–11. Goytisolo contrasts institutionalized Arab repression with the casual racism of Europe in 'Violencia de Estado y violencia social', *Cambio 16* (24 June 1991), 86.

machine', producing innumerable and continual relations between arbitrarily chosen terms. And if for the purposes of exposition I have presented the trilogy as a kind of homosexual dialectic (from Oedipus to phallus to anus) the irregular movement of the novels is more akin to the machine: thus the naturalism of *Señas de identidad* is incommensurable with the fantasies of *Don Julián* and the parodies of *Juan sin tierra*; and the random 'grouping' of desire is found in *Señas* as well as in *Juan sin tierra*, although it is given a more circumspect, less rhapsodic treatment.

Perhaps the most pervasive device linking the three novels is the use of the second-person pronoun 'tú'. As a 'sign of identity', an 'impersonal pronoun' (*Juan*, p. 146), it suggests that the subject is called into being by address, by linguistic interpellation. A sense of self is thus at once fragile and irreducibly material: both national and sexual identities are linguistic constructs. Goytisolo reveals once more the complex interplay of the literary, the political, and the subjective in the textual arena. And in his refusal to isolate homosexual desire from this general struggle he confirms Hocquenghem's suggestion that homosexuality is perhaps about to 's'achever' in the twin senses of the word: to reach a state of both perfection and conclusion. Hocquenghem goes on to invoke a favourite image of the annular:

But the revolts which [homosexuality] transmitted have disseminated themselves around it, forming one of those 'fairy rings' ['ronds de sorcières'] known to mushroom pickers, spreading out in concentric circles by means of an invincible movement towards the edges ['bords'], until the accidents of the terrain fragment and disperse them . . . and the ripples formed on the surface of water by the stone that has been thrown into it, constantly dilating, resonating, and cutting into one another, effacing one another, fragment the reflection of a homosexual character ['personnage'] weary of contemplating himself. (*La Dérive*, 20)

The notice of the death or dissolution of the homosexual subject was perhaps somewhat premature. But the image is common to Goytisolo: from the successive 'waves' of tourists and emigrés in *Señas de identidad* to the undulating flesh of *Don Julián* and the rippling sand dunes of *Juan sin tierra*. These decentred and acephalous fictions also chart the dissemination of circles of resistance, the interpenetration of lines of force. And they also serve, finally, to disrupt the narcissism of the same through the interference of the other, to fragment the reassuring image of a homosexual 'identity'. The question posed by and of homosexual desire thus receives no answer in the trilogy of treason: rather it finds expression in a continuing 'drift' away from the origin, in a textual spiral whose successive rings are at once linked and separate, parallel and discontinuous.

3
The Lesbian Body in Tusquets's Trilogy

I. LESBIAN BODIES

Esther Tusquets's trilogy of novels set in her native Barcelona is generally held to be the first substantial account of lesbianism in Spanish narrative: the first volume, *El mismo mar de todos los veranos* (*The Same Sea as Every Summer*) appeared in 1978, only three years after the death of Franco and the same year in which state censorship was abolished.[1] While critics have responded enthusiastically to the trilogy, they have seemed somewhat nervous of treating the theme of lesbianism at any length, and often prefer not to mention the word itself.[2] It is Tusquets's achievement, however, not merely to have given a complex and explicit account of lesbian desire, but also to have fused that account with a critique of class and nationality: the novels are set amongst the decadent *haute bourgeoisie* of the 1970s and juxtapose their received versions of Catalan history with the 'racial' myths of Europe and the New World.[3] The highly self-

[1] All three novels in the trilogy are pub. in Barcelona. Eng. trans. *The Same Sea As Every Summer*, trans. and afterword Margaret E. W. Jones (Lincoln, Nebr. 1990); and *Love is a Solitary Game*, trans. Brian Penman. The first gives an excellent rendering of Tusquets's labyrinthine syntax; the second version does not respect the Spanish original. There is as yet no Eng. trans. of *Varada*.

[2] Nina L. Molinaro, *Foucault, Feminism, and Power: Reading Esther Tusquets* (Lewisburg, Pa., 1991) is the only book on Tusquets's œuvre. It had not yet appeared when I wrote this chapter. Molinaro focuses on intertextuality, simulacra, time, supplementarity, and psychoanalysis. The most recent article is Mirella Servodidio, 'Esther Tusquets's Fiction: The Spinning of a Narrative Web', in Joan L. Brown (ed.), *Women Writers in Contemporary Spain: Exiles in the Homeland* (Newark, Del., 1991), 159–78. The only ref. to Tusquets and Wittig I have found is Stephen M. Hart, *The Other Scene: Psychoanalytic Readings in Modern Spanish and Latin-American Literature* (Boulder, Colo., 1991), 71–2. See also the same author's 'Esther Tusquets: Sex, Excess, and the Dangerous Supplement of Language', *Antípodas* 3 (1991), forthcoming.

[3] For lesbianism and colonialism or 'race', see the essays in *Hidden from History: Reclaiming the Gay and Lesbian Past*, ed. Martin Duberman, Martha Vicinus, and George Chauncey, Jr. (New York, 1990): Paula Gunn Allen, 'Lesbians in American

conscious form of these novels, their minute attention to psychological nuance, and their acute social satire immediately suggest to the critic three areas of concern: narratology, subjectivity, and social practice. I propose in this chapter that the question of the lesbian body (or bodies) problematizes each of these areas, prevents them from being penned into discrete territories, safely insulated from each other and from libidinal investment.

In each of the novels of the trilogy a central female figure, middle-aged and unhappy, confronts a crisis and seeks consolation with a young lover. Typically there is a triangle, in which the woman must choose between a female and a male partner. The names of the characters recur from one volume to another. Thus the first person narrator of *El mismo mar* is nameless; but the protagonists of both *El amor es un juego solitario* (*Love is a Solitary Game*) and *Varada tras el último naufragio* (*Beached after the Last Shipwreck*) (published in 1979 and 1980, respectively) are called 'Elia'. The name 'Clara' refers to the youthful lover in each book, although it clearly denotes different women in each volume. Tusquets's characters are, almost invariably, self-absorbed; and their narcissism is shown to render intersubjective relations (whether homo- or heterosexual) virtually impossible. The trilogy thus exhibits a compulsion to repeat: names, situations, and psychic traits recur in an oppressive circulation of the same. However, I shall suggest in the conclusion to this chapter that this insistent homogeneity implies not a neurotic restaging of psychic trauma, but rather a feminist subversion of identity, a denial of lesbian existence outside intersubjectivity.[4]

As we shall see in the next section of this chapter, the name of the youthful lesbian 'Clara' seems to imply an innocent or instinctive transparency that, on closer reading, is not borne out

---

Indian Cultures', 106–117; Eric Garber, 'A Spectacle in Color: The Lesbians and Gay Subculture of Jazz Age Harlem', 318–31; Lourdes Argüelles and B. Ruby Rich, 'Homosexuality, Homophobia, and Revolution: Notes toward an Understanding of the Cuban Lesbian and Gay Male Experience', 441–55, is an apology for Castroist repression. There is now a large number of studies on and by lesbians of colour. See e.g. essays in the collections by Cherríe Moraga and Gloria Anzaldúa, *This Bridge Called My Back* and Barbara Smith, *Home Girls: A Black Feminist Anthology* (both New York, 1983).

[4] For the sometimes competing demands of lesbian identity and community, see Bonnie Zimmerman, 'The Politics of Transliteration: Lesbian Personal Narratives', in *The Lesbian Issue: Essays from 'Signs'*, ed. Estelle B. Freedman, Barbara C. Gelpi, Susan L. Johnson, and Kathleen M. Weston (Chicago, 1985), 251–70.

by Tusquets's narrative. On the other hand, the name of the mature and nominally heterosexual 'Elia' ('ella' or 'she') suggests the violent hierarchy of sexual difference itself. Monique Wittig, the lesbian theorist and novelist whose work has been published in Spain in a collection edited by Tusquets herself, has suggested that the categories 'men' and 'women' are inherently political, and cannot be read as natural facts.[5] This chapter will interweave Wittig's radical and rhapsodic narratives of cultural feminism with Tusquets's more ironic and detached fictions.

In *Female Trouble: Feminism and the Subversion of Identity* (New York, 1990) Judith Butler gives a complex introduction to Wittig's theory of the lesbian body, concentrating on her polemical essays.[6] She begins by showing how Wittig refuses the binary of 'sex' (held to be anterior to a culturally determined 'gender'). Citing Wittig's paradoxical formula 'a lesbian is not a woman', Butler shows how 'the linguistic discrimination of "sex" secures the political and cultural operation of compulsory heterosexuality' (p. 113). If the oppressive category of 'sex' is discursively produced then the political task 'is to overthrow . . . the very grammar that institutes . . . "fictive sex" . . . as an essential attribute of humans and objects alike . . . without recourse to the pronomial differentiations that regulate and distribute rights of speech within the matrix of gender'. 'Sex' is thus a reality effect, produced by a violent process whose nature is to conceal itself (p. 114). In *Le Corps lesbien*, Wittig 'enacts the overthrow of the category of sex through a destruction and fragmentation of the sexed body'.

Butler goes on to argue that in Wittig there are two levels of reality: a 'pre-social ontology' to which lesbian subversion can gain renewed access; and a 'socially constituted ontology' iden-

---

[5] I cite the following texts by Wittig: *Les Guérillères* (Paris, 1969), *Le Corps lesbien* (Paris, 1973); and Sande Zeig, *Brouillon pour un dictionnaire des amantes* (Paris, 1976); 'Paradigm', in *Homosexualities and French Literature*, ed. George Stambolian and Elaine Marks (Ithaca, NY, 1979), 114–21 (p. 118). See also Diana Fuss, 'Monique Wittig's Antiessentialist Materialism', in *Essentially Speaking* (New York, 1989), 39–54; Namaskar Shaktini, 'Displacing the Phallic Subject: Wittig's Lesbian Writing', in *The Lesbian Issue: Essays from 'Signs'*, ed. Estelle B. Freedman, Barbara C. Gelpi, Susan L. Johnson, and Kathleen M. Weston (Chicago, 1985), 137–52; and the same author's, 'A Revolutionary Signifier: *The Lesbian Body*', in *Lesbian Texts and Contexts: Radical Revisions*, ed. Karla Jay and Joanne Glasgow (New York, 1990), 291–303.

[6] Judith Butler, 'Monique Wittig: Bodily Disintegration and Fictive Sex', 111–28.

tified with and produced by the 'straight mind' (presumptive heterosexuality)(p. 115). Language, then, does not simply interpret bodies, but rather effects physical violence against them (p. 116). The distinction between the real and the fictive (the concrete and the linguistic) is thus erased: the constructs of the dominant order are no less material for being culturally produced; on the contrary, they are ' "real" to the extent that they are fictive phenomena that gain power within discourse' (p. 119). The role of the (lesbian) text, then, is to act as a 'war machine . . . to universalize the point of view of woman [and] simultaneously to destroy the category of woman' (p. 119). Wittig's experimentation with pronouns (in particular her splitting of the 'I' into 'j/e') is part of this radically oppositional struggle against the 'heterosexual contract' (p. 120).

We have seen that, in spite of her stress on the constitutive force of language, Wittig still seems to appeal to a pre-cultural space or stage to be reappropriated by the disintegrative lesbian body. And Butler claims that her 'j/e' denotes not the necessarily divided self of a lesbian woman under patriarchy, but a 'sovereign subject who can wage war linguistically against a "world" that has constituted a semantic and syntactic assault against [her]' (p. 120). Likewise, Wittig conceives homosexuality as standing radically outside a 'heterosexual matrix' which is characterized by a systemic and hermetic integrity (p. 121). For Butler, then, Wittig's professed materialism gives way to idealism; her attempt to transcend 'sex' leads to an indefensible separatism; and her quest for bodily plurality returns the reader to yet another exclusive binary: the violent distinction between male and female is replaced by an equally seamless divide between hetero and homo. For Butler, however, 'lesbian and gay culture is . . . embedded in the larger structures of heterosexuality even as it is positioned in subversive or resignificatory relationships [to it]' (p. 121); and heterosexuality is 'both a compulsory system and an intrinsic comedy, a constant parody of itself' (p. 122). Elsewhere in her book, Butler associates parody with a new form of political agency, based on performance and masquerade. I shall suggest later that aspects of lesbian sociality such as costume and role-play also point (in Butler's words) to a 'subversive and parodic redeployment of norms . . . [a] site of parodic contest and display that robs compulsory heterosexuality of its claims to naturalness and originality' (p.

124). Disguises and play-acting are also vital to Tusquets's fictional enterprise, in which the (Wittigian) attempt to transcend power is shown to be impossible and the compulsive repetitions of theatrical performance become the only way out of the libidinal labyrinth.

Wittig and Butler would seem to agree that language and the body are the battlefields on which definitions of sex and gender are to be contested. However, Butler confines her analysis almost exclusively to Wittig's essays. And I would argue myself that texts such as *Le Corps lesbien* and its predecessor *Les Guérillères* (Paris, 1969) (texts which elude classification, which carry no generic marker) come closer to the ideal of parodic performance than might be acknowledged. Butler herself allows at one point that Wittig's 'fictions' (as opposed to her essays) enact a 'strategy of *dis*integration' in which the sex binary fragments and proliferates into the many sexes prized by theorists such as Deleuze and Guattari (p. 118). In Tusquets, also, sex is multiple and provisional.

A novel like *El mismo mar* is clearly quite different from *Le Corps lesbien*, which is a collection of prose fragments. In spite of their fluid syntax and fragmented exposition, Tusquets's novels do not abandon the naturalistic register and plot devices of narrative realism. Wittig, on the other hand, confronts the reader with a rhapsodic and oneiric text, a sequence of scenes which elude formal characterization and plot. However, both writers attempt to recreate a woman's space and language immune, temporarily at least, to male territorial aggression; and both combine a refusal to offer 'positive images' of lesbians with a suspicion of political programmes based on the Anglo-American model of 'individual rights'. More specifically, both also engage in the symbolization of female genitalia, the re-presentation in figurative language of vulva, labia, and clitoris.

I mentioned earlier that critics seem uncertain as to the status of the lesbian theme in Tusquets: is it primary or secondary, central or peripheral? They also tend to coincide in a number of other areas. First, there is the stress on mythical figures (Ariadne, Eurydice, Demeter), archetypes who can be read as idealizations of an eternal female predicament;[7] and the related attention to

---

[7] See Catherine G. Bellver, 'The Language of Eroticism in the Novels of Esther Tusquets', *ALEC* 9 (1984), 13–27 (p. 14); and Jones's afterword to her trans. of *El mismo mar*, 188, 190.

nature (plants, animals, the elements) as a pointer, sometimes ironic and disabused, to women's supposed closeness to the non-cultural world.[8] Second, there is the assertion that the novels are reflexive and intertextual, 'about' literature;[9] and that the textual references in them (to Homer and Aristotle, to the Bible and Shakespeare) reveal an erudite engagement with (mainly male) literary culture.[10] Finally, there are the intermittent appeals by critics to theories of *jouissance* and *écriture féminine* in French feminism,[11] combined with expressions of disappointment that Tusquets seems unwilling to offer politically 'correct' accounts of women's desire.[12] Her detailed accounts of heterosexual penetration and violation figure strongly in this argument; and I shall suggest myself that such scenes can now be read in the light of specifically lesbian debates around pornography and sado-masochism as 'threshold[s] of pleasure'.[13]

In the chapter that follows, then, I propose a new reading of all of these critical topics in the light of Wittig's challenging versions of the lesbian body. I read *El mismo mar* as a commentary on myth and nature; *El amor* as a critique of language and (male) culture; and *Varada* as a comedy or parody which rejects identity politics in favour of new, less direct, feminist strategies. The

[8] See Elizabeth J. Ordóñez, 'A Quest for Matrilinear Roots and Mythopoesis: Esther Tusquets's *El mismo mar de todos los veranos*', *CH* 6 (1984), 37–46 (p. 46 n. 5); Jones, 'Afterword', 189; Bellver, 'Language', 19.

[9] See Mirella Servodidio, 'A Case of Pre-Oedipal and Narrative Fixation: *El mismo mar de todos los veranos*', *ALEC* 12 (1987), 157–74 (p. 167); Linda Gould Levine, 'Reading, Re-reading, Misreading, and Rewriting the Male Canon: The Narrative Web of Esther Tusquets's Trilogy', *ALEC* 12 (1987), 203–17 (p. 204). For narrative and other 'codes', see Mirella d'Ambrosio Servodidio, 'Perverse Pairings and Corrupted Codes: *El amor es un juego solitario*', *ALEC* 11 (1986), 237–54.

[10] For the cult of literature, see Janet N. Gould, 'Reading the Love Myth: Tusquets with the Help of Barthes', *HR* 55 (1987), 337–46. For a comparison of Tusquets with Juan Goytisolo, see Geraldine Cleary Nicholas, 'The Prison-House (and Beyond): *El mismo mar de todos los veranos*', *RR* 75 (1984), 366–85 (pp. 381–2). For the male order, see Mercedes M. de Rodríguez, '*Para no volver*: Humor vs. Phallocentrism', *LF* 16 (1990), 29–35.

[11] See Nichols, 'The Prison-House', 367, 373; Servodidio, 'Pre-Oedipal', 173 n. 13.

[12] See Levine, 'Reading', 208.

[13] See Cherry Smyth, 'The Pleasure Threshold: Looking at Lesbian Pornography on Film', *FR* 34 (1990), 152–9; and in the same issue, Sara Dunn, 'Voyages of the Valkyries: Recent Lesbian Pornographic Writing', 161–70; Margaret Hunt, 'The De-eroticization of Women's Liberation: Social Purity Movements and the Revolutionary Feminism of Sheila Jeffreys', 23–46 (pp. 38–40); compare Parveen Adams, 'Of Female Bondage', in *Between Feminism and Psychoanalysis*, ed. Teresa Brennan (New York, 1989) pp. 247–65.

movement of the trilogy in my reading, then, is from a natural locus traditionally gendered as feminine, through the engagement with a 'masculine' cultural mode, to a hesitant and ambivalent woman's space, hard won and precarious.

The Spanish covers of these novels reinforce this movement: *El mismo mar* has a seagull flying into or out of a rectangle of sea; *El amor* has a window, half shuttered and covered by foliage, set underneath a fragment of another identical window that disappears out of the cover; *Varada* has a square of cloudscape above, and below it a seagull once more, but this time on a plain white background, outside the representational space. These covers (by Joaquín Monclús) not only suggest a movement from nature to culture and back again; they also imply a common concern for representation, for the necessary 'frame' or boundary that arbitrarily limits the frontiers of the narrative object: the gull is at once inside and outside the sea and sky it inhabits; the half-shuttered room both provokes and prohibits the voyeuristic gaze. The covers thus anticipate the main thread of my argument: that the lesbian bodies of Tusquets (and of Wittig) are not confined to the clearly delineated fields of physiology or essence;[14] that they are positioned on the liminal site or threshold between the physical and the linguistic, between desire and its representations.

2. *EL MISMO MAR DE TODOS LOS VERANOS*: MYTHS OF NATURE

El mismo mar begins with the words: 'I walk through the door.' The phrase is emblematic of a text which places liminality at the centre of the fictional space. The anonymous narrator returns to her childhood home, disappointed by her philandering husband's latest affair. She is 'submerged' in the gloomy entrance hall, the first of many internal spaces in the novel in which she will seek shelter or love. It is described as a church: a cool, damp refuge with light piercing the stained-glass windows (p. 7). Characteristically, the figurative term (the church) here precedes its literal referent (the former family home). As the narrator stands on the threshold, her eyes unaccustomed to the half-light, we have yet to be told where she is.

[14] My anti-essentialist version of Wittig thus coincides with Diana Fuss's (see n. 5 above).

If figuration precedes the real in this space, then art is preeminent: the narrator seeks out a classical statue (perhaps of Mercury) in the entrance hall;[15] and much of the rest of this first section of the novel (which is, like the rest, unnumbered and undivided into paragraphs) is devoted to a scene she may or may not have witnessed as a child: her 'blonde goddess' of a mother hiding the statue's bronze fig leaf amongst the shimmering crystals of the chandelier (p. 14). This game or 'ritual' of hide and seek, endlessly repeated in her childhood, came to an end when the leaf was definitively lost in one of its hiding places: the statue's penis, object of the mother's delighted laughter and the concierges' fearful distrust, now remains 'triumphantly' visible. This interplay of past and present, this shuffling of literal and figurative terms, will prove constant in *El mismo mar*. But so too will the references to a classical myth (Mercury and the Goddess) and the menace of male intrusion into a female space: the naked statue is an anomaly in a family in which men scarcely exist, in which women form a 'solid chain' (p. 141). The novel will raise the question of whether female desire must always refer back (as it does in this scene) to the phallus: the empty, but insistent, marker of sexual difference.

The narrator returns, then, to the large, gloomy flat where she had lived as a child. Abandoned temporarily by her husband, she receives little comfort from her 'divine' mother or distant daughter, who are unwilling to disrupt their travels or studies abroad. As the novel progresses she begins a brief affair with Clara, a Colombian student whom she teaches at the University; and we learn, indirectly and in disrupted chronological order, of the multiple betrayals of her life: of her husband's repeated infidelities; her mother's indifference; her father's affair with her beloved nurse, Sofía; and her own abandonment by an adolescent lover, Jorge, who had committed suicide. This sense of circularity, of repetition compulsion, is confirmed by the adjectives in the novel's title: 'same', 'every'. However, the 'sea' to which the title refers is metaphorical: it is the canopy of leaves that suddenly descends over the city in May, which the narrator remembers from her childhood. There follows an extended metaphorization of Barcelona (which remains, like the narrator, unnamed): the asphalt becomes pebbles, the cars fishes (p. 17).

[15] Cf. Rosa Chacel's suspension before the classical statue as a child (see Ch. 1).

But this process is also a feminine phenomenon: the trees sprout buds like adolescent nipples or hang heavy with leaves like matronly breasts (p. 18). The sequence ends with the child's fantasy of being whipped with bunches of mimosa in a church decked with phallic flowers (p. 19).

Such complex threads of imagery (skilfully woven together) invoke the classical locus of Mediterranean myth. Thus the 'Aryan' mother, so different from her dark daughter, is compared to Athene, stately goddess of wisdom, while the mysterious Clara is a nymph or siren (pp. 34, 66). But the most frequent mythical reference is to Ariadne: the narrator believed Theseus (her lover Jorge) would rescue her from the labyrinth and the Minotaur she had created in her solitude (p. 72). But Clara, the Aztec princess from the New World, is also Ariadne, dependent on the narrator's Theseus (p. 87). The masculist myth is thus feminized, reversed. Clara is also compared to Eurydice: the narrator leads her down the staircase to the dark booth at the opera where they will make love (p. 132). I return to this scene at greater length below. Finally, we have Demeter, telluric goddess of the harvest, the dark 'subterranean' image of the narrator, contrasting with the bright and shallow Apollonianism of her mother (p. 34). In these images (which are interwoven in a complex sequence) we thus find three contradictory representations: of the woman abandoned (Ariadne); recovered (Eurydice); and autonomous (Demeter). The important point about their use in the text, however, is that they are intersubjective or relativized, applied now to one character, now to another.

In Wittig, also, femininity is inseparable from classical myth. Thus the first fragment of *Le Corps lesbien* invokes a black and gold Gehenna in which the anonymous 'j/e' slowly dismembers her 'siren-voiced' lover (p. 7). Later, 'j/e' is retrieved from the Underworld by a feminine Orpheus, who does not flinch from a Eurydice whose flesh falls, rotten, from her bones (p. 11). As in Tusquets, myth and legend are feminized, in the persons of 'Ulyssea', 'Achillea', 'Ganymedea' (pp. 16, 30, 39). And once more these representations are not fixed archetypes, but rather are reversible and provisional: now 'j/e' seeks out the beloved, now she seeks out 'j/e'. Indeed Wittig's favourite myths stress plurality and metamorphosis: the lover has a thousand eyes (is she hydra or medusa?); two female sphinxes ('sphyngesses') reach union on the beach and disperse into grains of sand (pp.

10, 46). However, as we shall see later, reversibility does not imply that power relations have been transcended: in each of Wittig's 'scenes' (each of Tusquets's amorous encounters) one partner is dominant and the other submissive.

Myth is associated with costume. The narrator's grandmother, notoriously, attended fancy-dress parties dressed as an androgynous devil or siren (p. 148). It seems possible, then, that myth serves not to naturalize women's position (to abstract them from historical determination), but to offer them a relatively autonomous space within an oppressive social structure. Tusquets thus tends to confirm a recent suggestion that costume presents lesbian women with a means of exploring the complex contradictions in which they are placed. Thus when the narrator takes Clara to the opera house she is surprised to find the younger woman wearing a fur coat over her habitual jeans: what can it signify (p. 126)? Just as the opera house is at once a 'parody' of Catalan culture and the most 'authentic temple of [her] race' (p. 126), so Clara's gesture reveals she is both implicated in and excluded from the social codes of the fashion system. The relation between heterosexual high culture and lesbian costume is thus not one of original to copy, or primary to secondary: as Judith Butler says of men in drag, disguise 'subverts the distinction between inner and outer . . . sex and gender are denaturalized by means of a performance which . . . dramatizes the cultural mechanism of their fabricated unity' (pp. 137–8). When the norm is revealed as spectacle (the bourgeois audience is as theatrical as anything on the stage) then deviation can no longer be dismissed as inauthentic.

The archetypes of myth are thus displaced by the provisional impersonations of costume. But, what of nature, the other idealizing sphere of female representation? We have already seen that in Tusquets's image repertoire the green sea of vegetation is identified with the woman's body. And it is possible to read the novel in terms of a 'cultural feminism' which seeks to (re)create in nature a separate womanly space, innocent of male aggression. Thus the narrator's mother smells of the forest (p. 74); the narrator takes Clara to the 'green well' of the woods by her grandmother's house, where Demeter dances with the Minotaur (p. 81); and Clara is compared to vegetation or flowers (p. 90), her vagina a 'grotto' at the bottom of the ocean (p. 139). But if we examine the scenes which juxtapose the young lover and the sea, this naturalization of the feminine (this abstraction of the lesbian body) seems untenable. When the women go on a boat trip natural images are indeed prominent: the sleek lesbian bourgeoise who accompanies them is a 'black swan'; Clara, by comparison, is an 'ugly duckling' (pp. 105, 106). When the first removes her clothing she remains artificial, her nakedness a new disguise; the vulnerable Clara, however, seems to be the very essence of nakedness. Later that day the narrator and Clara embrace for the first time. The kisses are described in terms of the sea again: furious waves which 'crash' against the narrator (p. 112).

In spite of the power of this passage, the context in which it is placed tends to denaturalize, rather than idealize, lesbian desire. Thus the sea trip follows a party at which the 'black swan' (a predatory lesbian who attempts to seduce the narrator) is described as a precious object, purchased by her husband to adorn his house. The lovemaking of this 'object' with a stereotypical French girl is described, as if from a distance, as a 'strange struggle' (pp. 104, 114). And the embraces with Clara lead not to a fusion of the feminine principle and mother nature, but to a complex interplay of women's myths (Clara as a witch on a broomstick), male archetypes (the narrator as a captain on a ship that has run aground), and defiantly unlyrical physicality (Clara's body as a 'bog')(pp. 115–17). I would suggest, then, that Clara's supposed 'innocence' is by no means natural or transparent: Tusquets shows rather how Clara is constructed in such a way as to be vulnerable, as to be repeatedly open to the violence of fictive sex. This is not to deny the lyricism and eroticism of the depiction of lesbianism here. Rather it is to acknowledge that for Tusquets any escape from the rigours of patriarchy will be hesitant and provisional: the space where Clara first strips (and to which the two women return later alone) is a stretch of water marked out by a circle of rocks, a shifting and tenuous territory, one without fixed boundaries or defences.

In Wittig's separatist narratives also, the sea serves as the definitive locus for lesbian lovemaking: the lovers embark for Lesbos on the fluid that has flown from a woman's body (p. 20); sex on the beach leads to a literal merging of bodies (p. 52); and on the seashore 'you are alone as I [*j/e*] am with you opposite me' (*sic*, p. 71). Often this setting is combined (as in Tusquets)

with animal imagery: thus *j/e* plunges into the sea with a mare
(p. 110). However, even here on the classical island, nature is
scarcely innocent. If the sea is merger and fluidity, it is also
annihilation and death (p. 162). And if the earth is a telluric
woman, it is also the inescapable corruption of corporeality: a
woman retrieves the dismembered corpse of her lover from the
mud (p. 87); a couple's bones mingle in the cemetary (p. 172).
The scenes in which lovers are metamorphosized into she-wolves
or sea monsters (pp. 14, 43) suggest a minute defamiliarization
of the woman's body (an attention to the specificity of sensual
experience) rather than an absorption into a universal principle
of nature. Moreover, the utopian space of *Le Corps lesbien* is
thoroughly cultural, populated by women who fish or cultivate
the land. Likewise the female communities of *Les Guérillères* must
confront male aggression and contagion.

In Tusquets also (and more evidently) lesbianism is culturally
specific. Only idle bourgeoises possess the leisure, space, and
cultural resources required for a relationship such as that
between Clara and the narrator. And that relationship is
inextricable from the Catalan woman's fantasy of the Colombian
as a New World exotic. Lesbianism is thus by no means outside
the heterosexual world to which it remains invisible: it is the
narrator's garrulous married friend Maite who sets up the affair
between the two women in the first place; the 'black swan' or
'woman-object' is not presented as atypical of the decadent,
moneyed class to which she belongs. Most controversial, perhaps, is Tusquets's appeal to the language of motherhood to
describe amorous relations between women: thus Clara (the
narrator's student) is repeatedly called her 'daughter'; and the
women first make love in what was once the children's bedroom
at her grandmother's house.[16] This need not, as critics have
suggested, denote infantilization or the neurotic repetition of
childhood trauma. Rather the repeated references to 'rituals' or
'rites' in this context (frequent also in Wittig) point to a lesbian
reproduction or induction from one generation to another, a
process in which biological motherhood is deprived of the
privilege of primacy it is generally accorded. Just as in the

---

[16] See Elizabeth J. Ordóñez, 'Matrilineal Roots' (n. 7 above). Compare in a US
context, Rosemary Curb, 'Core of the Apple: Mother–Daughter Fusion/Separation
in Three Recent Lesbian Plays', in *Lesbian Texts and Contexts: Radical Revisions*, edd.
Karla Jay and Joanne Glasgow (New York, 1990), 355–76.

opening passage of the novel metaphor precedes literal term (church precedes family home), so here the pretended family relationship displaces its supposed origin: the narrator never received the passionate 'maternal' love she offers Clara from her cold and indifferent biological mother.

The reframing of mother-daughter relations within an erotic context thus serves to destabilize two previously discrete areas: Tusquets reveals both the repressed libidinal investments in the family and the often muted echoes of the family in libidinal relations. As Judith Butler puts it in a different context: 'The presence of so-called heterosexual convention within homosexual contexts . . . cannot be explained as chimerical representations of originally heterosexual identities . . . [but rather as] the denaturalization and mobilization of gender categories' (p. 31). The use of 'chimerical' is significant here. Even the most monstrous or evanescent of Tusquets's and Wittig's figures of the lesbian body cannot be dismissed as fantasy, as mere myth.

Let us turn now to a particular passage, one we have mentioned several times already: the lovemaking in the opera house. It offers a characteristic exploration of myth, nature, and corporeality. Reversing and feminizing the old narrative, the narrator has led Clara-Eurydice down into the opera booth which is the property of her family:

en esta oscuridad grana, en este cubil con aroma a mar y a cachorro, en esta guarida cálida y aterciopelada donde me he sentado año tras año a lo largo de casi toda mi vida, en este templo mío donde asumo todo lo que soy y lo que no soy y lo que amo y detesto a un tiempo, mientras suenan trémulos —siempre desafinados— los violines, y las princesas cisne, las muchachas abandonadas en la noche de bodas, las sirenas enamoradas, aletean, se estremecen, agonizan en los brazos de un príncipe de cartón, y quedan lejos, tan lejos las cabezas confusas de los espectadores, y estoy yo sola, aquí, en esta primavera polvorienta en que me he sentido tan exaltada y tan triste, en que he tenido por primera vez conciencia de empezar a envejecer, aislada aquí con esta niña grande y flaca, con esta muchacha loca loca, de largo pelo oscuro y ojos tempestuosos, que se queda ahora muy quieta, como adormecida —sólo un estremecimiento fugaz riza a ráfagas su piel suavísima—, mientras la tiendo sobre las pieles lustrosas —¿será para esto que las habrá traído?— y acaricio sin prisas las piernas de seda, me demoro en la parte tiernísima, turbadora, del interior de los muslos, para buscar al fin el hueco tibio donde anidan las alas, y, aunque la ondina ha salido hace ya mucho del estanque, el rincón de la gruta está extraña-mente húmedo, y la gruta es de repente un ser vivo, raro monstruo voraz de las profundidades, que se repliega y se distiende y se contrae como estos organismos mitad vegetales, mitad animales, que pueblan los abismos del océano, y después cede blandamente, y desaparecen los gnomos y las ninfas, y yo no siento ya dolor, ni oigo ningún ruido, porque he llegado al fondo mismo de los mares, y todo es aquí silencio, y todo es azul, y me adentro despacio, apartando las algas con cuidado, por la húmeda boca de la gruta. (pp. 138–9)

In this bood-red darkness, in this den smelling of sea and young animals, in this warm, velvety lair where I have been sitting year after year for almost my entire life, in this temple of mine where I take on everything that I am and am not and that I love and hate at the same time, while the violins—always out of tune—play tremolos, and swan princesses, girls deserted on their wedding night, mermaids in love, flutter their wings, shiver, and die in the arms of a cardboard prince, and the heads of the onlookers are indistinctly far, so far away, and I am alone here, in this dusty springtime in which I have felt so rapturous and so sad, when for the first time I have been conscious that I am beginning to age, alone here with this big, thin girl, with this crazy crazy girl with long dark hair and tempestuous eyes, who very still now, as if asleep—only the fleeting gust of a shiver ripples her smooth skin—while I stretch her out on the lustrous furs—could that be why she brought them?—and unhurriedly caress her silky legs, linger at that tender, exciting part of her inner thighs, finally seeking the warm hollow where the algae nest, and although the undine left her pond a long time ago a corner of the grotto is strangely moist, and the grotto is suddenly a living thing, a strange voracious monster from the deep that shrinks, swells, and contracts like those half-vegetable, half-animal organisms that live deep in the ocean, and then it softly yields, and the gnomes and nymphs disappear, and I no longer feel pain or hear any noise, because I have reached the very bottom of the seas, and here all is silence, all is blue, and slowly, carefully pushing the algae aside, I enter through the moist mouth of the grotto. (pp. 108–9)

Like the entrance hall at the start of the novel, the booth is an internal (vaginal) space that suggests both confinement and protection. There is a fluid merging of figurative and literal here, the scarlet velvet of the seats mingling with the metaphorical properties of nature: the sea and animals. This 'temple' of Catalan nationhood both is and is not the narrator's: just as the booth remains at once separate from the theatre and confined within it, so the lesbian woman lives inside and outside the dominant structures of the 'straight mind'. In this precarious space, culture precedes nature: the stereotypes of fictive sex (mermaids and princes) cannot be excluded from the scene of lesbian desire. However, the heterosexual public is left far behind as the narrator, pausing for a moment to mention Clara's costume once more, caresses her body and comes to rest between her thighs. Here the feminization of myth and nature recurs, as the nymph Clara's vagina becomes a hollow in which seaweed nests. The cave is suddenly a voracious sea monster, fluidly metamorphosizing. But, finally, all cultural images (gnomes and nymphs) are dismissed; and the narrator, carefully parting the seaweed-pubic hair, prepares to enter the wet mouth of the vulva.

In this passage, as so often, Tusquets exploits syntax to reproduce the continuing deferral of gratification which structures her erotic scenarios. It is only at the end of a sentence three pages long that narrator and reader are led to the brink of the feminine fold. Yet this private erotic sequence is juxtaposed with the public spectacle that follows it of the funeral of the narrator's grandmother, in which the women of the family are dressed 'like Sicilian widows' (p. 141). Lesbianism in this novel is thus at best an island surrounded by the ocean of cultural convention. The affair with Clara is quite literally central to the book, but it is framed by male-identified passages at the beginning and end; and it is presented as the narrator's mature choice (as opposed to her adolescent love for Jorge), yet it is incapable of articulation within the adult world; and, finally, it is integrated into social hierarchy (with the narrator's bourgeois friends serving as go-betweens or predatory rivals), but it cannot be acknowledged within that hierarchy. The confined spaces of the sexual scene (opera booth, deserted house, circle of stones) do not open out on to the wider world of public signification: Clara builds a 'cocoon' for the lovers (p. 184).

The narrator abandons Clara and returns to her husband as soon as he calls her. But heterosexuality has rarely seemed as compulsory as here: the narrator is 'ridden' by her husband like a mare, 'crucified' like the butterflies pinned to the wall of his apartment (pp. 216–7). Where lesbian sex engages a free play of natural and cultural associations, heterosexuality is wholly alienating: a 'film location' in which the narrator is positioned by her husband like a dummy (p. 214). But as he penetrates her with his 'red hot needle' or 'arrow', the narrator (stifling screams of pain and pleasure) reaches orgasm. This scene has led some critics to think that Tusquets has not freed herself or her character from male identification.[17] But the disturbing possibility of a woman taking pleasure in violation will recur in the second novel of the trilogy. Belying as they do the more decorous myths of a feminine nature, such sado-masochistic scenes will prove to be even more complex and disturbing than they seem at first sight.

3. *EL AMOR ES UN JUEGO SOLITARIO*: LANGUAGES OF CULTURE

The second volume of Tusquets's trilogy begins with the words 'Una oscura llamada'. The translation renders this as 'A mysterious message goes out'. It is spring in the jungle and there is a scent in the air of fleshy flowers, of decomposing orchids. The female monkeys are on heat; and each male responds to a biological call meant only for him. In this opening sequence (references to which will recur throughout the novel) Tusquets sets up a multiple analogy between nature and culture, human and animal, instinct and drive. The question raised by default here is that of sexual preference. Is the text to be read as a naturalization of 'fictive sex': of gender division and heterosexuality? Sexual aim and sexual object (which in Freud's terms are merely 'soldered' together) here seem to be fused in the brute call of animal instinct. Yet this passage must be read in context. The curious rhythm of the apes, the lazy way they sniff the air and move from tree to tree, is compared to a pantomime (p. 7). I shall suggest in this reading of *El amor* that language and culture are indeed the effects and instruments of a male, heterosexual order that seeks to reproduce the world in its own image; but that this order is reproduced not through natural expressivity but, rather, through fictive performance.[18]

The story of the passion of the apes is subsequently revealed to be taken from an adventure story which the protagonist Elia read as a child: it was illicitly interpolated by its bored author and read out aloud by one of Elia's male playmates (p. 8). We are told that this act of reading aloud confirms the marginaliza-

---

[17] Linda Gould Levine claims that Tusquets 'project[s] a male mentality on to a female character [and] . . . misreads . . . not just her narrator but women's sexuality' ('Reading', 208).

[18] This is Judith Butler's argument throughout *Female Trouble*.

tion of the character, already distanced from her bourgeois companions by her 'exotic' parents who (in the Spain of the 1950s) refuse to go to mass and are rumoured to bathe naked in the sea (p. 9). The adult Elia looks back on the scene and laughs (p. 11). But as the city metamorphosizes into a jungle (p. 12), this fantasy of an unculturated sexual desire (a wordless 'call' outside language) will be played out in Elia's forthcoming affair with the teenage Ricardo, a 'simian poet' innocent of erotic education. But as the 'game' of sexual initiation unfolds in the novel and its moves are inexorably recounted in chronological order, the coercive binaries of innocence and experience, instinct and language, will come under increasing pressure.

The intermediary between Elia and Ricardo is the former's young lesbian friend Clara: silent, passive, and infinitely vulnerable. Through her mediation the couple finally confront one another in a sordid bar: Elia, handsome, middle-aged, and self-assured; Ricardo, ugly, youthful, and easily embarrassed. This is the 'ape' who has perceived her scent across the forest. In this subtly ironic scene, Ricardo's surprisingly learned discourse is equated with the cold rationality of the syllogism; and he laments Elia's ignorance of Freud's study of Leonardo 'which would have saved us so much time' (p. 27). But if this language is literary, and dense with cultural allusion, it is also a rhetorical performance: the silent Elia, infinitely superior in her knowledge of the world, compares his speech to a school recitation made at a prize-giving ceremony (p. 26). Yet even here there are real psychological wounds 'infected with pus' (p. 27). Corporeality is merged with rhetoricity in Ricardo's narrative of his own misfortune in love.

As the couple's meetings continue, the literarity of heterosexual love is frequently stressed. Elia and Ricardo are a play of mirror images, reflecting perfect inventions of each other (p. 35). Their 'literary' relation is founded on the invention of stories in which no one but they could 'mime' the necessary roles with such subtlety (p. 36). Ricardo's eventual declaration of love is wholly foreseen, inevitably part of the game; but is also 'terribly real and sincere'. It is a 'pantomime' once more (p. 37) in which gestures of affection ('mimos') are acted out for oneself and for the other.

As we shall see, Ricardo's 'scripting' of the love narrative will extend to lesbian relations also. Tusquets would seem to bear

out Wittig's assertion in *Les Guérillères* that language is always
already appropriated to the masculine (p. 162). But in her
depiction of normative heterosexuality Tusquets shows quite
clearly the process by which this appropriation takes place and
the violence it inflicts on women. Thus Ricardo's pleasure is
pornographic: he superimposes images derived from illicit films
seen in France on the bodies of Clara and Elia, the women he
knows. And when Elia allows him to embrace her naked body,
his 'outrageous anatomical survey' ends with him licking her
feet, a gesture Elia recognizes from Buñuel (p. 42). Infantilizing
her lover, she has given him the 'magic key' to the sweetshop or
toy cupboard (p. 39), granted him the phallus that she is, but he
does not yet have. But there can be no pleasure yet, merely
appropriation: Ricardo 'establishes the territory' of the woman's
body, taking possession of each fetishized fragment in turn (p.
41). The fantasy, however, is not reciprocal. For Elia, men and
women are two different species, and young girls must be taught
by alternating cruelty and flattery to play the appropriate role
(p. 43). And Ricardo's image of the vagina as a 'bottomless trap'
(p. 44) can be cured only by the projection on to the female lover
of the maternal function: pliantly assisting male *amour propre*,
Elia defers consummation, allowing Ricardo to cast himself as
the hunter not the prey (p. 45).

Heterosexuality thus does not end with the male/female dyad.
It requires the third term of fantasy, representation, or external
voyeur to make it complete: Ricardo recounts in detail his
adventures with Elia to the Clara whom he knows is also
enamoured of Elia, making the young girl the unwilling audience
to the 'stage' that is their bedroom (p. 46). Indeed, when Ricardo
and Elia finally make love in the most theatrical location of the
novel (a labyrinthine house of assignation in whose 'literary
decor' Ricardo recognizes the pornographic scene), Elia also
feels the lack of an 'audience' other than the mirror above the
bed to observe the 'exquisite scene' they have enacted (pp. 72,
78). The vagina changes from a 'ferocious mouth' of filed teeth
into a 'warm, upholstered lair' (p. 75). But this 'literary adventure', this game without rules or repetition (p. 76–7) is but a
circulation of the same: Ricardo notes the taste of his own penis
when he kisses Elia's mouth (p. 112). Like the various hands of
a game, then, the heterosexual 'comedy' is at once new and
always the same, circling back on itself. Tusquets thus seems to

coincide with Wittig in viewing gender identity as one of the effects of a male language or culture which presents those effects as natural origins, untrammelled sources of identity. But rather than mounting a Wittigian 'war machine' against the straight mind, Tusquets stresses, in this first half of the novel at least, the woman's pleasure in participating in the game, in finding her own perverse possibilities in the 'grammar' of fictive sex.

One powerful, but ambiguous, example of the constitutive nature of language in the erotic scene is the act of naming. In Wittig's separatist utopia the name is uniquely powerful: thus, on the one hand, the name of the beloved can never be spoken, must be punished by the direst torture if uttered (*Le Corps*, 44, 149); but on the other, it is to be celebrated, endlessly repeated in the amorous text (*Les Guérillères* is punctuated by dense pages of women's names). As in Wittig, Tusquets's women are deprived of patronymics, male markers. And their first names hold a terrible power: at first Ricardo dare not say Elia's name; later, he repeats it as he believes she likes him to (p. 89). His appropriation of her name mirrors his increasing control over the love game, just as Clara's baptism of Elia as 'the Little Queen of Cats' denotes a different, but no less decisive, act of fictive appropriation. But the homophone of Elia is also the pronoun 'she'; and the narrator mockingly plays on this textual difference which splits the oral identity in such phrases as 'Ricardo thinks of her, of Elia' ('en ella, . . . en Elia', p. 111). The trouble of the homophone (which can be apprehended only in writing, which cannot exist in speech) is thus parallel to the disturbance of names and pronouns. Unlike other more stable linguistic items, the latter are shifters; that is, they have multiple referents according to context. In his (initial) fear of the name/pronoun, Ricardo thus anticipates the gynophobia which will become rampant at the end of the novel.

The act of naming is a good example of the performative: the speech act that does not describe the world, but effects a change in it. And we shall return to language as performance, rather than expression, later in this section. However, if (masculine) language is alienating, what possibilities does Tusquets hold out for feminine or lesbian discourse in *El amor*? In the second half of the novel, Clara, the unwilling voyeur, becomes (at Ricardo's suggestion) an active participant in the erotic triangle. When she and Elia finally make love the latter tells her 'terrible, secret words' that she has never told male lovers (p. 103). These words (which are not offered to the reader) stand perhaps as an impossible lesbian language, similar to the language without vowels, the new, harsh and rhythmic language of women, celebrated (but not reproduced) in one of Wittig's fragments (*Le Corps*, 116). Lesbian language is associated with nature (the cats again) and with totality: where for Ricardo Elia represents an aggregation of different attractions or body parts, for Clara she is the absolute and indivisible answer to the demand for love (p. 120). Lesbian love is based on domesticity (Elia teaches Clara such refinements as the proper way to make tea) and on speech rather than writing (it is with Elia's voice that Clara first fell in love).

Yet each of these elements is shown by the text itself to be divided against itself and thus unreliable: the scruffy, ravenous cats of the alley are contrasted with the sleek pedigree specimens in Elia's pink bedroom; the pleasures of lesbian domesticity are highly class-specific, derived from the Anglophilia and internationalism of the Catalan *haute bourgeoisie*; and the simple presence of speech cedes to the ambiguous pleasures of absence: Clara can only express her happiness when she has left her lover's 'lair'. She too indulges in fabulation, albeit less coercive and baroque than Ricardo's pornographic scenarios. On the first night Elia asks her to stay, Elia prepares a dinner which seems like that of a 'fairy tale' and cradles her like a child (pp. 102–3). Clara cannot avoid comparing this night to one long ago when she was invited to spend the night with a blonde schoolmate: but is this memory or invention, 'recordar' or 'fabular' (pp. 99–100)? Likewise the internal (vaginal) space of Elia's apartment can serve both as a refuge and as a trap, as Clara discovers to her cost (p. 125). The shadow of Ricardo, male stage manager, is always present between the two women (p. 120).

In this novel, Tusquets's description of lesbian lovemaking is considerably more aestheticized ('vanilla') than its heterosexual equivalent: Clara 'shudders' as Elia places her hand between the young girl's thighs and ends up asleep in Elia's bed like 'a good little girl' (p. 104). As in *El mismo mar*, however, these familial echoes are ambiguous. For if Clara is seeking from Elia the love she was denied by a heartless mother, then so is Ricardo: it is not lesbianism that is locked into a repetition of the same but desire in general. Moreover, the intermittent reversibility of lesbian love (Clara cradles Elia as she cradles her) is confounded by a failure of reciprocity: Clara cannot tell whether Elia is laughing or yawning when she hides her mouth with her hand; but she recounts her most intimate thoughts to the 'queen' who is sometimes indifferent to the gift she is offered (pp. 115–18).

When the lesbian body comes in contact with the social it stands revealed as textuality itself. Clara's brutish mother cannot 'correctly interpret the meaning' of the amorous smile on her daughter's lips (p. 114). Clara's 'most secret and reserved intimacy' is not to be uncovered. Yet this depth metaphor is not natural but culturally produced. If homosexuality is to remain 'deviant' it must be kept always on the edge of public exposure. In Alan Sinfield's words: 'It must not be allowed fully into the open, for that would grant it public status; yet it must not disappear altogether, for then it would be beyond control and would no longer work as a warning against deviance'.[19] The innermost space of lesbian intimacy is thus called into being by the 'straight mind' that casts it at the very limits (on the very threshold) of representation. Clara is at once thrilled and horrified by the possibility that her open secret (so plainly manifested in a 'unique' smile) might be 'read' by her family.

The constant scenes of dismemberment in Wittig can be read in a similar way. Thus when 'Patroclea's' internal organs have been consumed by the flame her body is 'surface . . . without depth', compared to the image of 'Christa' on Veronica's hand-kerchief (p. 30). Or again, when one woman 'garlands' herself with another's internal organs: 'I ["j/e"] see myself displayed [or "spread out": "étendue"]' (p. 34). The depth of the body stands revealed as an illusion, a fantasy which the lesbian 'war machine' can discard at will. Some women have complained that in her stress on mutilation, penetration, and (lesbian) rape Wittig is 'male identified', merely reproducing in a different mode the dominant and violent fantasies of the male (see Butler, p. 126). Such scenes clearly pose an uncompromising challenge to those radical or cultural feminists who see aggressive sexuality

---

[19] Review of Eve Kosofsky Sedgwick, *Epistemology of the Closet*, *GLAN* 1 (Apr. 1991), 8–10 (p. 10). For Sedgwick and lesbianism, see Terry Castle, 'Sylvia Townsend Warner and the Counterplot of Lesbian Fiction', *TP* 4 (1990), 123–35 (p. 232). Castle is citing Sedgwick, 'Across Gender, Across Sexuality: Willa Cather and Others', in *Displacing Homophobia: Gay Male Perspectives in Literature and Culture*, ed. Ronald R. Butters, John M. Clum, and Michael Moon (Durham, NC, 1989), 53–72.

as a site of women's oppression, to be displaced by a womanly space of joyful reciprocity.[20] But Tusquets's ambiguous reproduction of male (as opposed to female) sexual violence against women is perhaps even more difficult to stomach.

At the end of the novel, having encouraged the apathetic Elia in her affair with Clara, Ricardo manœuvres both women into bed with him together, having plied the unwilling Clara with champagne and marijuana. The first version of this scene is from Clara's point of view. As the ever-vocal youth strips off her clothes, uttering 'grotesque, terrible words' (p. 128), we are offered a nauseous anatomy of the male body: greasy hair stuck to the nape of the neck, muddy eyes, and purple acne on cheeks, chest, and back. Ricardo covers Clara with his sweaty hands and thick saliva; Elia cradles her in her arms once more, calling her 'my little cat, my little girl' (p. 132).

The narrative now shifts to Ricardo's point of view. It is an 'exquisite scene', a masturbatory fantasy like those on which he superimposed the face of a porn actress (p. 133). But these women obstinately refuse to play their part for the 'great master of ceremonies' or 'puppeteer', the manipulator of 'generic' characters (p. 135). The aestheticizing Ricardo offers a lengthy comparative anatomy of the two women's contrasting bodies: Elia's ripe abundance versus Clara's immature austerity (pp. 136–7). But when Clara screams to be let free, and Elia tells him, finally, to leave her alone, he turns once more on Elia and, beating her savagely, penetrates her as Clara looks on:

y da vuelta de golpe al cuerpo de la mujer a bruscos tirones, a rudos palmetazos, y le levanta las nalgas, las rodillas de ella hincadas en la sábana, su rostro sepultado en la almohada, y la monta y la cabalga como —está seguro— derribaban y montaban a sus hembras en plena jungla los simios superiores, de espaldas ellas, sin poder los dos mirarse, ni besarse, sin poder hablarse, infinitamente distantes y solitarios, aniquilada la más remota esperanza de comunicación o de ternura, una Elia sin rostro —sólo su cabello, rubio desparramado sobre la almohada—, una Elia sin voz, privada finalmente del don de la palabra, de las caricias en las mejillas y en las sienes, de los besos tan suaves, sólo sus nalgas soberbias, duras, espléndidas como los flancos de madera de una nave, sus nalgas de hembra en celo, de hembra en flor, sus nalgas que se mueven envolventes, totales, mecidas en el oleaje que la vence y la arrastra, perdida ya la brújula, quebrado ya el timón, desgarradas

[20] See Margaret Hunt (n. 12 above), 36–8.

PLATE 1. The Good Homosexual meets the electorate: José Sacristán (*second left*) with screen wife María Luisa de San José (*far left*). Eloy de la Iglesia, *El diputado* (1978).

PLATE 2. Reproducing the father: José Luis Manzano (*left*) and Javier García with political

PLATE 3. The habit of desire: Chus Lampreave as Sor Rata with Yolanda's red dress. Pedro Almodóvar, *Entre tinieblas* (1983).

PLATE 4. The frontal set-up: First Supper in the convent with (*from left*) Lina Canalejas (Sor Víbora), Carmen Maura (Sor Perdida), Julieta Serrano (Mother Superior), Cristina Sánchez Pascual (Yolanda), Marisa Paredes (Sor Estiércol), Chus Lampreave (Sor Rata). Pedro Almodóvar, *Entre tinieblas* (1983).

PLATE 5. Laws of desire: Antonio Banderas as obsessive gay lover. Pedro Almodóvar, *La ley del deseo* (1987).

PLATE 6. Heterosexual asymmetry: Victoria Abril (Marina) and Antonio Banderas (Ricky). Pedro Almodóvar, *¡Atame!* (1990).

las velas, y más arriba la cintura fina, conmovedoramente breve y
frágil, la espalda dorada recorrida por un surco tenue y en la que se
dibujan los huesos delicados, y más arriba aún la nuca de la cabeza que
desaparece en la almohada, entre una marejada ondulante de cabellos
rojo y oro, reducida la deliciosa, la detestable Reina de los Gatos a una
grupa magnífica y enloquecida, a un sexo babeante y ardiente que se
abre y lo apresa y lo oprime como un fruto maduro, elevada o
disminuída Elia a su calidad definitiva, insoslayable, de hembra en
primavera. (pp. 141–2)

He turns Elia around, roughly tugging and slapping her body, and
makes her kneel on the sheet with her rump in the air and her face
buried in the pillow. Then he mounts her and rides her as he imagines
that the great apes mount and ride their females in the jungle, from
behind, so that the two partners can't look at each other, or kiss each
other or speak to each other, each of them infinitely remote and solitary,
without the faintest hope of communication or tenderness . . . This is a
faceless Elia (he can only see her auburn hair spread over the pillow),
a voiceless Elia, who has finally lost the power of speech and has no
sweet kisses for him, no soft caresses for his cheeks, nothing but her
magnificent haunches, firm and splendid as the curving wooden sides
of a ship, the haunches of a female in rut, of a female in flower,
embracing, absorbing haunches, rocked in a powerful swell that carries
all before it; the compass is out of action, the rudder is broken and the
sails are in shreds . . . Her waist is slim and shapely, movingly fragile
in appearance; her back is a golden brown, with a slight furrow down
the middle and just a hint of the delicate bony structure beneath; and
finally her head vanishes into the pillow, beneath a sea of red and gold
curls. The delicious, detestable Queen of the Cats has been reduced to
a madly twitching pair of splendid haunches, to a moist, hot orifice
which opens up for him and takes hold of him and squeezes him, like a
ripe fruit. Elia has been elevated or degraded to her final, essential,
undeniable character—that of the female in the springtime. (pp. 134–5)

This passage raises complex and disturbing questions about
women's relation to the male language and culture reproduced
here. The scene of sadistic sexuality seems entirely appropriated
to the masculine: Elia is violently turned over by the 'wild male
of the jungle' and penetrated from behind like an animal. She is
deprived of both identity and language, reduced to the partial
objects of her body: 'splendid' haunches and 'dribbling' vagina.
The appropriation of the woman's (fragmented) body, this utter
helplessness, is imaged in the metaphor of the ship tossed by the
storm, all control lost. It is no accident that this performance of
male gynophobia should be completed with a desecration of the

name Elia had been given by her female lover: Queen of the Cats.

Elia is thus unambiguously returned to her place as the female of the species in the human jungle. But we saw at the start of the novel that the story of the apes is precisely a story, one printed in a children's book. The vengeful sex performed here is thus not natural, but cultural, the fruit of learned experience. This is not to diminish its violence. Unlike critics who have claimed that literature is the object of Tusquets's fiction, I do not suggest that these novels be read for their supposed hermetic reflexivity. Judith Butler claims that the gendered body is 'performative', 'has no ontological status apart from the various acts which constitute its reality' (p. 136). When Ricardo re-enacts the myth of the natural male he at once produces and reproduces a fictive role that has devastating material effects. By calling attention to the presence of myth and culture, even here at the moment of most uninhibited sexual activity, Tusquets may be implying a critique of those dominant fantasies.

Most disturbing of all, however, is the loving anatomy of Elia's body in the midst of violation: the golden waist, back, and hair. Tusquets tests the reader's 'pleasure threshold' here. For we know that the lesbian Clara is watching. To whom is the spectacle of Elia's rape directed? Sara Dunn has recently suggested that in lesbian pornography women can choose with whom they wish to identify; they may even take pleasure in the 'otherness' of sex involving men, recognizing the 'perversity' of such desire in a lesbian context.[21] While Dunn's view is highly controversial, she does break with the traditional view of male voyeur and female object: other combinations are also possible. And she is rigorous in denying that the mere representation of sexual matter is inherently radical; for her, this is as mistaken as to view the sexual scene as a uniquely privileged site of women's oppression. Judith Butler asks whether there are 'forms of repetition that do not constitute a simple imitation, reproduction, and hence consolidation of the law?' (p. 31) Wittig claims that any gesture can be an act of reversal or overthrowing: 'Tout geste est renversement' (*Les Guérillères*, p. 27). By repeating the figures of male language, miming the gestures of male culture, Tusquets treads a tricky and dangerous path to new forms of

[21] See n. 13 above.

female agency. We shall see in the next section where this emphasis on performance will lead.

4. *VARADA TRAS EL ÚLTIMO NAUFRAGIO*: A POLITICS OF PARODY

Varada begins, characteristically, with a sentence whose subject is not specified: 'S/he rests her/his head sideways on the towel, and the sun reaches him/her filtered through her/his dark hair . . .' (p. 7). Many of the fragments of which this lengthy novel are composed start with similar acephalous clauses, forcing readers immediately to confront the questions of agency and gender. The hair metamorphosizes into a 'dark jungle'; and its owner, now revealed as a woman, thinks back over the different shades it has turned during her life: from the blonde of childhood, to the dark brunette of maturity, and the silver threads of middle age. It is a sign of the body as an index of temporality, of the 'flow' or 'discourse' ('discurrir') of time. The woman, named once more Elia, is at the beach; and the barrier made by her hair, arm, and towel is described as a 'tent' (p. 8). Here, as so often in the narrative that follows, the woman's body serves as a fragile screen against the perils of the outside.

As the first section continues we learn that Elia, after breaking up with her husband Jorge, has returned alone to the 'same sea' that they have visited together for so many years. Stretched out like a 'lizard' in the sun, Elia is exiled outside of history, her hair a 'blind' ('celosía') (p. 13), or semipermeable boundary between self and world. And that world (of heterosexual normativity) is aggressively, if unselfconsciously, theatrical. As Elia watches the boys and men show off in front of the girls and listens to the 'professional' mothers call out to their heedless offspring, she notes how all the 'actors' are in their proper places: the generations succeed one another, the roles are exchanged, but the 'scene' or 'stage' of the beach remains the same (p. 17). Elia is thus exiled from reproduction as well as from time: on the birth of her son she had felt anything but maternal (p. 9).

The title of the novel is soon explained. Elia has been 'vomited up' by time and life, 'beached' after the shipwreck of her marital failure (p. 29). The result of this abjection (literally, 'throwing down' or 'away') is her wish to retreat to the preverbal state of lizard or stone (p. 30). Elia is a poet, someone who deals in metaphor (p. 32); and Tusquets describes her grief in strikingly visceral terms, reminiscent of Wittig's lesbian anatomies: although she suffers from a 'terrible wound', she dare not strip off the bandages, lest she reveal the gangrened bones, smashed skull, and amputated limbs beneath. Anaesthetized by pain and drugs, she cannot check which organs have been damaged (pp. 44–5). As we shall see, Elia claims to be wholly dependent on the absent Jorge, the 'key' who unlocked the closed chests of her potential and deciphered the secrets of her identity. We are told that her life before Jorge is but 'prehistory' and her current position that of a 'lost dog', dumbly awaiting a master who will not return (p. 61).

However, if this Elia is more submissive than the protagonists of *El mismo mar* and *El amor* (requiring the mediation of phallic law to gain access to language itself), *Varada* also offers for the first time an explicitly feminist character, engaged in the struggle for women's social and political rights. Eva is Elia's closest friend, a radical lawyer married to the listless Pablo. It is only together that the two women can talk freely, sharing once more a secret key or code (p. 24). The capable Eva's sphere is not metaphor, but the real. She runs a 'kindergarten' for lost causes: utopian politicians or impoverished poets, women raped by their husbands or bosses (pp. 32, 50–1). While this vocation is somewhat ironized by the normally impersonal narrator, Eva is undoubtedly a success in the professional arena, winning many of the cases thought by others to be impossible. Moreover, Elia's dependence on her husband Jorge is contrasted with Eva's independence of Pablo. Unlike Elia, Eva is sceptical of the motives for her husband's social 'performance': would he strive so hard to recreate the role of a young and fit man, would he dive into the sea so perfectly, if he did not know he was observed by the women on the beach (p. 19)?

The first quarter of the book thus sets up two contrasting models of heterosexual femininity: woman as absence, silence, and psychic dependence (Elia); and woman as action, discourse, and social autonomy (Eva). Both of these women are contrasted with a curiously anaemic male (Pablo), who shares Elia's adoration of Eva, but lacks both women's commitment to their respective careers. With the introduction of a third woman, the young lesbian called (as in the previous novels) Clara, Tusquets raises for the first time in the trilogy the question of the relation between feminism as a political strategy and lesbianism as a psychic challenge to the heterosexual norm.[22] It is a question that will not be resolved within the novel.

Clara's language is markedly different from that of the other women. It is a language wholly composed of figuration, fantasy, and viscosity. When we first meet her she is being driven by Eva from the small town she detests to the house by the sea where the other characters are staying. Clara has been raised by her hated aunt and uncle: their harsh voices are 'wasps' pursuing her; her aunt is a 'serpent', a wax or eyeless woman; her uncle a 'toad' (pp. 61–2). These reptilian relations are contrasted with the 'bird-like' Eva whom she loves, the white, warm, feathery woman; and her aunt's 'parody' of maternity with the real, lost mother, still cherished as a 'talisman' (p. 64). This family romance is of the body: in the village (Clara fantasizes) her viscera are visible beneath the skin to her prying aunt; on meeting Eva, her fantasy world becomes 'corporeal' (p. 63). Fearing the discovery of her 'marvellous secret' by the toad-uncle with his 'viscous body', Clara imagines a parthenogenetic matrilineage: now she has no father, but only Eva the 'feathery mother' (p. 67).

As in the previous novels, then, lesbianism is said to derive from childhood trauma, is conceived as a blind substitution of the lost maternal object. Moreover, in *Varada* it is also the space of abjection, of that nausea through which the hysterical subject seeks, in vain, to stake out the boundary between self and other, body and world.[23] Thus the defenceless Clara is described (like Elia) as a 'beaten dog'; she flushes and cries in the preverbal (corporeal) language of the infant; and Pablo lasciviously enumerates the parts of this mature female body rendered all the more attractive by its childlike unease: eyes, hair, mouth, breasts, and legs (p. 73). At night Clara becomes the hysterical subject, screaming out when she imagines muddy reptiles crawling over

---

[22] For lesbianism and psychoanalysis, see Diane Hamer, 'Significant Others: Lesbianism and Psychoanalytic Theory', *FR* 34 (1990), 134–51; Shirley Nelson Garner, 'Feminism, Psychoanalysis, and the Heterosexual Imperative', in *Feminism and Psychoanalysis*, ed. Richard Feldstein and Judith Roof (Ithaca, NY, 1989), 164–81; Joanna Ryan, 'Psychoanalysis and Women Loving Women', in *Sex and Love: New Thoughts on Old Contradictions*. ed. Sue Cartledge and Joanna Ryan (London, 1983), 196–209.

[23] For abjection and the constitution of the self, see Julia Kristeva, *Histoires d'amour* (Paris, 1983), 56–61

her body (p. 86). As unmediated physicality, she is unaware of
her own 'flesh'; and when pursued by men in the village 'vomit[s]
her disgust in interminable arcs' (p. 90). Her nightmares are of
'an architecture of smoke', or of a cemetery full of viscous mud,
insects, and rotten cadavers (pp. 92, 95).

Pablo makes a patronizing diagnosis of Clara's suffering,
claiming that she has mistaken her true sexual object and would
be cured by discovering 'authentic tenderness in the male' (p.
105). Rather than dismissing this rich fantasy life as infantilism
or error, I would suggest that it can be read as a lesbian strategy
which coincides with Wittig's anatomy of the erotic scene. Thus
in *Le Corps lesbien*, also, the lover is identified with a phantasmatic
architecture, a city walled up against 'j/e' (p. 35); and the
merging of self and other leads to the spitting out of the lover:
'tu m'es . . . je te crache'. Or again, the lover's body sinks into
mud, swims through algae, or falls into a pit (p. 49, 140, 157).
Most shockingly, one woman vomits up the body parts of the
lover she has ingested, only to devour them again; and another
is dissolved in fluid and absorbed through the proboscis of her
insect-lover (pp. 138), 172). Such scenes reclaim the visceral and
the viscous as spheres of erotic fantasy, in a queasy oscillation
between introjection and projection. They suggest a new mor-
phology of the woman's body based on a desire that recognizes
no corporeal limits, refuses to be limited to the part objects of
conventional fetishism. Likewise, Clara, the lesbian lover, suffers
an 'insatiable avidity' (p. 123). Like Wittig's classical tableaux,
Tusquets's metamorphic 'fairy-tales' take place in an atemporal
zone which cannot be reduced to the strict chronologies of the
unforgiving, heterosexual Eva (p. 118). And, as in Wittig once
more, the sexual scene is unremittingly asymmetrical: Clara's
gift of herself to the unresponsive Eva is absolute and uncompromising; she wishes to be used 'like an ashtray or nailbrush' (p.
140). The abjection of the lover is thus predicated on the utter
indifference of its object.

As the novel proceeds Clara is progressively marginalized.
While both Elia and Pablo initiate heterosexual affairs, Clara's
passion for Eva remains unrequited. Moreover, heterosexual
love is frequently described in banal, clichéd terms. Thus Elia
states repeatedly that Jorge had 'given her the moon'. Sometimes
Tusquets offers a male, heterosexual viewpoint whose status is
unclear. Thus when Pablo initiates his affair with a teenage girl

we are told that the time he has sex with her in his car is one of those 'rare moments when life is worth living' (p. 169). The treatment of this nameless young woman is particularly disturbing, suggesting as it does the stereotypes of male fantasy. She is animal-like, her nipples compared to 'twin blind beasts'; ignorant, apparently unaware of the identity of poet Antonio Machado; infantile, clutching a teddy bear in the 'doll's house' where the illicit lovers have made their temporary home (pp. 169, 180, 198). Most of all she is adoring, innocent of artifice and wholly enamoured of the paunchy Pablo. Yet even here there are signs that heterosexuality is no natural phenomenon, but rather a cultural and psychic performance: the girl is very conscious of her power, first entering the sea in a 'pantomime' of graceful movement addressed to the watching Pablo (p. 137). And Pablo (like Clara) is compulsively repeating a pattern established many years before: the unnamed girl is the image of an English girlfriend whom Eva cruelly compelled him to abandon.

And if we return to Elia and Eva once more, we find that although lesbianism is depicted as hysteria, heterosexuality is also (in Freud's phrase) a 'casualty ward', a staging post for the 'walking wounded'.[24] Thus Elia once saw herself as Antigone, the plain sister chosen by the handsome stranger; and as Sleeping Beauty, the woman whose sexuality must be awakened by a man (p. 100). Now she has been abandoned in the viscous place of abjection: 'the marshy bottom of a pond, a muddy abyss of weed and sand' (p. 101). And Eva, the independent woman, is no less alienated from her role: she has been educated from childhood to assume responsibility, forced to play the part of the 'strong woman' invented for her by others. Now it has become a 'shroud' (p. 130). Heterosexual love is repeatedly described as a 'farce' (p. 145, 201). The word is also used of Elia's lovemaking with the stranger she invites to her bed. As he toils over her zombie-like body she can feel only nausea and horror (p. 184).

Tusquets shows, then, that heterosexual experience is socially constructed for women and at a considerable psychic cost to them. And it is constructed in part through the fictional genres of narrative and drama: the grieving Elia laments her 'novelet-tish' style; the jealous Eva addresses Pablo as if in the alexan-

---

[24] Freud's essay is '"Civilized" Sexual Morality and Modern Nervous Illness', cited by Hamer (see n. 13 above), 139.

drines of French tragedy (pp. 184, 202). This drama of gender identity is based on repetition. As Judith Butler puts it: 'As in other ritual social dramas the action of gender requires a performance that is *repeated*. This repetition is at once a reenactment and reexperiencing of a set of meanings already socially established; and it is the mundane and ritualized form of their legitimation' (p. 140). In just such a way the traditional roles of femininity (loyal daughter, tender lover, abandoned wife) are repeatedly rehearsed in the novel. And it is only in their repetition that their claim to legitimacy lies.

Tusquets shows, then, that the identities women are compelled to adopt may be catastrophic for them: Antigone-like, they embrace the shroud. And she does so through parody, another form of repetition. Thus the discourse of each of the characters is ironized by the commentary of the others: Eva decries Elia's second-hand romanticism; but Clara is well aware of the limitations of Eva's heartless rationalism. Or again, Pablo mocks Clara's obsessional love; but she scorns his smug satisfaction at his affair with the young girl. The roles may be fixed, but the people occupying them are not. Tusquets's parodic narrative is thus disturbingly intersubjective, inviting the reader to identify now with one character and now with another and to ironize the discourse of each. The successive re-enactment of these various 'roles' reveals they have no ontological status outside the parodic 'scenes' in which they are played out. The fictions of gender identity are no longer tenable.

I would suggest that this knowledge can be political. Tusquets satirizes and pathologizes Eva's feminist commitment: she endlessly rehearses the role of the little girl who wishes to please her parents by taking on responsibility for others. But while Tusquets's dismissal of activism may be glib, it points the way to a different politics that is no longer based on female identity. In the final part of this section I hope to show that even in *Varada* lesbianism can be read (in Wittig's formulation) as a 'culture through which we can politically challenge heterosexual society on its sexual categories.'[25]

I have already suggested that for Tusquets, lesbianism is associated with abjection, in the twin senses of subjection to the beloved and projection from the body. But the term may also be

---

[25] 'Paradigm', 118.

used in its botanical sense, as an expulsion of spores from the parent plant. Thus, although in *Varada* lesbian desire remains unconsummated and marginalized, it is scattered throughout the novel in amorous visions of the female body ascribed to nominally heterosexual women. Thus Elia's first sight of Pablo's future girlfriend provokes a lengthy description of the latter's body from the older woman's point of view: the girl shifts from foot to foot; leans her head to one side with her red hair covering her face; and displays her 'impeccable, golden body, absolutely protected by her beauty, shielded by her extreme youth' (p. 147). This is the epiphany that first lifts Elia's depression, albeit momentarily and in a way which disavows any sexual pleasure. Elia is simply 'extremely sensitive to beauty' whatever the person's sex (p. 148). In spite of these qualifications, however, it is significant that there is no comparable scene in the novel in which Elia sings the praises of male beauty: Jorge, with his loping gait, reminiscent of the Pink Panther, inspires no such reverie. This is not, of course, to argue that Elia is 'really' lesbian. Rather it is to suggest that the lesbian desire that is not allowed expression in the novel is displaced or expelled into tableaux of erotic femininity set up for the pleasure of heterosexual women and men.[26]

But at one point in the novel we also find a rare example of the lesbian look. On hearing Pablo and Eva return to the house, the sleepless Clara, longing for her goodnight kiss, leaves her bedroom and makes her way quietly to theirs. She fantasizes on her childhood fear of burial alive (of cockroaches and spiders on her body) and the horror stories she heard as a child (of corpses and insects also). When she reaches the open door the couple are making love, the man's head between the woman's thighs:

Y ahora está petrificada aquí, acurrucada en el pasillo, con progresivo miedo a que la descubran, a que Pablo levante un momento la cabeza y la descubra, sin querer mirar ella y sin lograr no hacerlo, como no podía de pequeña dejar de escuchar las terribles historias que contaban las viejas en el cuarto de la plancha, fascinada y horrorizada, como no consigue tampoco en el cine dejar de seguir la película por entre los dedos por más que se haya tapado la cara con las manos, con miedo ahora a que la sorprendan y la riñan —dios, ¡si fuera Eva quien se

---

[26] This is rather similar to the 'metaphorical' lesbianism I cite in ch. 1; see Elizabeth Meese, 79.

incorporara y la descubriera!—, pero también progresivamente indignada, porque ¿cómo han podido olvidar estos dos la puerta abierta?, las sienes latiéndole con furia, el corazón desbocado, sofocándose y ahogándose en el pasillo oscuro, y la mirada fija, inmovilizada en esta imagen tan extraña —parece en realidad la fabulosa criatura de un bestiario imaginario, una araña enorme con dos únicas pinzas doradas y entre ellas la cabeza peluda y gris—, y después las piernas se agitan, se crispan, se contraen, le rechazan, y surge del lugar donde queda la almohada una voz alterada, desfigurada por la emoción —¡ven, oh ven, por favor, ven ahora, ven!—, que es sin embargo imposible confundir con la voz de Eva y . . . es la voz de una mujer desconocida, que se ha incorporado y ha aferrado a Pablo por los hombros, lo ha agarrado por la espalda y lo ha forzado a levantarse, a darse vuelta, a cubrirla, a penetrarla, y los dos cuerpos se agitan crispados, torpes, feos —de nuevo piensa Clara que se trata de un animal fantástico, de un ser repulsivo pero imaginario, que manotea histérico con sus ocho patas y deja oir unos sonidos cada vez más inarticulados, menos humanos—, sólo que a Clara ha dejado de importarle lo que parezcan o lo que graznen o lo que hagan, son únicamente una muchacha desconocida, un hombre al que detesta, copulando asquerosos y violentos en la cama . . . (pp. 197–8)

and now she is petrified here, crouching in the corridor, more and more afraid that they'll discover her, that Pablo will raise his head for a moment and discover her, without wanting to look and without being able not to look, just as she couldn't stop listening when she was small to the terrible stories told by the old ladies in the ironing room, fascinated and horrified, just as she can't stop watching in the cinema from between her fingers, however well she has covered her face with her hands, afraid now that they'll discover her and scold her—God, what if it were Eva who sat up and discovered her!—but also more and more indignant, because how could these two forget that they'd left the door open?, with her temples beating madly, her heart in her mouth, suffocating and choking in the dark corridor, and her gaze fixed, immobilized on this strange image—it really does seem like a fabulous creature from an imaginary bestiary, an enormous spider with just two golden claws and between them the grey hairy head—and next the legs move, tense, contract, push him off and there comes from the place of the pillow a voice that is altered, disfigured by emotion—'come, oh come, please, come now, come!'—which is none the less impossible to confuse with the voice of Eva and . . . it is the voice of an unknown woman, who has sat up and seized Pablo by the shoulders, got hold of his back and forced him to sit up, turn around, cover her, penetrate her, and the two bodies move tense, clumsy, ugly—once more Clara thinks that they are a fantastic animal, a repulsive but imaginary being which gesticulates hysterically with its eight limbs and emits sounds that are more and more inarticulate, less and less human—only it no longer matters to Clara what they look like or what they croak out or what they do, they are just an unknown girl, a man she hates, copulating disgustingly and violently in bed . . . (*translation mine*)

In this voyeuristic scene, the repulsive insects of Clara's infantile fantasy are transposed onto the bodies of the heterosexual couple. The fascination and horror of such a spectacle is mediated, as so often in Tusquets, by narrative: the precedents are the old ladies' stories Clara heard in her youth and the horror films she sees now. Heterosexuality becomes at once archaic and incredible, a 'monstrous' coupling derived from a bestiary. The body is fragmented, recomposed, replicated: the head placed between the legs, the two legs becoming eight. The movements of this double body are 'clumsy', its sounds inarticulate, even inhuman.

The reader is here invited to adopt a lesbian perspective, to share Clara's nausea and fascination before the bizarre spectacle of heterosexuality. Her attitude is not, of course, presented as authoritative: rather it is offered quite explicitly as a limited point of view (the reader, unlike Clara, already knows about Pablo's affair). However, as a monstrous portrayal or parody of love between men and women, it serves a political end which is perhaps inherent in the novel: to denaturalize sexual identities, make visible their specificity, and thus render them subject to historical change.

The final section of the novel is set apart syntactically from the rest of the trilogy. As Elia drives to meet her son Daniel, Tusquets abandons the carefully crafted, infinitely extended sentences that are her trademark for shorter clauses in the first person, unpunctuated, and juxtaposed without grammatical linking. This move from hypotaxis to parataxis suggests a final accession to unmediated personal experience in the quest for the object, the mother's reunion with the male child: 'I'm coming to get you, Daniel' (p. 250). However, Elia refers to herself mockingly as 'rotten with literature', and in an ironic self-reference on Tusquets's part reiterates the title of the first volume in the trilogy: 'the same sea'. Until now travel had been merely a quest for 'backdrops' for Elia's love, for 'sets' in which to place her husband. Now the heterosexual dyad of life *à deux* must be broken and Elia must reclaim a 'corporeal self' which is no longer a 'pretext' (p. 251). Elia remembers a photograph glimpsed in a newspaper, of a South American child whose pet dog is about to be clubbed to death during an epidemic of rabies. It symbolizes for her the defencelessness and vulnerability of the other (p. 253). Now maternity, which for her has been merely a 'return' to her husband's past, must become not an extension of the self/same but an acknowledgement of an other who is not reducible to his parents (p. 269). Elia's future will thus be a quest for new relations with the world (with her son and with writing) which are unmediated by men (p. 271). This, she believes, is happiness.

Lesbian Clara has been summarily dismissed from the novel: we are told in an aside that she has been 'stupidly' run over by a motorbike and has returned to her uncle's home to recover (p. 267). As a primary example of the defenceless victim, however, she should be a target for Elia's new ethics of alterity. While the return to maternity may not be as conservative as it appears (requiring as it does the establishment of an autonomous female subjectivity), the exclusion of lesbianism remains worrying. Wittig has some difficulty in relating her feminine communities to a patriarchal outside: *Les Guérillères* ends weakly with a call for men to join women in their struggle for self-realization (p. 192). Tusquets also seems to find the relation of lesbianism to the outside problematic. Unlike the other characters, Clara is without history or sociality, has no love interest outside the single obsession with Eva. Lesbian sociality is thus unrepresentable within the novel because one woman's love for another is offered as a singular predicament which resists universalization, an imaginary discourse of bodily fantasy which cannot accede to the symbolic. Within the novel itself, sexual-object choice is a matter of indifference: even Pablo registers no surprise that Clara is in love with his wife. However, the narratological impasse created by the lesbian character (whose story cannot be resolved, who is simply abandoned) points to a return of the repressed social context of lesbianism in Spain. In the privileged space of the holiday home by the sea, the political question of lesbian emancipation can be avoided, but not transcended.[27]

---

[27] Nor does Tusquets examine class differences between her characters. For a fascinating account of material factors of class and labour in the USA, see Kathleen M. Weston and Lisa B. Rofel, 'Sexuality, Class, and Conflict in a Lesbian Workplace', in *The Lesbian Issue: Essays from 'Signs'*, ed. Estelle B. Freedman, Barbara C. Gelpi, Susan L. Johnson, and Kathleen M. Weston (Chicago, 1985), 199–222.

In *Brouillon pour un dictionnaire des amantes* (Paris, 1976), Wittig and co-author Sande Zeig leave an empty page beneath the name Sappho, suggesting the irreparable loss of a lesbian culture (p. 213).[28] In Tusquets, however, the absence of such a culture is symptomatic of a failure to acknowledge and to address the intersubjective nature of lesbian experience. While *Varada* offers a critique of the fictive sex purveyed by the straight mind, it makes no gesture towards the lesbian 'war machine' that would help to repair the damage inflicted on women's bodies. The politics of parody have their limits.

5. TOWARDS THE FEMINARY?

We have seen that lesbian characters come under increasing pressure in the trilogy: thus in *El mismo mar* the first Clara takes leave of her faithless lover with some dignity; in *El amor* the second is feared to have attempted suicide; finally in *Varada* the third does indeed make a pathetic attempt at suicide when faced by the utter indifference of the woman she loves. If, for Wittig, lesbians are not women (because 'women' are defined only through their relations with men) then Tusquets's women are not 'lesbians' (because they barely achieve a measure of self-realization). The central characters of the trilogy invariably return to husband or son at the close of each novel.

Tusquets seems to be hinting that lesbian separatism is impossible because all of those subject to the violence of 'fictive sex' are branded by the male symbolic order. And she tends to confirm Margaret Whitford's[29] recent suggestion that there are only three positions for women within that order: they can either adopt a masculine role, or they can exist 'for men' in a state of helpless alienation, or they can opt for a marginal identity, and thus risk being labelled witch or lesbian (p. 153). These three categories correspond to the three women in *Varada*: the high-performing Eva is male-identified; the doting Elia exists only through her absent husband; and the lovelorn Clara is marginalized (by characters and narrative) because of her lesbian passion. The novels can thus be read, in an inversion of Sedgwick's schema,

---

[28] *Brouillon* is the text pub. in Spanish by Tusquets's own publishing house, Lumen.

[29] *Luce Irigaray: Philosophy in the Feminine* (London and New York, 1991).

as heterosocial triangles: erotic relations between women serve merely to obscure a continuing engagement with men which both precedes and succeeds abortive lesbian affairs. As *Varada* shows quite clearly, in Tusquets only heterosexual women are allowed a transcendental project in which to realize their freedom: Elia will continue the adventure of writing which Clara dare not even attempt.

Tusquets, then, cannot conceive a relation between lesbianism (understood as the product of psychic and familial circumstance) and feminism (understood as women's accession to the social and linguistic sphere). The two remain confined to separate territories. Her emphasis on the personal thus risks repathologizing lesbianism as a psychic disorder; and her indifference to the social context of female homosexuality makes her blind (after *El mismo mar* at least) to the class relations that underwrite the amorous games of her bourgeois lovers. Tusquets herself would no doubt argue that lesbianism is incidental to her fictional project: whatever their object choice (indeed, whatever their gender), all her characters are locked into the repetition compulsions of the neurotic. But her refusal or unwillingness to represent a lesbian symbolic (a social space between-women) points perhaps involuntarily to a truth that is itself social: the inability of lesbian women to transcend the private sphere unless the public arena is transformed to admit them. Tusquets's trilogy reveals the extreme difficulty of thinking through that desire which is situated on the very borders of the social and which is repeatedly displaced from the centre of narrative interest.

The longest entry in the lesbian dictionary *Brouillon* is 'Histoire' (pp. 123–9). And I have tried to show that for all its utopianism, Wittig's project is defiantly cultural. Many of Wittig's images happen to coincide with Tusquets's: cats, monkeys, black swans, and labyrinths all occur in both writers. And in *El mismo mar* Clara fantasizes that she and her lover will become female 'guerrillas' (p. 185). But such coincidences, close as they are, do not suggest an essential lesbian language, the 'feminary' evoked by Wittig in *Les Guérillères* (p. 17). For both writers reveal that identity is radically temporal, always constructed in time. For example, *El mismo mar* recounts the narrator's quest for the child who was innocent of adult role-playing, 'if she ever existed' (p. 30). The qualification is vital here: for it hints that there can be no access for women to a presocial ontology before patriarchy, no language uncompromised by past precedent.

The solution to this dilemma lies once more in the body. For the irreducible materiality of the body reveals (in Judith Butler's words) that 'to be *constituted* by [male] discourse is not to be *determined* by [it]' (p. 143). If constitution 'is not opposed to agency [but] is the necessary scene of agency' (Butler, p. 147), then Tusquets's appeal to citation and parody need not signal helpless repetition. In particular, the apparently random duplication of names in the trilogy would suggest that (lesbian) identity is not hermetically private and individual but is rather 'a diffuse corporeal agency . . . that comes not from within the individual but [from] exchanges between bodies . . . beyond the categories of identity' (Butler, p. 127). By foregrounding the status of the name as intersubjective shifter (with her multiple 'Elias' and 'Claras'), Tusquets gestures towards the instability at the heart of the linguistic constitution of the subject: the name that functions as if it were uniquely related to the individual is in fact subject to repetition and deviation. Butler claims that for Wittig, 'to become a lesbian is an *act*' (p. 127). In Tusquets's (and Wittig's) erotics of the performative, names can be adopted and discarded at will.

Diane Hamer[30] has recently proposed that lesbianism be understood not as a (Wittigian) rejection of the category of woman, but as a reworking of that category (p. 149). This would seem close to Tusquets's position. We have seen that Tusquets's rearticulation of femininity involves an engagement with a largely male corpus of classical myth and psychology of love. One pre-text I have not mentioned earlier is Proust. In *À la recherche du temps perdu* we find such motifs as the transformation of the theatre into a marine grotto, the drama of the goodnight kiss, the exploration of lesbianism itself.[31] What is more, we also find Tusquets's characteristic syntax: the interminable sentences that remain, none the less, grammatically impeccable. It is no contradiction to suggest, finally, that the lesbian body of Tus-

---

[30] See n. 22 above.

[31] For the transformation of the opera into grotto, see *À la recherche du temps perdu, II: Le Côté de Guermantes* (Paris, 1954), 38–44. This scene, in which the narrator first catches sight of the Princesse de Guermantes as a 'nereid' in her opera-box-grotto, has many points in common with the love scene in *El mismo mar*. To my knowledge, neither critics nor the author herself has drawn attention to such close parallels.

quets lies not in her problematic representation of subjectivity or social practice, but in her richly textured and highly idiosyncratic language. With its slow, circling movements, its neglect of linear development, and love of deferral, Tusquets's Proustian prose reduplicates the multicentred languor of her lesbian love scenes. A recent account of Sappho's poetry[32] is equally applicable to Tusquets: 'The accumulation of topographic and sensuous detail leads us to think of the interconnection of all the parts of the body in a long and diffuse act of love, rather than the genital-centred and more relentlessly goal-oriented pattern of love-making which men have been known to employ' (p. 186).

While it is clearly dangerous to designate plurality and diffuseness as unique characteristics of a lesbian text, Tusquets also coincides with Sappho in her references to the hidden 'fruits' or 'flowers' of the beloved's sex. To take just one example, in *El mismo mar* Clara is said to be indistinguishable from the exotic pattern of the carpet on which she lies (p. 89). This is not merely a rhapsodic symbolization of the female genitalia reminiscent of Wittig. It also suggests a slow search for the hooded or hidden object which resists representation, which remains ever on the margins of visibility. It is Tusquets's achievement to have traced that quest for the reader in uniquely subtle and sinuous prose. As lesbian body, as textual performance beyond its manifest content, Tusquets's trilogy reenacts this interminable but necessary quest for the impossible object of the feminary.

[32] John J. Winkler, 'Double Consciousness in Sappho's Lyrics', in *The Constraints of Desire: The Anthropology of Sex and Gender in Ancient Greece* (New York, 1990), 162–87.

4

Eloy de la Iglesia's Cinema of Transition

I. HOMOSEXUALITY, REGIONALISM, AND MASS CULTURE

The cinema of Eloy de la Iglesia is by no means academically respectable. One standard reference work rehearses the majority view that the criteria motivating his films are wholly commercial: sensationalism, crude topicality, melodrama.[1] Yet de la Iglesia's films of the mid-1970s and early 1980s not only mark the first extended representation of gay men in Spanish cinema, they also stage an explicit and complex examination of the interplay between homosexuality, Marxism, and separatism.[2] Thus *Los placeres ocultos* ('Hidden Pleasures', 1976) has its bourgeois hero fall in love with a working-class youth; *El diputado* ('The MP', 1978) has a Socialist politician engaged in a similar affair with a youth in the pay of the ultra-right; and *El pico* ('The Shoot', 1983) plots the complex relationships between a bisexual youth, his friend and fellow heroin addict, and their respective fathers (a Civil Guard and a Basque separatist politician). Homosexuality is thus invariably qualified by factors such as class, national politics, and regional identity, and not exiled to some ideal space outside history. Moreover, these works were the most successful Spanish films of their day at the box office. They represent what is perhaps a unique moment during the transition to democracy when the topic of homosexuality and the mass audience coincided in the Spanish cinema. De la Iglesia's exclusion from both national and regional histories of film is thus all the more troubling. As we shall see, his very visceral films raise questions

[1] Augusto M. Torres, *Cine español 1896–1983* (Madrid, 1983), 256.
[2] This connection is stressed by George De Stefano in one of the very few pieces in English on de la Iglesia: 'Post-Franco Frankness', *FC* 22 (June 1986), 58–60. De Stefano gives a brief account of de la Iglesia's career and an interview with him when *Los placeres ocultos* opened the 1986 New York Gay Film Festival. The only other films available with English subtitles are *El diputado* and the teenage gangster movie *Colegas* (1982)

of taste and value that must prove unsettling to those who would promote cinema as 'the seventh art'. In order to address such a body of work at all we must confront problems of genre (exploitation) and historicity ('shelf life').

In a 1983 interview, de la Iglesia himself called for a cinema that would be 'like a newspaper'.[3] And it is clearly impossible to consider his films outside the immediate context of the transition to democracy within which they were made. The model of the newspaper, however, has further implications. First it suggests an ephemeral medium, one that does not aspire to lasting value; second, it suggests actuality, the immediate irruption of the real into the text; and finally, it suggests political engagement: the film will not flinch from editorializing, from making wholly explicit its political bias.

In spite of his espousal of the newspaper form, de la Iglesia's treatment at the hands of the press during this period was brutal. While the initial banning of *Los placeres ocultos* may have motivated relatively kind reviews from those (such as Fernando Méndez-Leite,)[4] opposed to the continuing censorship one year after the death of Franco, later films received bitter attacks from all sides of the political spectrum. To read the accumulated press files in the Filmoteca is to be exposed to an extraordinary catalogue of abuse, some of which is clearly homophobic. Interviewers constantly circle around the question of the director's own sexual preference (the secret that would 'explain' the films) and repeatedly ask why he is so interested in homosexuality.[5] Some of the abuse is also motivated by anti-Basque racism: one squib mocks de la Iglesia for a project (later to metamorphose into *El pico*) featuring a gay love story set in the Basque country complete with dialogue in *euskera*.[6] The anonymous journalist states that other countries seek to conquer the international

---

[3] 'No cerrar el pico: el director Eloy de la Iglesia lleva 20 años escandalizando', interview with Miguel Bayón, *Cambio 16* (14 Nov. 1983).

[4] 'Ultimo veto de la censura: *Los placeres ocultos*', *Diario 16* (26 Jan. 1977). Méndez-Leite praises the cast's performances in this film. See also the anonymous review in *El pueblo* (19 Apr. 1977), which says that the film treats the 'sad problem' of homosexuality, but with 'little scandal'. For the banning, see Angeles Maso, 'La luz roja a *Los placeres ocultos*: Eloy de la Iglesia no piensa alterar la integridad de su película', *La vanguardia* (15 Feb. 1977).

[5] See e.g. 'Eloy de la Iglesia: el homosexualismo en el cine', interview with Monty Padura, *Catalunya Expres* (19 Oct. 1977).

[6] *El pueblo* (3 Oct. 1981).

market, implying that Spanish directors waste their time on such minority projects. This was a curious complaint to make against the most commercially successful director of his time: homosexuality and regional identity would thus always seem to be marginal even when placed at the centre of a mass culture.

Fernando Trueba's review of *El diputado* in *El país* (27 January 1979) is a good example of vitriol from the socialist side. Trueba begins by accusing de la Iglesia of a double servility: to leftist propaganda and commercialism. The boldness of the director's themes is no defence for this 'cinema of excess', which tolerates the grotesque and ridiculous just so long as they are profitable. The film's overt references to actuality (recent political events) fail to disguise a story which is wholly false. This is not cinema: the characters are inauthentic, the dialogue unintentionally humorous, the aesthetics amorphous. The main character is nothing but a puppet. Trueba claims that de la Iglesia has not made one good film. Not only is he a bad director, he is also a bad trickster (no one will be taken in by this film).

The title of Trueba's review is 'Sex and Politics: A Cocktail that Sells'. Confronted by this very physical cinema, critical response is often physiological, evoking food and drink: ingestion, digestion, or expulsion. More noticeable here, however, is the stress on the inauthentic: references to falsity, disguise, trickery. And if we briefly compare this review with one of *El pico* from the extreme right *El alcázar* (15 October 1983), much of the same language and arguments recur. Thus Félix Martialay stresses the lack of 'art' in the film, which is linked to its mendacity: it contains no truth or authentic feelings, but rather reflects the 'deficiencies' of its director. Martialay finds particularly offensive the scene in which a father takes his son to a brothel in order to celebrate his coming of age. Such a scene reveals that the director knows nothing about what it really means to have a son. Disturbance in the reproduction of familial relations is indeed a recurrent theme in de la Iglesia's work, and one which this hostile critic clearly finds worrying. For Martialay, the characters are wholly 'unreal', subject as they are to the threefold political programme of the director: attacks on the army, scorn for the Civil Guard, praise for the queer ('maricón').

As in the leftist critic, then, the question of aesthetics is also immediately a question of ethics: there is an unacknowledged shift from formal inadequacy to moral turpitude (the director is motivated either by base commerce or culpable 'anti-milita-rism'). Yet the extremity of language used in both cases suggests something more is at stake: the attempt to expel the abject, that which the body cannot tolerate. One critic accuses de la Iglesia of the 'aesthetics of the Y-front' ('estética del calzoncillo'). It seems likely, then, that what threatens critics in these films (in which naked male bodies are exposed to the viewer, in which the same youthful actors constantly recur) is the unmediated irrup-tion of homosexual desire into the mass form of commercial cinema. It is this desublimation that is intolerable.

John Hopewell has recently given a brief but suggestive account of the emergence of new forms of sexuality in Spanish cinema of the transition.[7] The early 1970s saw a curious combi-nation of Catholic morality and European-style consumerism in Spanish film. Extramarital sex was permissible only in certain special circumstances: if the female character was raped, if she was the object of a classical 'Spanish passion' (as in a biopic of Goya), if she was an actress, foreigner, or prostitute (pp. 165–7). After the death of Franco, sex was no longer the other and three shifts took place: the gradual abandonment of the virgin/whore dichotomy; the shift from the family to the couple as the basic narrative and ideological unit; the emergence of active (hetero-sexual) women and gay men as subjects of desire. While the first films in this final category tended (like Hopewell himself) to confuse homosexuality, transvestism, and transsexualism, they adopted a liberal viewpoint, claiming that gays were 'just like you and me'. For Hopewell both *Los placeres ocultos* and *El diputado* display a fatally abstracted representation of homo-sexuality, which is conceived as a 'democratic right', but not a 'democratic desire'. Citing Steve Neale's *Genre*, Hopewell sug-gests (after Freud) that the occultation of homosexual desire is the basis of the scopic drive, and hence of dominant visual narratives. To desublimate homosexual desire would thus be to challenge the basis of mainstream cinema, to assert that gay men have a specific difference and cannot be represented by the liberal tag 'the same as you and I'.

---

[7] *El cine español después de Franco* (Madrid, 1989) is an expanded and substantially revised version of *Out of the Past: Spanish Cinema after Franco* (London, 1986). The section I cite here ('Del sexo de los ángeles a sexos angélicos', 164–78) does not appear in the English version. Hopewell discusses de la Iglesia in 'Dando en los cojones: Eloy de la Iglesia y el populismo radical', 233–42.

In one of the very few articles on the representation of homosexuality in Spanish film after Franco, Eduardo Haro Ibars also rejects de la Iglesia's formulations in these films.[8] In *Los placeres ocultos* he finds not a Marxist analysis of sexual repression and class struggle but a novelette ('folletín') full of stereotypes: the rich queen and castrating mother (p. 88). In *El diputado* José Sacristán, who plays the eponymous hero, is 'unrealistic', a 'cardboard cutout'. No one, Haro complains, has told the life of the *true* homosexual, he who is neither rich nor a politician, but is forced to live his life as best he can (p. 91).

Haro argues for the same criterion of authenticity as the straight Spanish critics, albeit from a different position: the characters must be (felt to be) real. Hopewell, on the other hand, in his sympathetic account of de la Iglesia, argues that the films reveal a subtle account of homosexuality and the ambivalence of familial relations (pp. 236–8). While most Spanish film makers are 'localist', trusting to the domestic audience's knowledge of the historical background of their work, de la Iglesia problematizes the relation of his work to the real by directly discussing that relation within the fiction: thus when the Civil Guard father in *El pico* speculates as to the frequency of corruption in the force, the question of whether this highly coloured narrative can serve as an allegory of the national predicament is openly confronted (p. 240). Hopewell argues that the film's relation to the real is thus necessarily mediated by its genre, in this case melodrama. Just as in melodrama the social stability of the family is undermined by a sexual desire which reaches beyond it, so in the narrative of national history minority groups (ethnic or sexual) can be absorbed only with difficulty into the new democratic order. Critical abuse of de la Iglesia has thus been motivated by an inability to 'read' his use of genre: the rough texture of the film surface is taken to be neorealism, and the films criticized for failing to live up to criteria which they do not themselves recognize. More particularly, Hopewell argues, the depiction of gays as 'queers' ('maricones') in these films is also determined by the melodramatic genre, which requires stock

---

[8] 'La homosexualidad como problema socio-político en el cine español del postfranquismo', *Tiempo de Historia*, 52 (Mar. 1979), 88–91. Raúl Contel's, 'Cine de homosexuales', *Cinema 2002*, 56 (Oct. 1979), 54–6 is on 5 QK,s (*sic*), a Catalan collective who made 'anti-machista' parodies of pop culture.

characters, not documentary style representation of the real (p. 240).

Hopewell goes on to make an interesting point about de la Iglesia's preferred hero, the youthful hooligan. Such figures both concretize class conflict in the films and, by representing a life lived only in the present, comfort Spanish audiences of the period, who were equally afraid of past suffering and future uncertainty (p. 242). However, Hopewell's insistence on the determining nature of genre (the fact that we should not 'ask for pears from an elm tree') seems over schematic. The particularity of de la Iglesia, I shall argue, is precisely that he subverts classical genres in *auteuriste* fashion while remaining within the confines of mass culture. Indeed the very choice of a homosexual hero in these films must pose a challenge to those codes of representation and structures of identification inherent in dominant cinema practice. Moreover in the films I treat, de la Iglesia explicitly rejects stereotypical images of gay men, who are invariably described in the scripts as 'worthy' or 'manly'. I shall call these figures (played by sympathetic actors such as Simón Andreu and José Sacristán) 'Good Homosexuals'.

What Hopewell does, briefly, sketch out is the possibility of a reading of these films which addresses both formal and historical questions; indeed, which relates the former to the latter through the mediation of narrative genre. During the period the films were being made the only comparable critical account they received was from an unexpected source: the pioneer journal of film theory in Spain, *Contracampo* ('Countershot'). In 1981 the pages of *Contracampo*, more accustomed to Godard or Ozu, ran a special feature on de la Iglesia.[9] It consists of a dense article by Javier Vega, a lengthy interview by Francesc Llinàs and José Luis Téllez, and a fragment of the script for *Galopa y corta el viento* ('Gallop and Cut through the Wind'), the unmade feature on the affair between a Civil Guard and a Basque separatist.

Javier Vega's 'The (Ideological) Apparatus of Eloy de la Iglesia' (pp. 22–6) is the most developed of successive *Contracampo* pieces on the director. As its title suggests Vega's position derives initially from Althusser: cinema is one of those institutions through which the dominant class 'inoculates' its ideology into the subject masses. The role of an engaged cinema would

---

[9] 'Eloy de la Iglesia', *Contracampo*, 25–6 (Nov.–Dec. 1981), 21–41.

thus be to eschew avant-garde aestheticism and challenge the apparatus through a 'direct engagement with temporal reality'. This politicized cinema will reject all pretensions to art, and thus risk rejection by those critics of the left who prize cinema most highly (p. 21). In a culture of mass spectacle such films will no longer be of interest as an 'object of pleasure', but only as an 'object of struggle'; the aesthetic criterion will cede to that of political efficacy. De la Iglesia's transgression of 'codes of dominant cinema' will thus prove as challenging as that of the more rigorous (and intellectually respectable) formalists. Hence the angry responses his cinema has inspired (p. 22). It does not express the viewers' feelings (their desires, fears, or obsessions); rather it forces them to take up a position for or against the thesis of the film. The latter's power is thus based not on exquisite images, but on the exposition of ideas. *Mise en scène* is reduced to the strictly functional.

Citing an earlier piece by his colleague José Luis Téllez, Vega compares de la Iglesia's films to pamphlets. Their exalted tone, conjunctural discourse, and Manichean approach to characterization resemble written tracts (p. 24). De la Iglesia's originality lies in adapting this medium to the cinema; but unlike in the case of the printed pamphlet, the aesthetic poverty of his films does not result from lack of finance. The peculiar expression of the genre he has created thus makes it particularly difficult to 'read'. These tendencies have been stripped down, refined: in his later films clarity of exposition and the use of emblematic characters prevent the spectator from getting lost, in spite of unexpectedly intricate plots; references to the real are increasingly emphatic and dialogues openly schematic; the acting, apparently naturalistic, is strewn with redundancies and repetitive gestures pointing unambiguously to the function of the character in the plot. Such apparent clumsiness or vulgarity serves to prevent the viewer from being distracted from the topic in hand. These are 'closed' films, without 'noise' (superfluous interference in the transmission of the narrative message)(p. 25). They constitute a shameless manipulation which (because of its very transparency) Vega can call 'honourable', even 'ethical'. De la Iglesia, cineaste of the people, is thus an *auteur malgré lui*: through theoretical reflection on the cinematic medium, he has evolved his own narrative style which subverts conventional forms and conflates disparate genres (*film noir*, melodrama, agitprop, pornography). He thus reveals that auteurism is just another genre (p. 26). Through this final theoretical twist, Vega ensures that the Marxist director is not reinstalled in the privileged place of the bourgeois artist.

As we shall see, *Contracampo*'s wilfully perverse and sometimes ironic praise of de la Iglesia extends to specifics of filmic practice, such as the use or abuse of the close-up. More generally however, their important account provides a precedent for the analysis of the central paradox of the director's work: the curious combination of mass technique (sex and violence) and personal, indeed idiosyncratic, obsessions. In the rest of this chapter I hope to chart the strange configurations that occur when the homosexual hero takes up his place in three of Eloy de la Iglesia's films. In the final moments of the fragment of the script for the unmade *Galopa y corta el viento*,[10] Basque separatist Patxi and Civil Guard Manolo, stranded in the countryside, are caught in the lights of the other's motorcycle and car. 'The image', we are told by de la Iglesia and co-writer Gonzalo Goicoechea, 'starts to take on a magical hue' (p. 41). It is a fitting icon of the emergence of the gay man into Spanish cinema: caught in the light, exposed to view, illuminated by his relation to the other.

2. *LOS PLACERES OCULTOS*: THE EROTIC TRIANGLE

A medium long shot of a naked youth in the shower; the camera follows him to the bedroom, where he starts to dry himself. Cut to medium shot of a middle-aged man in dressing gown, looking off screen to the right. A framed photograph can be seen behind his shoulder. Cut again to a medium long shot of the boy dressing with his back to the camera. Crosscuts between watching man and dressing youth lead to a medium shot of the man taking money from his dressing gown to give to the youth. The camera follows them in medium close up to the door. As the youth leaves, the credits start to roll. The camera then follows the man back from the door and cuts to a low angle, long (establishing) shot of the room. We look up at the man as he relaxes in a chair, listening to choral music. A slow pan over

---

[10] I cite the extract pub. by *Contracampo*. See also the outline held in the Biblioteca Nacional, Madrid, 'Galopa y corta el viento: argumento para una historia cinematográfica escrito por Eloy de la Iglesia y Gonzalo Goicoechea' (Madrid, 23 Jan. 1980). The title is taken from the campy, popular song 'Mi jaca'.

framed photographs in a curious ghostly light leads to a close up of the man wearing eye goggles: he is basking in the light of a sunlamp.[11]

The dialogue in this first sequence of the film is as follows:

CHICO: ¿Estará abierto el portal?
EDUARDO: Sí . . . se abre por dentro.
CHICO: ¿Me puedes dar algo suelto para el taxi?
EDUARDO: Venga, toma. . . . A ver si nos vemos otra vez . . . ¿eh?
CHICO: ¡Vale! . . . Dame tu teléfono y te llamo . . .
EDUARDO: No . . . es que yo casi nunca estoy en casa, ¿sabes? Bueno . . . ya nos veremos por aquí.
CHICO: Yo paro mucho por los billares. Así que ya sabes . . .
EDUARDO: De acuerdo. Un día de estos me pasaré.

BOY: Will the front door be open?
EDUARDO: Yes . . . it opens from the inside.
BOY: Can you spare some change for the taxi?
EDUARDO: OK . . . here you are . . . Maybe we'll get together again some time.
BOY: Fine . . . Give me your phone number and I'll call you.
EDUARDO: No . . . the thing is, I'm hardly ever at home. Well, see you around.
BOY: I hang around the billiard halls a lot. So you know . . .
EDUARDO: Agreed. One of these days I'll drop by.

The opening sequence of *Los placeres ocultos* is a good example of the way in which Eloy de la Iglesia economically establishes a visual regime which transcends an impoverished, even banal, dialogue. Thus the gradual shift in framing (from medium long to close-up) draws the viewer's attention to the principal character's narcissism and isolation; the cross-cutting suggests his ambivalent relation to an erotic object which fascinates him; and most particularly, the delayed suggestion that the opening shot of the naked youth is actually a 'POV' (a shot from the older man's point of view) implicates the spectator in a traffic of homosexual voyeurism which is overtly commercial. The man and the audience have paid to look; the boy is paid to be looked

---

[11] *Los placeres* is briefly referred to in Hopewell, *El cine*, 178, 236; and De Stefano (see n. 2 above) where de la Iglesia presents it as the first of a projected 'gay trilogy' (with *El diputado* and the unmade *Galopa y corta el viento*). In his generally hostile 'Los límites de Eloy', *Destino* (3 Aug. 1978), Jorge de Cominges concedes that *Los placeres* was the first Spanish film to treat homosexuality 'with dignity'. I have referred to the script by de la Iglesia and Goicoechea, which has the working title 'La acera de enfrente' (Madrid, n.d. [1975?]).

at. According to the script, Eduardo (Simón Andreu: 'distinguished and manly, intelligent and cultivated') watches the youth 'half indifferent and half tired, without being able to avoid a certain pleasure' (p. 2). The spectator, asked to identify with a gay male gaze, must also choose to make a response.

The opening sequence thus sets up a series of binaries which the narrative will violently disturb: subject and object, rich and poor, private and public. It is no accident that the sequence should lead up to a doorway, the liminal site of transition between domestic and social space. Homosexual affect is the privileged factor that will upset these initially static binaries. When Eduardo experiences not lust but love for a youth, then the separate and stable territories mapped out by class and capital will be thrown into disarray. Perhaps the most interesting point about this opening moment, then, is that (commercial) sex between men, far from subverting the existing social order, is shown to be safely (if discreetly) submerged within it. De la Iglesia thus neatly reverses one of the traditional techniques of melodrama mentioned by John Hopewell above: the dissolution of the family (and of narrative equilibrium) is effected not through erotic desire for an external object, but through a sublimated affect which is doomed to dissatisfaction.

As the narrative develops, the relation between homosexuality and a number of different areas is explored. Eduardo is a banker, and parallels are drawn between the different modes of exploitation effected by prostitution and capitalism. He is also a devoted son to his clinging mother: the first cutaway after the opening sequence in his flat is to the family apartment in the upmarket Barrio de Salamanca in Madrid. Here, as so often, *mise en scène* is wholly functional, works solely as an index of social value: Eduardo's studio is 'modern and functional', his mother's home crammed with pictures and carpets. The first time we see her, a crucifix is prominently displayed on the wall behind her. At a time when the continuing modernization of Spain was much debated, homosexuality is here offered (curiously perhaps) as the essence of modern, secular society in opposition to the old Spain of family and religion: Eduardo's office with its steel table and sleek executive toys is also emphatically marked as 'modern'.

On one of his regular cruising sessions in the University area, Eduardo meets (and fails to pick up) a youth, Miguel. The latter has a girlfriend Carmen and a married lover Rosa (Charo

López). Eduardo finds the impoverished Miguel a job in his office, confesses his love for him, and attempts to build a new family for himself with Miguel and Carmen. The spurned Rosa wreaks revenge on both of them: she arranges to have Eduardo beaten and robbed by male prostitutes and Miguel shamed by putting about the rumour that he too is gay. The amorous conflict (with hetero- and homosexual lovers competing for the same youth) is clearly beyond resolution; and, as we shall see, the ending of the film is left disturbingly open.

Los placeres ocultos offers a series of contradictory images of homosexuality which are distributed schematically amongst the characters. Thus Eduardo is the Good Homosexual: a loving son, respected employee, and devoted (platonic) lover who gives up commercial sex for unconsummated but passionate romance. The Bad Homosexuals are Eduardo's camp friends whom he neglects on meeting Miguel. Sipping lurid cocktails in an improbable gay club ('a luxurious and sophisticated atmo-sphere'), they mock him for his chaste devotion, claiming he must have become a socialist or a nun. The queens' scorn for politics is set against the political engagement of another variety of Good Homosexual: Eduardo's colleague and ex-lover Raúl, who encourages him to join in the collective struggle against homosexual oppression. The saint, the queen, and the liberation-ist: these, then, are the three models of male homosexual life offered by the film.

At times *Los placeres ocultos* offers explicit apologies for the characters' behaviour. Thus in one scene Eduardo dutifully explains to the bemused Miguel that, no, homosexuality is not an illness and that, yes, each person has the right to be as he or she really is. But elsewhere apologetics are compromised by an awareness of the inextricability of homosexuality and capital. Thus when Miguel exclaims to Raúl that he will not allow gay men to take advantage of his poverty, the latter suggests (improbably for a banker) that he should place homosexual prostitution within the context of capitalist exploitation: 'Learn how to struggle, but not just against a queer ["marica"] who offers you 500 pesetas to sleep with him . . . Think that you may be selling more important things than your arse and you haven't even realised that's what you're doing. That's why I say to you: learn how to struggle.' In this utopian dialogue the revolutionary homosexual exposes the false consciousness of the proletarian heterosexual.

More interesting than these schematic exchanges are the curious, indeed irreconcilable, contradictions that accumulate at the level of the plot. Most of these contradictions involve women. Charo López's Rosa is a voracious man-eater. In an early sequence she devours cream cakes with Miguel as they make love, a sign of her rampant sexuality; and in the most purely melodramatic scene of the film she pleads with Eduardo to make Miguel return to her, before threatening him with blackmail. Inversely, Miguel's bland and initially virginal girlfriend, Carmen, pliantly accepts Eduardo's amorous interest in her fiancé. In a montage sequence the three thrill to the delights of the funfair before swimming together in a deserted lake: the amorous triangle can flourish only in the non-cultural spaces of play and nature. Finally, Eduardo's long-suffering mother reveals (on her deathbed) that she knew her son's secret but was compelled to remain silent: women of her class are obliged to play the fool in order to make their men feel proud of them. These three examples of womanhood (the *femme fatale*, the pliant virgin, and the bourgeois mother) are all marginalized by homosexual desire: Miguel prefers the 'father figure' Eduardo to his female ex-lover or girlfriend (both of whom are abandoned by the narrative before the end of the film); the mother can only acknowledge her son's homosexuality as she lies dying. De la Iglesia thus both reconfirms and inverts the 'homosocial triangle' which Eve Kosofsky Sedgwick has identified in the nineteenth-century novel.[12] Women continue to serve in traditional style as a vehicle through which two men explore the relationship between each other; but unlike in the classic texts, this relationship is desublimated, openly acknowledged to be based on erotic desire. The problem remains, however, that the woman is still effectively excluded from the 'base line' of the founding male relationship; and can adopt only the thankless roles of shrewish harridan (Rosa) or long-suffering victim (Carmen, the mother). As long as male homosexual desire is presented as a disturbance in existing heterosexual and familial relations, there can be no re-evaluation of female desire, whether hetero- or homosexual.

Los placeres ocultos offers no example of a reciprocal relationship

---

[12] *Between Men*, 21 and throughout.

between men of equal status. Even Eduardo's colleague Raúl, as cultivated and bourgeois as his ex-lover, was once, like Miguel, a poor youth illicitly introduced into the workplace by Eduardo. We have seen that this asymmetry in the homosexual relation is reinforced by class and financial inequality, but the asymmetry is bizarrely underlined here by the heterosexuality of the love-object. At one point Raúl attacks Eduardo: once he merely bought boys' bodies; now he buys their lives. The latter replies that he is trying to form a 'kind of family' with the youthful couple, to feel like a father or grandfather to their future children. By doing so he will avoid a lonely old age. Raúl, the sexual revolutionary, replies that he and his comrades will not be alone either 'at the time of struggle'; it is useless to rely on individual efforts.

Homosexuality is here presented both as a mimicry of the heterosexual (an attempt to recreate its structures) and as a deviation from it (a perversion of the natural order). Yet, as Jonathan Dollimore has suggested, the problem of the perverse is inextricably linked to the normal; that far from constituting the other to the 'normal' same, it is already inherent in it from the very beginning. Initially negative and patronizing, Eloy de la Iglesia's idiosyncratic decision to have his gay hero love a straight man thus reveals the necessary coexistence of homo- and heterosexuality in the same social space, and under the same economic laws. As a narrative it may perhaps be more subversive than one set in the hermetically sealed space of an all-gay sociality. In interviews of the period, de la Iglesia claimed that what interested him in this film (and in his next, which treated bestiality)[13] is not a specific sexual practice, but the general social process by which certain groups are marginalized. Through a somewhat indirect (deviant) route he may well have achieved that result here.

But how do these ideological fissures reveal themselves at the formal level of the filmic text? The fundamental disorder of heterosexuality (and the horror of female sexuality) is vehicled by grotesque shock cuts or rhythmic crosscutting. Thus when Rose and Miguel have sex, we cut from a close-up of her breast

---

[13] *La criatura* ('The Creature/The Baby') (1978), starring Ana Belén as the wife who leaves husband Juan Diego for a dog. For the supposed feminist implications of this film see the interview with L. Fernández Ventura, 'Eloy de la Iglesia: lo popular y lo político', *Diario 16* (13 Dec. 1977).

to a religious print on the bedroom wall. Or again when Rosa
seduces the hooligan who will attack Eduardo we crosscut from
the sexual act to a scene in which she washes the youth's hair.
Camera angle is used emphatically to reiterate class positions:
Eduardo is often shot from below, as he sits in his chair or car,
as he surveys the workers from his glass-walled office. The
impoverished Miguel is shot from above; at one early point the
camera looks down from the ceiling on the tiny bedroom that he
shares with his brother in the family shack. These devices rarely
draw attention to themselves. Cinematography and editing, like
mise en scène, are reduced to a functional, emblematic level.

More important, however, than editing and camera angle is a
more emphatic mannerism pointed out by *Contracampo*: racking
focus (shifting the area of sharp focus from one plane to another
during a single shot). Thus when Eduardo spies on young lovers
Miguel and Carmen in the park, the blurred green matter at the
front of the image is revealed (with a change of focus) to be the
leaves behind which Eduardo is hiding. Here, as in the opening
sequence, the spectator is implicated in the homosexually motivated voyeurism of the protagonist. Or again, when Miguel and
Carmen first have sex in Eduardo's apartment, the focus shifts
from a framed photograph of Eduardo in the foreground to the
naked bodies of the lovers in the background. This literal change
of perspective within a single shot is an emphatic means of
underlining the irreconcilability of the two gazes in the film: the
man's amorous regard for the youth, and the youth's erotic
pleasure in his girlfriend.

By the end of the film this homosexual gaze has been (overtly
at least) de-eroticized: as Eduardo looks at the naked and
inviolate Miguel lying on his bed, the script tells us that this is
not a 'lascivious observation . . . he contemplates him . . . as if
he was seeing the most beautiful landscape or the most brilliant
work of art' (p. 77). He caresses Miguel's lips with his fingers.
The only scene in the script of explicit sexual activity between
the two men (when Eduardo reaches orgasm as he clutches the
heedless Miguel on a motorbike) was omitted from the film itself.
I would suggest, however, that this improbable relationship is
perhaps more revealing of the relationship between gays and
Spanish society in the period than a more plausible, reciprocal
love affair might have been. The exaggeration of Eduardo's
predicament (which permits no resolution) is not inept but

strategic. It points indirectly to the impossible position of gay Spaniards in the transition: at once intimately linked and profoundly separated from their heterosexual partners at work and in the family. *Los placeres ocultos* does not reflect the real, but it might claim to typify it (to act out its contradictions with heightened intensity). Such a reading is clearly consistent with both the Marxist sympathies of the director in the period and the Lukácscian enthusiasms of his protectors at *Contracampo*.

At the end of the film the long-suffering Eduardo has been beaten by hooligans and exposed as a homosexual by Miguel at their place of work. In a visual echo of the opening sequence he relaxes in a chair listening to music, alone with the sunlamp. The bell rings and the camera follows him to the door. As he looks through the spyhole a smile comes to his face. The frame freezes on a close-up as he opens the door.

Los placeres ocultos was initially banned *in toto* by the censor: no provision was made, as was usually the case, for editing the film into an 'acceptable' form.[14] For the Francoist censor, then, the very topic of homosexuality was taboo, and would inevitably contaminate every inch of the film. The defiantly open ending, however, broaches a final taboo which cannot be resolved by the logic of the narrative: it is only the return of Miguel that can satisfy Eduardo; but the latter refuses to impose his sexual demands on the youth. A happy ending is required, but cannot be represented. Like the formal and ideological discontinuities we have seen elsewhere in *Los placeres ocultos*, the final freeze-frame points symptomatically to meanings which the referential level of the film dare not acknowledge: if homosexuality is depicted (as it is in the film) as a disturbance in existing heterosexual relations, it will necessarily be doomed to failure; but if it is also a 'democratic right' to 'be as one really is' (as the film also proposes), then in the new Spain of the transition homosexuals can no longer be punished for their sexual-object choice. The impossible, open ending of *Los placeres ocultos* (so inimical to its melodramatic form) is thus the final, paradoxical result of a compromise formation between genre and history: between the formal desire for aesthetic resolution and the political requirement for social change.

[14] See Méndez-Leite (n. 4 above).

3. *EL DIPUTADO*: THE GOOD HOMOSEXUAL

Roberto ('40 years old, square glasses, intelligent, and elegant in his sports jacket and shirt without a tie') sits in his car outside the police station in Madrid's Puerta del Sol.[15] We hear a voice-over:

Yo no tengo nada que temer. Soy un político legal, un parlamentario elegido democraticamente, un representante de la voluntad popular y, aunque esté en la oposición, de alguna manera también soy parte del poder. Pero han sido tantos años de clandestinidad, de persecuciones. ¿Como será mi ficha political? . . . ¡Cuantas defensas he hecho en mi vida! Y, sin embargo, ¿seré capaz de defenderme ahora a mí mismo?

I have nothing to fear, I am a legal politician, a democratically elected MP, a representative of the popular will and, even if I'm in the opposition, in some ways I'm also part of the power structures. But there were so many years of clandestinity, of persecutions. What can my police file be like? . . . How many times have I defended others in my life! And, yet, will I be able to defend myself now?

As in the opening sequence of *Los placeres ocultos*, the dialogue at the start of *El diputado* is unremarkable. However, it sets up the dilemma of the main character with stark clarity. An MP belonging to the recently legalized 'Partido Radical Socialista' (a fictional amalgam of the real Socialist and Communist Parties), he is haunted by his past experience of oppression under Franco. Thus from the very beginning of the film there is an implicit contrast between the recent emergence of Marxist activists into the political arena and the continuing 'clandestinity' of homo-sexuals: both kinds of people will be described in similar terms throughout the film. And as in *Los placeres ocultos*, *mise en scène* is strictly functional: Roberto's casual but elegant clothes epitomize his class position as a progressive intellectual (*progre*). Even more schematically, he is defined by a single object: his heavy, square glasses, icon of 'straight' respectability (Plate 1). In the poster

---

[15] For *El diputado* as a continuation of *Los placeres*, see the interview by Pirula Arderius, 'Eloy de la Iglesia: "Aún no hay libertad de expresión"', *Información* (23 Feb. 1978). Richard Dyer mentions *El diputado* as one of those European films of the 1940s in which 'positive images [are] curtailed by social repression': *Now You See It: Studies on Lesbian and Gay Film* (London, 1990), 267. He is not quite right in saying that this film (like the others he treats) ends with the death of the gay protagonist: it is the youthful lover, not the eponymous MP, who is killed. I have consulted de la Iglesia's script: 'El diputado: título provisional' (Madrid, 1978).

used to advertise the film the glasses recur: the contrast between public rectitude and private deviance is expressed by having the husband, wife, and lover reflected in the dark lenses of Roberto's spectacles as they embrace.

As the opening sequence continues, Roberto (the mild-mannered José Sacristán) narrates in flashback the story of his continuing homosexual tendencies, to the accompaniment of *vérité* images such as a press photo of the Carretas Cinema in Madrid, a famous gay rendezvous. Attempting to reason with himself 'in a scientific and Marxist way' he marries, convinced that homosexuality was a 'bourgeois and counter-revolutionary deviation'. But erotic obsession transcends rational analysis: while imprisoned for illicit political activities in the last days of Francoism, he encounters Paco, a tattooed male prostitute; and in a voyeuristic scene typical of Eloy de la Iglesia watches as Paco's erect penis emerges from beneath a sheet. As in the opening shower sequence of *Los placeres ocultos*, this is not simply a scandalous challenge to the censor. It is also a direct assault on the mass audience, who find themselves encouraged to identify with the sympathetic Roberto's voyeuristic fascination.[16]

Homosexuality irrupts, then, as the random encounter that eludes rational analysis and disturbs correct political positions. But the irony here is that the object of sexual and political interest is identical: the exploited proletarian represented by a lumpen youth. The marginality of the Marxist before political reform and of the homosexual before sexual liberalization is thus both similar and different. In a speech to his fellow militants Roberto exclaims 'Legal or not, we're here to stay.' And his words clearly apply also to the gay constituency yet to emerge into the political arena.

In interviews on the film's release de la Iglesia repeatedly claims that *El diputado* sets out to show the contradictions between homosexuality and Marxism, between the struggle for sexual freedom and the class struggle. But he also invokes 'individual' freedom, inciting one interviewer to ask him leadingly if the film is autobiographical.[17] Within this framework of the individual 'case history' (enhanced by the privileged access

[16] The film found a new mass audience (of some three million) when shown on national television for the first time on 15 Nov. 1985. See De Stefano (n. 2 above).

[17] See n. 5 above.

of internal monologue or voice-over) the narrative will progress through schematic oppositions: the noble Roberto falls in love with Juanito (José Luis Alonso), a youth in the pay of a sinister conspiracy of the ultra-right. But this Manicheism, so scorned by critics at the time, conceals the complex relation between gay liberation and leftist politics which was also being explored outside Spain in the same period.

In his excellent 'Gays and Marxism', Bill Marshall explores the relationship between the two terms in Britain, France, and the USA in the 1970s.[18] He begins by identifying certain strands of (non-leftist) gay political activity in the Seventies:

An emphasis on the struggle for 'rights' of 'gays' as an identified sexual (analogous with racial) minority within the status quo of property relations; an emphasis on the fundamentally revolutionary/dissident position of being gay; an emphasis on personal liberation with wider political pretensions: 'the personal is political'. These positions, some-times distinct, sometimes interlinked, are clearly inimical to Marxism. They lack a *global* project, whether political (the transformation of class society) or intellectual (a theory of historical development, and within it, the oppression of gays); and they eschew a call to arms against capitalism. (p. 259)

This 'personalist' tendency shares with Marxist approaches of the same decade a lack of interest in material conditions and an unwillingness to consider the 'gay community' within the context of the distinct professions and class positions it actually occupies. In particular, it 'neglects the way in which class oppression intersects with the oppression of gays' (p. 263).

If we examine *El diputado* more closely we shall see that (coming from the very different context of the Spanish transition) *El diputado*'s account of gays and Marxism does not assume the existence of a homogeneous gay community; and indeed it insists constantly on the intersection of sexual and class interests, on the determining force of material (economic) conditions on libidinal relations. I will argue that the personal narrative of Roberto in the film is indeed political, but that politics is inseparable from the global project of the emancipation of the working class from capitalism.

Male prostitution is recurrent in the film. We first meet the

[18] In *Coming On Strong: Gay Politics and Culture*, ed. Simon Shepherd and Mick Wallis (London, 1989), 258–74.

angelic Juanito ('pinkish skin, blue-green eyes') at an orgy where his presence has been paid for by older men. And there is a continuing parallel between political and (homo)sexual corruption: thus when Roberto asks the *chapero* (male prostitute) Ness why he is now in the pay of the extreme right, the latter replies: 'You found it easy to buy me; so did they.' Roberto's leftist, internationalist culture is contrasted with Juanito's less sophisticated tastes, through schematic contrasts: Roberto recites a poem by Cernuda to his young lover, reads to him from *Capital*, or plays him a song by Georges Moustaki. Juanito initially reacts with scorn. But while such moments can be taken as stages in the progressive education of a lumpen youth, other sequences are more disturbing. Thus when the two men first make love in the secret apartment where the party faithful had met under Franco, de la Iglesia edits the scene with a series of shock cuts between the two bodies and the revolutionary posters on the wall of the flat. Or again at certain points the characters seem to parody Marxist vocabulary by repeating formulae in inappropriate contexts. Thus after considering her reaction to her husband's revelation of his gay affair, Roberto's wife (the perfectly poised María Luisa de San José) says that she 'has made a concrete analysis of a concrete situation'. On the film's release, critics chose not to recognize the overtly ironic tone of such comments (an irony which is confirmed by the script), reading them as unintentionally humorous.[19] But it remains the case that at key moments such as this one, political and affective discourses are imperfectly matched, and often flagrantly contradictory.

But in a Marxist reading it would be foolish to attempt to erase such inconsistencies of tone. For contradiction is of the essence. In an interview on *El diputado*'s release, the director claims that he has set out a problem, but not attempted to resolve it.[20] And at the close of the film, as we shall see, Roberto prides himself on having borne with his contradictions to the bitter end. The problem is that it is not simply the predicament of the character that is contradictory, it is also the texture of the film surface itself. Thus at times the narrative is interrupted and José Sacristán is required to deliver unashamedly expository

---

[19] See the anonymous review in *Arriba* (24 Jan. 1979), which gives the film a rating of 'zero'.

[20] Antonio Egido, '*El diputado*, político y homosexual; Eloy de la Iglesia: "Los partidos políticos no deben marginar la libertad sexual"', *El periódico* (19 Jan. 1979).

dialogue. A good example is an exchange with Juanito as they share a tent in the countryside, the location which serves (as in *Los placeres ocultos*) as the privileged site for illicit pleasure. Juanito asks Roberto why he's a communist: surely they are all manual labourers or people without cash; and of course none of them are queer. To this Roberto gamely replies that socialists like himself are attempting to build a new country which will offer a better future for all. As a 'Good Homosexual' Roberto is properly patient with his youthful lover's political education. To say that his character is implausible or a cardboard cutout is to miss the point. De la Iglesia claims to have chosen Sacristán for the part because he represented the 'standard' Spanish man. And he contrasts the old-style depiction of the homosexual in Spanish cinema (a heterosexual who disguises himself as a 'mariquita' in order to have greater success with women) with his own representation of him ('a man who sleeps with men because he likes it, and that's it').[21] The curious anaemia of Sacristán's performance is thus a significant part of the film's ideological message: as a strictly representative character (the typical Spaniard, the ordinary homosexual) he cannot be allowed any particularities of character or behaviour. To do so would be to put into jeopardy his value as an emblem of a particular social and political conjunction.

It is perhaps instructive to compare de la Iglesia and Sacristán's somewhat pallid creation with a literary precedent, Jordi Viladrich's *Anotaciones al diario de un homosexual comunista*, published in Madrid in 1977, the year before the release of *El diputado*. The text purports to be the diary of a gay Marxist who sends it to the (safely heterosexual) author in order to have the benefit of his sage commentary. The lurid cover, showing a hairy-chested figure whose head has been replaced by a hammer and sickle, sets the tone for the 'diary', which recounts 'Roberto''s flight from the monastery where he had sheltered and his descent into the Communist cells and gay bars of the big city. It is interspersed by Viladrich's ludicrous commentary (for which 'Roberto' expresses great thanks) in which he 'proves' that 'Roberto''s condition derives from an unresolved fixation on his

---

[21] A.M.M. (Angeles Maso), 'Llegó con *El diputado*: Eloy de la Iglesia: "La izquierda ha heredado una moral que no es la suya", *La vanguardia* (24 Oct. 1979); Diego Galán, 'Eloy de la Iglesia: la ambición de un cine popular', *Triunfo* (14 Feb. 1979).

mother. The end of the volume contains a joint lexicon of gay and Marxist terminology, proof (if any were needed) that homosexuality and Communism are linked, alien discourses, to be deciphered only with difficulty by the common reader.[22]

Against such a background, de la Iglesia's MP seems something of a revelation: the somewhat laborious stress on his morality and normality was no doubt necessary in the period. But what is striking about *El diputado* is that in spite of its 'personalized' depiction of politics and its autobiographical narrative (complete with 'intimate' voice-over), Roberto is never set up as a (pseudo-medical) case-history, and indeed never thinks to ask himself the cause of his homosexuality. Presented and experienced as a social relation which brings him into contact with men outside his own class, it is necessarily expressed through the discourses of ethics or politics, not those of psychiatry or medicine. Roberto's 'superficiality' (Sacristán's pale, blank face is like a reflecting screen) thus has an ideological as well as a narrative value: it suggests that once their sexual-object choice is acknowledged, homosexuals carry no psychic enigma or secret within them, are just 'men who like to sleep with men'. The demonstrative quality of de la Iglesia's cinema (its tendency to point things out to the audience without risking superfluous 'noise') would tend to vindicate just such a functional conception of characterization in film.

But such formal and conceptual clarity can be deceptive. An excellent critique in *La calle* ('The Street')—the journal that billed itself as 'the first on the left'—suggests that criticism should address itself to the clear and 'diaphanous' text if it is to draw out its ideological presuppositions.[23] *La calle* acknowledges that de la Iglesia's objective was to analyse the confrontation between leftist politics and homosexuality. However, the anonymous writer ('F.L.')[24] claims that the film ends at the very point this confrontation begins: when Roberto is about to reveal his private dilemma to the party conference. Genuine debate is avoided because the contradiction is interiorized (played out

---

[22] The copy in the Biblioteca Nacional, inscribed with marginalia correcting mistakes in the supposed 'gay lexicon', proves that the readership for sensationalist and homophobic works of this kind was not exclusively 'general'.

[23] '*El diputado* de Eloy de la Iglesia: a por los 300 millones' (30 Jan.–5 Feb. 1979).

[24] Probably Francisco (Francesc) Llinàs. (In Catalan, unlike in Castilian, 'll' is not a distinct letter.)

within the character's mind) or expressed only through his relationship with his wife. De la Iglesia thus fails to examine the bourgeois sexual ideology of the left, as he does not show the party reacting to Roberto's declaration.

What is more the film relies on three simplistic narrative devices: schematic simplification, sentimentality, and crude topicality. Thus José Sacristán's character must be adorned with positive attributes in order to make the audience 'forgive' his homosexuality; and this positive pole must be opposed by the equally monolithic evil of the far right. But this schematicism (the division into goodies and baddies) capsizes the picture: the dualistic structure does not permit the insertion of any contradictory factor (such as Roberto's wife) or any character who evolves towards a new consciousness during the course of the film (such as the youthful Juanito who discovers his own homosexuality and his commitment to his leftist lover). The audience's sentimental identification with the protagonist is thus achieved only at the cost of abandoning the political analysis which was the initial objective of the film. Without the 'spice' ('pimienta') of the sex scenes and the obtrusive references to actuality, the melodrama would prove unpalatable.

'F.L.''s account is the most substantial of those critics of the left who clearly felt themselves to be threatened by the film; and it should be added that *La calle* itself subsequently published a defence of *El diputado*.[25] But for 'F.L.' de la Iglesia's main sin is commercialism: the feature is entitled 'Out for 300 million', a reference to the number of pesetas the film was aiming for at the box office. What is more, *La calle* neglects the filmic texture of the work, reducing it to manifest content. José Luis Téllez in *Contracampo*, however, offers a more adequate reading.[26] His review is the text which first proposed that de la Iglesia's cinema be read as a pamphlet. Téllez argues that, taken in this generic context, the supposed defects of *El diputado* (archetypical characters, exaggerated situations, implausible dialogues, clumsy cinematic technique) are precisely the virtues of de la Iglesia's work. The role of such 'defects' is to communicate the moral of the film to the audience with the greatest efficacy: the moral being that Spain has been freed from dictatorship only to achieve

[25] Encarnación Andany, 'En defensa de *El diputado*' (13–19 Feb. 1979).
[26] No. 1 (Apr. 1979), 51–2.

a precarious and shameful parliamentarianism. Téllez draws attention to a particular technique: from time to time, one of the characters pretends to address another and, looking into the camera, expresses one of the salient points about the transition. In this coarse, Brechtian way political analysis is made to predominate over the plot which is merely the vehicle for it. The audience is directly addressed, invoked as the countershot to the close-up. But if this cinematic pamphlet draws on melodrama, its position is not that of the bourgeois noveletta, but rather the opposite: love is not a 'bridge' which permits the character to transcend class struggle, but rather a mechanism through which class struggle becomes visible and is made more conflictory. Thus Juanito's transformation from enemy and prostitute to comrade and lover leads inevitably to his death: a final emblem of the inexorable nature of (political and sexual) destiny.

At the end of the film (as so often in Eloy de la Iglesia's work) the youth is sacrificed: his former fascist paymasters murder him in revenge for his betrayal of their cause. Previously, however, he had been curiously integrated with the heterosexual couple in an ersatz family. Roberto's wife claims that she feels Juanito could be their son; and she comes to share Roberto's passion for the youth. Hence the triangle of *Los placeres ocultos* is reiterated with a twist: here the older man's passion is sexually gratified and indeed reciprocated. Juanito finally admits that he is no longer doing it for the money: the homosexual relation transcends financial motives for a moment, only to be destroyed by its implacable opponents.

In the final scene Eduardo, about to be elected leader of his party, resolves to tell his comrades the story that we have just seen narrated in the film. The script tells us that 'slowly he starts to clench his fist and he raises it firmly, angrily, hopefully. But he cannot stop his eyes filling with tears' (p. 213). The frame freezes as the 'Internationale' is played. It is an implausible, even derisory moment. But it is also a defiantly utopian image of a radicalism transformed by libidinal investment, of a Marxism inflected by homosexual affect.

4. *EL PICO*: REPRODUCING THE FATHER

A medium shot of two youths (Paco and Urko) sitting on a bridge, smoking marijuana. The camera tilts up as the boys stand: the industrial landscape of the port comes into view behind them. There are distant hills beyond. The camera follows them as they move right and a political poster comes into frame: it shows the head and shoulders of a smiling man with the words 'ARAMENDIA PARLAMENTURAKO'. The first youth holds the other next to the poster, comparing his image to that of the man who is his father, Basque separatist candidate in the forthcoming elections. Behind the (unremarkable) dialogue we hear the external diegetic sound that will recur throughout the film: a distant police siren[27] (Plate 2).

This early sequence of *El pico* maps out the narrative and ideological space within which the action of the film will unroll. In the foreground are the two youths, played by Pasoliniesque José Luis Manzano and elfin Javier García, respectively. Their relationship will be the main one in the film. In the middle ground is the symbolic or public space of paternal authority: Paco's father is a Civil Guard; and Urko's (as we have seen) a politician. And in the background the city of Bilbao: a site of political conflict, industrial decline, and inclement weather (the characters always seem to be huddled up against the cold or sheltering from the rain). This early image, then, suggests that the film will be concerned with relations between men: both horizontal (between friends of the same age) and vertical (between fathers and sons). As a narrative of genealogy or filiation, it will trace both the threats to the patriarchal order and the exclusion of women from that order. Like *Los placeres ocultos*, *El pico* is the story of a dying mother; and like *El diputado* it is the story of a female partner excluded from a relationship between men.

It was *El pico* that made *Diario 16* say that de la Iglesia's cinema had 'the aesthetics of the Y-front'[28] and made *El alcázar* claim one of his political aims was to 'praise queers'.[29] However, as we shall see, the theme of homosexuality is less prominent in this film than in the earlier two, in which the audience is

---

[27] *El pico* was highly controversial on its release; see José Arenas, '*El pico*, una película de Eloy de la Iglesia que se presenta polémica', *ABC* (7 Sept. 1983); however, 6 years later, when shown on television, critics decried it as 'pastiche' and 'melodrama': see anonymous previews in *Diario 16* (11 Aug. 1989) and *ABC* (11 Aug. 1989). I have also referred to the script: 'El pico: guión (título provisional)' (Madrid, 14 Feb. 1983).

[28] Manuel Hidalgo, 'Arrojarse a los pies del "caballo"', *Diario 16* (18 Sept. 1983).

[29] 15 Oct. 1983.

encouraged to identify with an unambiguously gay hero. I shall argue, however, that the explicit homosexual romance of de la Iglesia's unmade Basque melodrama *Galopa y corta el viento* recurs in sublimated form in the various relationships between men in *El pico* and in the central theme of heroin addiction, presented here as an eroticized spectacle of the male body. On the film's release, the still most frequently reproduced in the press was of the bare-chested Javier García injecting himself in the arm.

Critics have noted the information overload in de la Iglesia's narratives, the desire to 'tell it all' in each film.[30] This reaches a climax in *El pico*, which has at least five main themes: the Civil Guard, the family, homosexuality, drugs, and Basque politics. Newspapers at the time of its release stressed the topicality of these elements: de la Iglesia had hoped to have a real-life politician (José María Bandrés) play the part of the Basque separatist, just as he had had film-maker Juan Antonio Bardem play himself in *El diputado*.

In his excellent review-article in *Contracampo* Ignasi Bosch confirms that it is not the form but the referent of de la Iglesia's cinema that has proved so controversial: during the transition he unerringly chose to address those topics (such as homosexuality) which most Spaniards chose to ignore.[31] With transition now achieved and a Socialist government in power, political change would require both thematic and formal changes in de la Iglesia's cinematic practice. Bosch claims that those insistent (even hectoring) devices of earlier films (such as the racking focus we saw in *Los placeres ocultos*) are no longer appropriate. He calls attention to a very different technique which features in this film, the use of long takes without camera movement, more characteristic of art film than the exploitation genre. I shall return to one such sequence (Paco's birthday party) a little later.

De la Iglesia claimed that this was his most ambiguous film to date; and critics seemed uneasy as how to 'read' it. An extreme case is the literalism of *El alcázar*, which accused the film of promoting drug abuse by citing such lines as 'drugs give you peace' out of context.[32] Other critics, taking the opposite line,

---

[30] See Ignasi Bosch, '*El pico*: lo viejo y lo nuevo', *Contracampo* 34 (Winter 1984), 52–60 (p. 55).
[31] '*El pico*', 53.   [32] See n. 29 above.

attacked the film for excessive moralizing.[33] Less hostile pieces vindicated fertile contradictions within the film's modes and genres. Thus Ruiz de Villalobos noted twin tendencies to auteurism (a 'fabulous' *tremendismo*) and commercialism.[34] This conflict inspires an unprecedented intensification of narrative form. José Luis Guarner notes a similar conflict in the tone of the film, which switches between solemnity and irony: de la Iglesia is a 'journalist with the soul of a writer of novelettas [*folletinista*] . . . with a particular capacity to capture what is novelettish in real life'.[35] For Guarner, therefore, there is no simple opposition between melodrama and documentary, fiction and the real. Indeed, *El pico* may come closest to the real where it appears to be most fantastic.

El pico sets the central (non-sexual) relationship between the two boys in a number of different contexts: ethnicity, the family, homosexuality. We can consider each of these in turn. The youths (repeatedly described as 'intimate friends') are separated by ethnic difference: Paco is the son of a Castilian newcomer, the Civil Guard father who has been posted to a combat zone; the *euskera*-speaking Urko is 100 per cent autocthonous: the script tells us that he has 'unequivocally Basque features ["rasgos euskaldunes"]'. From the very beginning, then, the body is marked by the trace of cultural or ethnic difference and by its relation to a clearly defined territory. But *El pico* does not allow its audience the luxury of a belief in the untouched purity of Basque culture. When the two youths drift into heroin dealing to support their habits they are shown making a connection with a film director. He is shooting a youth in national costume dancing to the *txistu* or Basque flute. The incongruity is deliberately grotesque, demonstrating to the viewer that even the innocence of rural tradition has been corrupted by urban vice. Much later, when Paco resolves to leave Bilbao, the alien scene of his addiction, he tells his lover and protector the gay sculptor Mikel (bug-eyed Quique Sanfrancisco) that the Basque country is not his home-

[33] See Jorge de Cominges, 'Una historia que se permite todas las osadías', *Noticiero universal* (1 Oct. 1983); Francisco Marinero, review of *El pico*, *Diario 16* (8 Oct. 1983).

[34] '*El pico*: el fabuloso cine tremendista de Eloy de la Iglesia', *Diario de Barcelona* (25 Sept. 1983).

[35] Review of *El pico*, *El periódico* (4 Oct. 1983). This is one of the very few sympathetic reviews the film received.

land; the latter replies, 'This land belongs to all those who wish to live here.' But the exchange merely shows that the relationship between the youth and sculptor (like that between the two youths) is unavoidably marked by ethnic division. Homosexual desire can cross that divide but cannot erase it.

As always in de la Iglesia, such differences are reinforced unequivocally by *mise en scène*: Mikel drinks *pacharán* (the Basque liqueur); Betti, the Argentine prostitute who introduces the boys to heroin, sucks on *mate*. Or again, the cluttered vulgarity of the Civil Guard's home contrasts with the white walls and more modern tastes of the Basque politician's.

But if characters are representative of ethnic (and class) positions, they are also inextricably 'placed' within their families. One important early sequence here is Paco's eighteenth birthday. In a single long take with only slight adjustments of the camera, the family members and maid walk in and out of frame, eating and drinking, each speaking in turn on the phone to the grandmother who has called to congratulate her grandson. The soundtrack is muddy, with overlapping dialogue and background noise from the television. Film theory has often suggested that single takes such as these demand a more active response from the spectator, who is at liberty to move at will within the frame without the coercive direction of continuity editing. Ignasi Bosch,[36], however, suggests that this may not be the case here: the 'freedom of the look' is exercised not by the audience but by the cineaste who does not allow us to avert our gaze from the scene (p. 57). Through this 'violence', de la Iglesia points to a strictly political reading of an apparently banal set-up: through purely filmic means (that is, without recourse to explanatory dialogue) he suggests that in spite of the recent election of Socialist government in Spain, real change must take place at the concrete level of everyday life, far from the parliamentary assembly. The space of the family is thus implicitly presented as an ideological space, the point of struggle between new subjectivities and old power structures.

The crowded sequence shot of the party is followed by a scene between father and son in which editing also conveys meaning. The emblematically named Commander Torrecuadrada ('square tower')(played by the stolid José Manuel Cervino)

---

[36] See n. 30 above.

paints a moustache like his own on Paco's face and questions him about his sex life. A police siren is heard in the distance. When Paco claims (falsely) to be a virgin, his father commiserates: Basque women are all slags and their men queers. He thus proposes to give his son the same gift his father gave him: a visit to a high class brothel where his 'first time' will be a good one. Here the editing is more traditional than in the previous party sequence, moving from a medium two-shot of the men together, to reverse angle close ups of each as they speak in turn. However, the visual rhyme ('graphic match') of the shots (the new similarity of the son to the father effected by the false moustache) heightens the sense of symmetry inherent in the shot/countershot of continuity editing: it is a moment of homosocial reproduction, in which the father attempts to transmit heterosexual practices to his son.

This bonding of men is over the bodies of women: the female members of the family excluded from this 'man to man' conversation; the prostitute women whom the father regales with tales of his potency when he takes Paco to the brothel. However, the filiation process is disturbed: Paco is with Argentine prostitute Betti and is more engaged by her drugs than her sex. Naked on the bed, he passively allows himself to be caressed: the camera moves in to focus on the syringe that lies on the table beside the lovers.

This scene with *femme fatale* Betti is typical of the way in which the film graphically juxtaposes sex and drug abuse even as it acknowledges the loss of libido produced by heroin. The most fetishistic sequence of this kind occurs later in the film: Paco and Urko have weaned themselves off heroin, but return to Betti's for a sexual threesome (once more, male relations are effected quite literally over the body of the woman). As the youths horse around offscreen in the shower, a medium long shot shows Betti on the sofa in her flat (posters of David Bowie and Marilyn Monroe),[37] languidly preparing her fix. Paco enters naked and stands behind the sofa on the right; Urko does the same on the left. Medium close-ups of the two youths looking out of frame towards each other are followed by POV shots over Betti's

[37] Such references in the *mise en scène* allude to an international pop culture which is not presented as being at odds with the stress on regional identity also affected by de la Iglesia's young rebels.

shoulder as she syringes the solution from the spoon. The camera pulls in for extreme close-ups of the two boys and a final 'primerísimo plano' of Betti's black-nailed fingers squeezing the syringe until a pearl of the liquid drips from the end. A heartbeat is heard on the soundtrack.

The eroticization of drug abuse here does not arise solely from the nakedness of the actors or the phallic angle of the syringe. It is also inscribed in the filmic grammar that imposes an increasing identification with the youths' 'point of view'. It is interesting to note that de la Iglesia chooses to break the 180 degree rule (to 'cross the line' of the axis of action) precisely in order to give us the boys' POV shots. What is more, the boys look at each other, but not at the woman who has her back towards them. Just as vertical bonding between men (father and son) is achieved through the exchange of women (prostitution), so horizontal bonding is effected through the mediation of a prostitute who is excluded once more from the traffic of the male look.

It is not too far-fetched, then, to see drug abuse as a displacement of the homosexual romance in the original Basque project for which de la Iglesia failed to find funding. The ethnic conflict between the lovers of *Galopa y corta el viento* (a non-Basque Civil Guard and a member of ETA) recurs in the relationship between the two junkie sons and between the two mismatched fathers, who are forced to join forces in order to save their children. As secrets which must be confessed to the father, as creators of a clandestine community which is invisible to the dominant culture it inhabits, homosexuality and heroin addiction share a similar (culturally constructed) narrative space. In each clandestinity is dangerously combined with proximity: both are found in the heart of the family, in the centres of political power. And on a graphic level the male body is offered as an object of sacrifice to a mystic *jouissance*: the script tells us that Paco's face takes on an 'otherworldly glow' when he speaks of the peace brought by heroin (p. 35); Urko's white arm, held out horizontally by a police officer to display its tracks and illuminated by a table lamp, is reminiscent of Christ's on the cross. When towards the end of the film, Urko dies of an overdose, the two fathers meet over his dead body in the morgue. The Civil Guards keeping watch outside are silhouetted against the windows, their black outlines contrasting with the deathly pallor of the youth.

Homosexual desire is thus displaced or sublimated into conventional, homosocial relations. But *El pico* does indeed contain an openly gay character, Basque sculptor Mikel. Initially presented as an outcast (sitting on his own in a bar or park), Mikel later takes over the functions of the family which Paco's authoritarian father and dying mother are respectively unwilling and unable to provide. Thus, although Mikel's interest in Paco is unequivocally sexual (and we are told that Paco does not dislike his embraces) as a Good Homosexual he shelters Paco in his studio and lovingly nurses him during his attempt at withdrawal. In an ironic inversion, then, it is the (non-reproductive) gay man who takes over the nurturing, protective function of the family.

The contradictions between radical politics and homosexuality central to *El diputado* are here confined to a marginal character. Mikel (who prides himself on the fact that people such as himself will never be trusted by the Civil Guard) must also confront the ambivalent reaction of *abertzale* (separatist) politicians: Urko's father is proud of Mikel as a 'great national artist', but embarrassed by his declaration of homosexuality. When Paco leaves the studio intending to set out for a new life in Madrid, Mikel is left alone, in long shot, standing against a dark, rainy window: Paco tells him that he could never give him what he really wants. As in *Los placeres ocultos*, the gay man is condemned to dissatisfaction and solitude; but as in the earlier film again, the homosexual relationship is more markedly affective, even sentimental, than its heterosexual equivalents. The music swells as Paco takes his leave.[38]

In his interview with *Contracampo* some two years before *El pico* was made, Eloy de la Iglesia complained of a new economic censorship, more subtle than the Francoist political censorship, which had prevented him from making his Basque, gay melodrama (p. 34). However, we have seen that the dispersal or displacement of homosocial desire amongst the varied characters of *El pico* raises, perhaps inadvertently, questions which the original, inert plot of *Galopa y corta el viento* would not have addressed: the sublimated bonding of men in all-male structures (of family, friendship, profession) from which women are definitively excluded; the eroticization of the male body in the travail of heroin addiction. At the end of the film father and son confront

---

[38] Elsewhere the music is disconcertingly incongruous, as when a cheerful tune plays over the final credits.

one another on top of a cliff: before his overdose, Urko had killed a dealer with a gun which Paco had stolen from his father, Commander Torrecuadrada. The latter places the gun and stolen heroin in his three-cornered hat and throws it into the sea: the script says that it flies through the air 'like a UFO', scattering a cloud of white powder. The pun in the title of the film ('pico' refers to both the fix of heroin and the corner of the Civil Guard's hat) is thus visualized in this final image. As John Hopewell comments, it is a salutary irony that the father chooses to protect the honour of his family rather than that of the Civil Guard (he has just destroyed the only evidence that could convict his son of complicity in the murder). For as father and son go off embracing, the audience is left with the feeling that, as an institution, the family may be more insidiously oppressive than the military police (p. 238). Paco's liberation is illusory and cannot be sustained: the sea has served the symbolic function of nature and absolved him of his contradictions; but now he must return to the cultural and historical space of the city.

5. THE FAMILY ROMANCE

When de la Iglesia's *La semana del asesino* ('The Week of the Assassin') was shown at the Berlin Film Festival in 1972, the distributors handed out sick bags to the audience (*Contracampo* interview, p. 29). While the violence in these films no longer seems as graphic as it once did, their sexual content would make distribution difficult in Britain and the USA today. In Spain to speak of de la Iglesia is to risk ridicule or worse: there can be few film-makers whose work seems to be so marked by the period in which it was made, in this case the transition to democracy. In terms of distribution, his cinema profited from the brief period (1977–84) between the end of censorship and the establishment of 'Salas X', cinemas licensed to show hard pornography. It was the time of the *destape* or 'strip' when actors (overwhelmingly female) first appeared naked in Spanish films.[39] Once the shock value attached to the disrobing of bodies or the presentation of taboo topics had died away, the market for de la Iglesia's cinema was bound to diminish. Times were changing, and on the same

---

[39] On the problematic end of censorship after the death of Franco see Hopewell, *El cine*, 140–7.

day that *Diario 16* slammed *El pico* (8 October 1983) it named
Almodóvar's *Entre tinieblas* ('Dark Habits') film of the week.

De la Iglesia himself was very conscious of the problems of
exhibition his films had even at their most popular, telling
Contracampo how *Colegas* ('Mates' 1982) was removed from the
upmarket Cine Fuencarral (in spite of its success) by a manage-
ment fearful of the suburban hooligans it had drawn into town.[40]
But by 1985 he had distanced himself from his earlier sympathies: abandoning the Communist Party, berating the Basque
Nationalist Party for its provincialism, and rejecting homosexuality for an erotic 'pluralism'.[41] His most recent film *La
estanquera de Vallecas* ('The Lady in the Vallecas Kiosk' 1987)
contains familiar low-life elements and stars the now adult José
Luis Manzano, but is couched in an uncertain comic tone.

In the introduction to this chapter I suggested that what was
interesting about the films I have discussed here is the combination of homosexuality and mass culture. And it is significant that
the emergence of gay men into commercial cinema in Spain in
the 1970s parallels the experience of British and East German
film in the 1960s and 1980s, respectively. Thus the British *The
Leather Boys* (1963) and the German *Coming Out* (1989) both
confront us with Good Homosexuals whose existing relationships
with women are disturbed by their attraction to men. This would
suggest that plots such as that of *El diputado* are to be expected
at moments of social and political transition comparable to that
of Spain (the liberalization of post-war Britain, the disintegration
of Communism in East Germany). In these films (as in de la
Iglesia) female desire is presented as an obstacle, and lesbian
desire inconceivable.

In the sequel to *El pico* (1984) Paco is sent to jail, where his
beauty makes him the object of a quarrel between jealous male
lovers. As John Hopewell describes, his adoptive 'family' in the
prison cell is finally replaced by his father's 'family': on his
release Paco joins the army. He ends the sequel with a son, still
dealing heroin from his outwardly respectable position. In the
new democratic Spain, styles may change, but patriarchal structures (fatherhood, police, army) remain the same. It is de la

---

[40] In the special section (see n. 9 above), 30.
[41] Interview with Carel Peralta, 'Eloy de la Iglesia: "El *PNV* tiene un concepto
aldeano de la moral"', *Interviú* (30 Oct.–5 Nov. 1985).

Iglesia's achievement, however, to have desublimated these homosocial institutions, to have laid bare the libidinal investments implicit in the same-sex communities of banking, politics, the armed forces, and prison. It is a dangerous knowledge which mass audiences (and most critics) would prefer to ignore.

The Spanish critics who reviled Eloy de la Iglesia (including those such as Fernando Trueba who went on to make films of their own) argued from art-house criteria. Unsympathetic to the genre theory which had made critics in France or the USA re-evaluate B-movies or exploitation pictures, they failed to acknowledge that 'quality' cinema was itself a category that was historically constructed. The endemic anaemia of Spanish film making under the Socialists (the reliance on literary adaptations and decorative *mise en scène*)—an anaemia challenged most forcefully by Almodóvar—owes much to this middle-brow respect for 'art'. The time is clearly ripe for a re-evaluation of de la Iglesia's œuvre from the twin perspective of *auteurisme* and genre theory: while the former would account for the idiosyncratic topics and filmic language of his cinema, the latter would approach its narrative structure unimpeded by bourgeois notions of good taste. The vindication of once-neglected genres such as the horror movie or the woman's picture clearly serves as a precedent for the reappraisal of de la Iglesia's *tremendista* melodramas.

At the end of *El diputado*, the José Sacristán character says 'I signed up to change history; I ended up suffering it.' This line sums up de la Iglesia's career to date: his politically engaged cinema once sought to change Spain and has now been abandoned by it. But the line also points to the essence of his characters in these films, who at once act on and are acted upon by history. Stephen Heath refers to two modes of subjectivity in cinema: the subject-process, which charts the development of character through metonymic displacement; the subject-reflection, which marks the point at which the character stops to look back at him- or herself.[42] The ceaseless displacement of the process can lead to chaos; the frozen reflection of the position to stasis. In classic (Hollywood) narrative the two modes are sewn (or 'sutured') together so that no join is visible. I would argue

[42] 'Film Performance', in *Cinetracts* 1/2 (1977), 9; cited in Steve Neale, *Genre* (London, 1987), 26–7.

that the discontinuity of de la Iglesia's cinema derives precisely from an unwillingness or inability to stitch together the fabrics of process and reflection, which remain distinct and jarring. Thus at some points in his films the dynamic rhythm of the plot leads to chaos; and at others the totemic nature of the characters leads to stasis. A good example here is *El diputado*, in which the extravagant complexities of the plot fail to mesh with the simple schematicism of the characters: Roberto's *prise de position* is massively over-determined. Such inconsistencies can no longer be dismissed as simple incompetence. Rather they should be interrogated for what they tell us of a cinematic practice and its relation to a historical moment.

What characterizes de la Iglesia's cinema, finally, is a nostalgia for the family and for the reproduction of the real. Both are rendered impossible by his continuing commitment to the representation of gay men. For, according to these films, homosexuality exists primarily as a disturbance in heterosexual and familial relations; it thus follows that a homosexual hero must be a special case, cannot be representative of the totality of social circumstances at any moment in a nation's history. Moreover, this disturbance at the heart of the family resists naturalistic expression, is best served by the conventions of melodrama. For all their love of the referent and passion for topicality (*El pico* begins with Felipe González's inauguration) these films are also small-scale romances of the private sphere. Thus the cinema of Eloy de la Iglesia is transitional in all senses: it chronicles the historical period of the shift from dictatorship to democracy; it exploits the distribution hiatus between the end of censorship and the legalization of pornography; and it depicts in the struggles of the homosexual hero the emergence of a new figure in Spanish film: the gay man who was to speak for and of himself.

5
Pedro Almodóvar's Cinema of Desire

I. HOMOSEXUALITY, POSTMODERNISM, AND SELF-PUBLICITY

It was Guillermo Cabrera Infante who rebaptized Almodóvar 'Almodollar'.[1] But it is worth remembering that the director who is currently the most commercially successful Spanish film-maker of all time only achieved that position in 1988 on the release of his seventh feature, the screwball comedy *Mujeres al borde de un ataque de nervios* ('Women on the Verge of a Nervous Breakdown'). His previous film, the gay melodrama *La ley del deseo* ('The Law of Desire', 1987) had been pointedly passed over when it came to nominating films for the Spanish equivalents of the Oscar awards.[2] Critical respectability also came late: the first (English) version of John Hopewell's classic study of post-Franco cinema (1986) devoted only two pages to Almodóvar; the second (Spanish) version (1989) boasted twelve.[3]

As a commercial and cultural phenomenon the cinema of Almodóvar is inextricably bound up with such 'external' factors as press coverage, marketing, and 'style'. Thus (unlike Eloy de la Iglesia) Almodóvar benefited from generally favourable reviews, and he showed from the very beginning a determination to manipulate the press. An interview in *Contracampo* on the release of his first feature *Pepi, Luci, Bom, y otras chicas del montón* ('Pepi, Luci, Bom, and Other Girls on the Heap', 1980) already carries the warning that it has been 'revised' by its subject.[4] And Almodóvar's particular graphic sense has been diffused through print as well as film: thus a feature in *Tribuna* ('Madrid: Court of the Moderns', 18 May 1986) placed his cinema in the context of

---

[1] Augusto M. Torres, 'Entre el super 8 y el Oscar', *El país* (30 Apr. 1989).

[2] The 'Goyas', chosen by the Academia de las Artes y Ciencias Cinematográficas de España.

[3] *Out of the Past*, 238–40; *El cine*, 444–55.

[4] Juan I. Francia and Julio Pérez Perucha, 'Primera película: Pedro Almodóvar', *Contracampo* 23 (Sept. 1981), 5–7.

the capital's fashion (Sybilla) and pop music (Alaska); the lavish press kit for *Mujeres* (which reproduces the stylish credit sequence in full) owes much to the graphic design of Studio Gatti; more recently the glossy *El europeo* (January 1989) produced a lavishly illustrated special feature on the director's œuvre, with articles by distinguished critics such as Vicente Molina Foix.[5] The distinction between film and design was further blurred by the announcement that, with the release of *¡Atame!* ('Tie me up! Tie me down!', 1990), Almodóvar's production company was diversifying not just into publishing, but also into the marketing of jewellery and leatherware.[6] A great deal of the Spanish press coverage on Almodóvar and his entourage has focused on their presence at glamorous parties, first in Madrid and Barcelona, and latterly in New York and Los Angeles.[7] It would be naïve to dismiss such journalism as somehow indifferent to the films themselves. For the figure of the *auteur* is here indistinguishable from his œuvre: Almodóvar's practice of cinema goes beyond production, into distribution and exhibition.

The narrative of Almodóvar's own biography (from childhood in La Mancha to telephone-operator and underground film-maker in Madrid) is endlessly repeated in interviews, and need not concern us here. However, uniquely in Spain, that narrative has always been openly homosexual. But while earlier interviews reveal an open pleasure in kitsch, camp, and homoerotic fantasy,[8] later pieces display an increasing disavowal of homosexuality, whether it is understood as a cultural identity, a recognizable sensibility, or a specific filmic tradition. Thus Almodóvar has angrily rejected comparisons between his own work and that of Cukor or Fassbinder; and claims in an interview with Lola Díaz (*Cambio 16*, 18 April 1988) to hate 'obvious homosexual expressions . . .[and] gay sensibility'. A writer such as Genet 'transcends' his subject matter: he could be writing about any subject; it just happens to be men (*tíos*). Almodóvar goes on to cite Luis Berlanga as an example of a Spanish director who is

[5] 'Almodóvar: bordeando el borde', *El europeo* 8 (Jan. 1989), 65–87.

[6] Gloria Selo and Emilio Garrido, 'Almodóvar monta un imperio amenazado por sus enemigos', *Tribuna* (5–11 Feb. 1990).

[7] For a more considered account of Almodóvar's reception in the USA, see Vicente Urbistondo, 'El triunfo de Almodóvar: forasteros en Hollywood', *El país* (20 Dec. 1988).

[8] See Angel S. Harguindey, 'Pedro Almodóvar: toma la fama y corre', *El país semanal* (29 Sept. 1984). Harguindey plays the cameo of a journalist in *Entre tinieblas*.

heterosexual, but whose work has a 'feminine' quality none the less.[9] As we shall see, when he speaks of *La ley del deseo* (his only feature to centre on a gay male relationship) he repeatedly denies it is a film 'about' homosexuality: it is purely incidental that the main characters are gay.

This attitude is clearly disingenuous: there is little doubt that Almodóvar's work would not have achieved its success abroad without the support of the gay press and gay audiences: his films still tend to be shown in cinemas known for lesbian/gay programming (the Scala and Metro in London) or in areas with large gay/lesbian communities (Greenwich Village). However, some commentators have suggested that Almodóvar's claim that homosexuality is purely 'incidental' in his cinema is quite simply a reflection of the social reality of contemporary Spain. Thus David Leavitt notes in the London *Guardian* (23 June 1990) that in *La ley del deseo*, 'one never has the sense that the characters' homosexuality in and of itself is the main subject. The only "law" that concerns the film's hero and his two lovers is desire itself.' Leavitt goes on to suggest that this is because 'the characters in the film live, like Almodóvar, in an atmosphere in which homosexuality is so taken for granted that the choice between making a film with homosexual or heterosexual protagonists becomes a purely artistic one'. In a gesture characteristic of press coverage of Almodóvar, Leavitt cites the party for the première of *¡Atame!* as evidence, claiming of the guests that 'some are gay and some are straight; as in *Law of Desire*, no one seems to care much one way or the other.'[10]

The problem with this sanguine view of contemporary Spain (based, of course, on a tiny, Madrid-based sample) is that it colludes with those who would deny homosexuality any specificity, who also believe that the artist (like Almodóvar's Genet) 'could be writing about any subject' when s/he chooses to represent lesbians or gay men. One example of the disavowal of specifically homosexual themes in Almodóvar's work is the critical neglect

---

[9] See Lola Díaz, 'Pedro Almodóvar: "Cuando me comparan con Fassbinder me parece una pesadilla"', *Cambio 16* (18 Apr. 1988); for a more recent and sympathetic interview, see Ryan Murphy, 'A Spanish Fly in the Hollywood Ointment: Gay Director Pedro Almodóvar Refuses to be Tied Up by Censorship', *The Advocate* (19 June 1990), 37–40.

[10] David Leavitt, 'Almodóvar on the Verge', *Weekend Guardian* (23–4 June 1990), 12–16.

of the theme of lesbianism in films such as *Pepi, Luci* and the convent comedy *Entre tinieblas* ('In the Dark/Dark Habits', 1983). Thus in his review of the second film (6 May 1988), the *New York Post*'s V. A. Musetto congratulates Almodóvar on the absence of the 'homosexual obsession so prevalent in [his] other films', while failing to inform his readers that the film is a lesbian love story. While Almodóvar's fear of being pigeon-holed as a 'gay director' is understandable (and *¡Atame!* in particular has suffered at the hands of critics who seem unable to believe that a gay cineaste can direct a heterosexual narrative), we need not conceive homosexuality in the cinema as a unified identity, much less a particular filmic style, handed down from one director to another (from Cukor, to Fassbinder, to Almodóvar), and thus innocent of historical change and cultural difference. In *Now You See It: Studies on Lesbian and Gay Film* (London, 1990), Richard Dyer traces the historical construction of different (and often mutually exclusive) identities and styles, the emergence of new subjectivities and new modes of expression in North America and Europe.[11] One aim of this chapter will be to measure Almodóvar's representations of lesbians and gay men against these foreign forms, to see to what extent they defer to or differ from cultural models outside Spain.[12]

[11] I cite Dyer's book throughout this ch. as it is the fullest and most recent work on the topic; it is also the only one which covers cinema and criticism in languages other than English. As Dyer draws the line at 1980, he does not treat Almodóvar's work. For female friendship and lesbianism, see Lucy Fischer, *Shot/Countershot: Film Tradition and Women's Cinema* (London, 1989), 216–68. Previous books on 'gays and film' in English include Dyer's early pamphlet of that name (London, 1977), which has essays by the editor, Caroline Sheldon, and Jack Babuscio; and Vito Russo, *The Celluloid Closet: Homosexuality and the Movies* (New York, 1981). For Hollywood, see 'When the Gaze is Gay', special section of *FC* 22/2 (Apr. 1986), 31–50. In the 'Coda' to this ch. I refer to Andrew Ross's more recent work on camp and pornography: *No Respect: Intellectuals and Popular Culture* (New York, 1989). Fiorenzo Lancini and Paolo Sangalli, *La gaia musa* (Milan, 1981) is a skimpy survey, with some interesting Italian material. Jean-François Garsi (ed.), *Cinémas homosexuels* (Paris, 1983), is a collection of short pieces which include an interview with Guy Hocquenghem (46–8); Bertrand Philbert, *L'Homosexualité à l'écran* (Paris, 1984) is a fuller account from a social constructionist viewpoint, excellently illustrated. I know of no equivalent volumes in Spain.

[12] Other Spanish films with gay themes in the early 1980s include Ramón Fernández's *Gay Club* (1981), in which the rhetoric of 'gay rights' is combined with gross stereotyping; and Imanol Uribe's lugubrious *La muerte de Mikel* ('Mikel's Death', 1984), in which Imanol Arias plays a Basque nationalist ostracized by his fellow politicians only to be murdered by military police. For the former see the review by M. Vidal Estévez, *Contracampo* 21 (Apr.–May 1981), 69.

Dyer charts the emergence in the USA of a specifically homosexual film (made by and for lesbians and gays) in symbiosis with the North American underground cinema of the Sixties (pp. 102–74). And Almodóvar's early work would seem to coincide with this model. Madrid (like Warhol's New York) benefited from a 'cross-over' between the art and fashion worlds and the gay scene; and a film such as *Pepi, Luci* reveals formal and thematic characteristics similar to those of Warhol and his coterie: the rejection of the mainstream virtues of 'finish' and 'clarity' in favour of an aesthetics of the ugly ('feismo'); the movement of hitherto marginal subject-matter and characters (practitioners of drug abuse and homosexuality) to the centre of the frame. As Dyer claims for Warhol once more (pp. 152–4), the growing commercial success of these films, their move into the mainstream, meant that suddenly they seemed representative of a moment in national history. Warhol's 'freaks' concretized the urban decay and growing uncertainty of American society; Almodóvar's fabulous eccentrics signalled the definitive break with a dictatorship which now need no longer be mentioned. The lack of reference to Franco in his films was thus a conspicuous absence which signalled the end of the transition. In Hopewell's phrase, Almodóvar moved from 'post-war' to 'post-filth' ('De la posguerra a la posguarra', 444), a reference to the increasingly 'clean' aesthetic pleasures offered by his later films.

One problem with approaching Almodóvar's work is the difficulty of finding a tone appropriate to discuss his very particular comic sensibility. In his rather patronizing review of two recent books on the director (*El país* 30 April 1989), Augusto M. Torres attacks these pioneering studies for being excessively respectful to the œuvre and for failing to give a properly critical acount of it.[13] For Torres, the Almodóvar 'phenomenon' is more interesting than the films themselves, which cannot be considered (as the books suggest) 'a complete, perfect and harmonious whole'. But if it is indeed the case that respectful

---

[13] See n. 1 above. The books are Nuria Vidal, *El cine de Pedro Almodóvar* (Barcelona, 1988) and María Antonia García de León and Teresa Maldonado, *Pedro Almodóvar: la otra España cañí* (Ciudad Real, 1989). The first is a useful collection of interviews; the second a dogged, sociological study with a useful filmography and selection of edited reviews. The humorous and incisive prologue is by John Hopewell (pp. 13–20). For a review of the Eng. trans. of this book see Peter W. Evans, *BHS* 67 (1990), 311–12.

academicism is inappropriate when dealing with films as anarchic and irreverent as those of Almodóvar, this problem of the
tone or register of critical discourse raises complex questions of
genre and identification. For example, the three films that I
study in this chapter all suggest a playful, self-conscious attitude
to questions of narrative: in *Pepi, Luci* the main character
(Carmen Maura) is planning to make a film of the action we are
seeing, and indeed instructs her 'actors' on how to be more real,
more perverse; in *Entre tinieblas*, Sister Rat (Chus Lampreave) is
a writer of sleazy novels whose plots are transcriptions of the
'real-life' stories of the fallen girls she has welcomed into her
convent; in *La ley del deseo* the main character Pablo (Eusebio
Poncela) is a cineaste writing the script for a film curiously
similar to the one we are watching. In each of these cases, then,
narrative is internalized as the object (not the means) of representation. However, such a device could be taken by the critic
either as a serious account of the role of fabulation in human
life[14] or as a cheerful gesture of complicity with the audience, an
acknowledgement that 'it's only a movie'. I shall argue, however,
that this difficulty in reading the films is precisely one of the
qualities defining the Almodóvarian 'atmosphere', which is now
as unmistakeable as that of Genet.

In linguistic terms, the consummate conjunction (linking
device) in Almodóvar's work is the 'as if . . .'. Thus a punk can
urinate on a housewife during her knitting class (*Pepi, Luci*), a
nun can trip on LSD (*Entre tinieblas*), and a transsexual return to
the seminary s/he attended in her/his youth (*La ley del deseo*) *as if*
it were perfectly natural. For all the scandal surrounding the
initial exhibition of these films, within the narratives themselves
the bizarre is wholly taken for granted. This places the audience
in a position of complicity with the film-maker: the spectator
must take the hermetic film world on its own terms or leave the
cinema. Richard Dyer asks whether it is possible to represent
homosexuality as 'incidental' in film without condemning it to
marginality (p. 166). And this is the fundamental problem in
examining the lesbian and gay interest of Almodóvar's cinema.
It is possible that the 'as if' places the spectator in a position of
indifference or disinterest with regard to homosexuality within

[14] For fabulation as the space of postmodern philosophy and culture, see Gianni
Vattimo, *La fine della modernità* (Milan, 1985).

the film, without necessarily challenging her or his attitudes towards the subject outside the cinema.[15]

The wilful generic confusion of these films will also unsettle audiences (and indeed actors: Carmen Maura recounts her distress at the amused response of a Canadian audience to a scene in which a naked man attempts to rape her in a shower).[16] And it seems the (homosexually loaded) terms of camp or kitsch (or the more neutral Spanish 'hortera') are of little help here. Indeed Susan Sontag's well-known definition of camp as 'failed seriousness'[17] is reversed by Almodóvar: the gravely hopeful ending of *Pepi, Luci* and the openly tragic conclusions of *Entre tinieblas* and *La ley del deseo* suggest rather a seriousness that it is fully achieved, but which remains articulated none the less within a comic context. And here performance is of the essence: Carmen Maura's particular significance as the most prominent actor in Almodóvar's work is to have added a defiant pathos to female characters placed in absurd and humiliating positions.[18]

As in the case of Eloy de la Iglesia, then, the *auteurisme* of Almodóvar (the fact that each of his films is immediately recognizable as his) is both compromised and facilitated by a contradictory engagement with genre. And as with de la Iglesia, once more, the two most significant genres are *cinéma vérité* and melodrama. Thus the *vérité* of the underground (as in Warhol) relies for its effect on actuality, on the unmistakable (but often repressed) knowledge that the events happening before the camera really did take place, in a particular place and at a particular time. The notorious 'meada' ('peeing') sequence of *Pepi, Luci* exemplifies this; as does the meticulous attention to the fashion and nightlife of a subculture in the early films. For novelist and columnist Francisco Umbral (writing in *El mundo*, 25 January 1990), Almodóvar is the quintessential chronicler of

---

[15] It is thus not my aim to argue that Almodóvar's representations of homosexuality (whether as everyday reality or exotic spectacle) are inherently progressive.

[16] See Richard Guilliat's interview, 'Maura the Merrier', *20/20* (June 1989), 70–3 (p. 73).

[17] 'Notes on Camp', in *Against Interpretation* (London, 1967), 275–92; see also Andrew Ross, 'Uses of Camp', in *No Respect*, 135–70; for 'black camp' (in Joe Orton) see Dollimore, *Dissidence*, 315–18. Eve Kosofsky Sedgwick and Michael Moon, 'Divinity: A Dossier' (on drag star Divine), *Discourse* (Winter 1991) [forthcoming].

[18] Almodóvar has frequently stressed his love for what is culturally coded as feminine; see e.g. the interview in *Dunia* with Charo Izquierdo, 'Pedro Almodóvar: "Ahora está de moda el placer"' (29 Nov. 1983). This does not, however, absolve his films from charges of misogyny (see 'Coda' to this chapter).

Madrid, the film-maker whose work could never be dubbed, so immediate is its (literal and filmic) language.[19]

On the other hand, Almodóvar's deliriously complex, screen-plays (written of course by himself) plainly draw on melodrama. But this does not in itself make the films less serious. Melodrama is rather a traditional way of incorporating fantasy and desire into narrative. And as a genre gendered as 'feminine', it is of course associated with the family.[20] I shall argue that (unlike de la Iglesia) Almodóvar reveals no nostalgia for the heterosexual family, but rather takes for granted the existence of homosexual 'pretend families': lesbian mothers, communities of women, looser groupings of same-sex friends. More particularly, melodrama provides a precedent for a non-linear narrative based on repetition and reversion which Tania Modleski identifies with 'woman's (non-phallic) time'.[21] I shall return to Modleski's discussion of the obsessive structures of melodrama when I treat *La ley del deseo*.

It is a commonplace of cultural theory that mass culture is based (like melodrama) on repetition, on the reproduction of an original object now definitively lost.[22] Popular cinema thus endlessly reduplicates 'simulacra'[23] of formulae long since deprived of artistic 'aura'. It seems likely that this sceptical, ironic reading of mass culture is already integrated into Almodóvar's cinematic practice and accounts for another aspect of his distinc-tive tone. To take just two examples, advertising and popular music (especially the bolero) are intrinsic parts of the Almodóvar-ian filmic repertoire and not external elements 'appliquéd' to the filmic surface. John Hopewell has offered a brief and somewhat ironic sketch of just such a (postmodern) reading of Almodóvar,

[19] *¡Atame!* has indeed been released on video in a version dubbed into North American English (see 'Coda').

[20] See *Home Is Where the Heart Is: Studies in Melodrama and the Woman's Film*, ed. Christine Gledhill (London, 1990), esp. Thomas Elsaesser, 'Tales of Sound and Fury: Observations on the Family Melodrama' (43–69). For changing images of the family and masculinity in US film and television, see Andrew Ross, 'Cowboys, Cadillacs, and Cosmonauts: Families, Film Genres, and Technocultures', in James A. Boone and Michael Cadden (eds.), *Engendering Men* (New York, 1990), 87–101.

[21] 'Time and Desire in the Woman's Film', *Home* (see n. 20 above), 326–38. For more on the problems of representation see, in the same volume, Annette Kuhn, 'Women's Genres: Melodrama, Soap Opera, and Theory', 339–49.

[22] For an early account of this argument (derived, of course, from Benjamin), see Frederick Jameson, *Marxism and Form* (Princeton NJ, 1971), 60–83 (esp. p. 76–7).

[23] The term simulacrum is mainly associated with Jean Baudrillard: see 'Simula-cra and Simulations', in *Selected Writings*, ed. Mark Poster (Cambridge, 1988), 166–84; and my *Representing the Other*, ch. 6.

couched (appropriately perhaps) in the form of a comic dialogue.[24] For Hopewell, Almodóvar's early work bears all the distinctive marks of postmodernism: the erasure of the distinction between high art and subculture; the appeal to allusive citation; the mixing of genres; the use of unmotivated images, sound effects, or shots. He also mentions a specific device: the absence of establishing shots at the beginning of sequences, a technique typical of pop videos (introduction to García de León and Maldonado, pp. 17–18). This last detail is particularly interesting: few critics have paid much attention to the formal structure of Almodóvar's work. For Hopewell, the later films reveal not only an increasingly assured technique, but also a characteristic he does not hestitate to call 'moral': the serious investigation of desire (and particularly of feminine and homosexual desire) (p. 19).

This general concern remains for Hopewell a personal matter, the province of Almodóvar's uniquely individual style. And (like postmodernism), as a moral ethos it is difficult to reconcile with political engagement.[25] Almodóvar has sometimes been criticized (particularly outside Spain) for repressing Spanish history, for failing to refer to the Civil War and dictatorship so important to an earlier generation of Spanish film-makers.[26] I will argue that there is none the less an implicit political and historical emphasis in his work, particularly in relation to homosexuality; and that this critique is embedded in the filmic texture of his work, not openly voiced in its dialogue. When Almodóvar presents two women cooking together or amorously miming a love song to each other (*Pepi, Luci, Entre tinieblas*) when he shows a male film-maker urging a youth to masturbate for the camera (*La ley del deseo*), he engages the spectator in a traffic of homosexual reflection (of voyeurism and identification) which requires an urgent and immediate response. It is this response that we shall now examine.

2. *PEPI, LUCI, BOM*: LESBIAN COMEDY

A medium shot of two women knitting indoors: Pepi (Carmen Maura) is thirtyish and wears a dress with black, white, and red

[24] See the introd. to García de León and Maldonado (n. 13 above).

[25] See Christopher Norris, 'Lost in the Fun House: Baudrillard and the Politics of Postmodernism', *TP* 3 (1989), 360–88.

[26] See the survey of US responses to Almodóvar in Urbistondo, n. 7 above.

stripes; Luci (Eva Siva) is 'fortyish and submissive' (script, p. 12) with sculptured hair and a neat blue cardigan. They quarrel over the knitting, and Pepi, now in close-up, eyes her companion lasciviously and strikes her on the arm. In a series of reverse angle shots Luci modestly explains to the admiring Pepi how she likes to be dominated. Pepi pricks her arm with the needle, with a smile of complicity; and, on hearing the doorbell, disappears out of frame.

Cut to medium long shot from Luci's POV of Bom (Alaska), a teenage punkette in a black dress and a leopard-print coat. We see a close up of Luci's reaction, her mouth gaping in wonder at this vision. In medium long shot, with Luci still sitting in the centre, Pepi moves into frame on the left, Bom on the right. The latter lifts her leg towards the wall. A match on action shows her completing the gesture from the side: now her leg arches over the top of the frame; Luci's hesitant face is below on the right; and the admiring Pepi is in the centre. A stream of urine crosses the screen and bathes the now ecstatic Luci.[27]

Almodóvar has proudly called *Pepi, Luci* his 'dirtiest' film, claiming that he wanted to show behaviour typical of pornography within a naturalistic and everyday atmosphere, free from exhibitionism (*Guía del ocio*, 3 November 1980). And it is clear that the humour of this scene lies in the contrast between banal, domestic reality (knitting classes) and perverse sexual practice: after urinating on her new-found partner Bom asks politely which part of Spain she is from. But this early sequence in the film is not merely important for the incongruity it suggests between bodily function and social convention. It also sets up a triangular structure which will operate throughout this lesbian comedy: the relationship between housewife Luci and punk singer Bom (the only one which will last the length of the film) is mediated for the viewer by Carmen Maura's Pepi, who serves both as an identification figure (we see most of the action through her eyes) and as a proxy for our voyeurism. Pepi does not take

---

[27] For urination and sadomasochism see the account by Antoine de Baecque of a sequence parodying television commercials, '"Pipi [*sic*], Luci, Bom": Pedro Almodóvar joue avec les signes de la pub[licité] sur fond d'instruction sado-maso', *CaC* 437 (1990), 88–9; see also reviews on the French release of this film by Philippe Royer, *Positif* 358 (1990), 79; and Jacques Valot, *RC* 465 (1990), 28. Neither of these reviewers mentions the lesbian theme of the film. I have also consulted the script: 'Guión original' (Madrid, 28 Nov. 1981).

part in the sex action, but is shown to initiate it and to take pleasure in watching her friends. This triangular structure ('top', 'bottom', and mediating voyeur) raises particular problems for the heterosexual male spectator, whose quest for pleasure in the pornographic scene is continually disrupted by banal, material detail (knitting needles and polite conversation).[28]

Pepi, Luci is Almodóvar's first feature, shot over a period of eighteen months (1979–80) on a minuscule budget. The coarseness of the image (16 millimetre blown up to 35) and the muddiness of the soundtrack are immediately apparent. One problem with discussing this film, then, is the extent to which its cinematic qualities result from deliberate technique or the exigencies of financial necessity. In his interview with *Contracampo*,[29] Almodóvar claimed that he adapted the material to suit the budget: for example, he could not afford a lighting engineer, but wrote the project in such a way that the quality of image was not important (p.7).

On its release *Pepi, Luci* was praised for its 'spontaneity' and 'freshness' by influential critics such as Diego Galán (*El país*, 30 October 1980).[30] However, if we look at the opening scenes (which take place just before the 'meada' examined above) we can see that this effect is by no means natural and is rather the result (conscious or otherwise) of a deviation from the norms of continuity editing. Thus in the first sequence, Pepi—played incongruously by Carmen Maura as a schoolgirl nymphette—is raped in her flat by a policeman (Félix Rotaeta). But in the next, she has changed into black-leather trousers and a rhinestone top, as she paces up and down plotting revenge. Immediately afterwards (with no signal that story time has elapsed) she visits the room where Bom's punk group are rehearsing. Now she wears jeans and a pink satin jacket. The lack of attention to continuity extends from clothing to characterization: Pepi's rape changes her instantaneously from a lewd child into a scheming woman. As the punks, on Pepi's instructions, beat up the man they believe to be the policeman (it is in fact his identical twin

---

[28] See Ross, *No Respect*, 188, for the multiple and complex reception of pornographic images. For lesbian S/M, SAMOIS, *Coming to Power: Writings and Graphics on Lesbian S/M* (Boston, 1982).

[29] See n. 4 above.

[30] See also Noam Ciusqui, 'Pedro Almodóvar: sexo y ganas de divertirse', *Diario de Barcelona* (2 Nov. 1980).

brother), they are dressed in nineteenth century costume as if 'for the *verbena* [street festival] of San Isidro' (script, p. 9). The beating (which Pepi spies on with conspicuous pleasure) inexplicably takes place to the sound of the *zarzuela* or Spanish operetta, 'La revoltosa'.

Without taking this sequence overseriously, I would suggest that it demonstrates to the audience from the start of the film that the virtues of classical cinema (plausibility, psychology) will be subverted by anti-naturalistic techniques (incongruity of sound and image, discontinuity of character). The film would thus seem to place itself generically as a 'crazy comedy', one in which anarchic humour derives from a subversion of the cinematic mechanism itself (Neale, p. 24). However I will suggest that, as *Pepi, Luci* continues, it also draws on the equally canonic genre of 'situation comedy', which relies on the disturbance of social hierarchies plausibly represented to the viewer. Thus we must believe in the possibility of the ill-fated lesbian romance between Luci and Bom if we are to respond to its subversive and comic properties. Lesbian desire thus serves as the trouble in representation, that element which makes the film hesitate between two mutually exclusive comic modes.[31]

The grainy look and informal narrative of *Pepi, Luci* give the impression of *cinéma vérité*: sequences at a party, in a nightclub, and in a concert hall seem improvised, although in fact they often correspond closely to the original script. In his review in *Contracampo*, Alberto Fernández Torres criticizes the film for the way it relies on the spectator's knowledge of an actual referent (the Madrid 'new wave' *demi-monde*) which lies 'beyond the camera'.[32] Fernández argues that Almodóvar's attempted rupture with the formal logic of cinematic discourse (his reduction of narrative to a 'disconnected babble') is itself an artificial device, no less mannered than the self-conscious minimalism of another first feature released in 1980, Fernando Trueba's *Opera prima* ('A Cousin in Opera/First Works'). Fernández takes it for granted that *Pepi, Luci* has no 'message' or 'analysis' beyond the surface of its anecdotal narrative. I would suggest, however, that in its representation of lesbianism, as elsewhere, it carries an

---

[31] Cf. Teresa de Lauretis, 'Sexual Indifference and Lesbian Representation', *TJ* 40 (May 1988), 155–77.
[32] In *Contracampo* 18 (Jan. 1981), 73.

implicit social commentary which transcends the film's undeniable concern with modish documentation.

Indeed, *Pepi, Luci*'s dialogue is thick with references to contemporary history and politics. Félix Rotaeta's policeman (rapist of Pepi, abandoned husband of Luci) is a caricature Fascist, complete with dark glasses, who complains over breakfast that he doesn't know what the country is coming to 'with so much democracy'. When Luci walks out on him for Bom, she claims to be a victim of 'the wave of eroticism sweeping Spain'. The problem with such references is that they are, of course, parodic, clichés stripped of their normal context. Like Pepi's pornographic provocations ('What do you think of my saucy little rabbit?') political discourse in the film is shown to be secondhand, an empty repetition of propositions which have lost any claim to truth value that they may once have had. In this (loosely postmodern) mode Almodóvar coincides with Richard Dyer's account of gay underground cinema in the USA; and *Pepi, Luci*'s explicit references to North America (the use of English-language pop music on the soundtrack; the appearance of a drag queen claiming—implausibly—to be from New York) suggest we should look more closely at the relationship between gay cinema in the two countries.

For Dyer, underground film is defined not so much by its formal properties (which vary from one cineaste to another) as by its marginal relation to mainstream production and distribution networks and its tendency to break down social (and particularly sexual) taboos (p. 102). From the Forties to the Sixties (from Kenneth Anger to Andy Warhol), gay underground film in the USA moved from a celebration of the film-maker himself as subject to an impersonal style, in which authenticity and fidelity of representation gave way to a desire for the inauthentic, the cult of plastic (pp. 103, 154). Like pop art, the camp sensibility of the time may have been morally and politically neutral, but it was 'not socially inexpressive' (p. 144). While assertions of a lesbian or gay identity are dependent on an 'illusory unified sense of self', the films of the underground offered in contrast 'fragments and surfaces, authenticity [mixed with] theatricality'; in short a 'fiction of identity' which questioned whether selfhood was even compatible with cinema (p. 173).

In spite of the transparent differences between the films of

Warhol and Almodóvar, I would argue that *Pepi, Luci* shares a similar underground ethos to that which flourished in New York in the Sixties. Thus the film was produced (like Almodóvar's previous Super-8 shorts) under unorthodox conditions: shooting took place when the director had the time and the money left over from his day job at the Telefónica. Unlike Warhol's films, however, it achieved immediate commercial distribution and was not subject to censorship, except by local authorities.[33] We have seen that the breaking of sexual taboos is a constant in the film, as is the matter-of-factness with which (porno)graphic material is presented to the audience. More specifically, Almodóvar and Warhol share an interest in figures whom Dyer claims as the epitomes of the underground: male prostitutes and drag queens. And while Almodóvar's personality already seems to dominate *Pepi, Luci* (and he makes his most extended screen appearance as the master of ceremonies in a penis-size competition), the film does not present itself either as the authentic expression of the *auteur* who has produced it, or as the faithful representation of a social reality it claims to reflect. Rather it manifests a cult of the surface and of the artificial, juxtaposing images and sounds from a bewildering range of secondhand popular culture: *zarzuela*, comics, and television advertising. Traditional Spanish motifs here collide with transnational youth culture, as when Bom combines a Spanish fan and *peineta* (ornamental comb) with a lurex microdress.[34]

The final question posed by Dyer is that of lesbian or gay identity, which he claims is problematized by (North American) underground cinema. To see if this is also applicable to *Pepi, Luci* we must look more closely at the central relationship between the punkette and housewife. After leaving her husband, Luci moves into the flat Bom shares with two gay painters (Enrique Naya and Juan Carrero). The paintings that hang on the walls of their flat (of classical Spanish ladies complete with mantillas) suggest both the postmodern cult of the ready-made and the underground cross-over of painting, music, and film. The script tells us that Luci has knitted covers for Bom's

---

[33] See the interview with Francia and Pérez (n. 4 above).

[34] This clash between national and international is superficially similar to that found in Eloy de la Iglesia; but, whereas *mise en scène* in the latter functions simply as a 'reality effect', Almodóvar's flamboyant costumes and decor are characteristically superfluous to the reproduction of a plausible sense of place.

punchball and weight-training equipment, 'a deliciously feminine touch' (p. 57).

In a long and poorly framed take, broken only by a disorienting cut to a mirror reflection, Pepi visits the lesbian couple, offers them cocaine, and informs them that she has decided to make a film based on their story. As Luci fetches the drinks in a properly submissive manner, Pepi explains excitedly that 'representation is always somewhat artificial'. For example, she has seen Luci peed on and beaten as if it were perfectly natural ('como si nada'); she has seen her eat Bom's snot 'as if it were a piece of bread'. In cinema, this is impossible: the spectator requires proof of (woman's) pleasure: if she doesn't moan in ecstasy, then people won't believe she's enjoying it, even if she really is. Everything must be exaggerated a little. What's fun about the women's relationship is that one is the 40-year-old wife of a policeman and the other a 17-year-old pop singer. It is thus necessary for Bom to act up her perversion: Pepi knows Bom is a true sadist, but at first sight she simply looks unsympathetic.

There are multiple levels of irony, here. For example, the monotonous performance of Bom (played by the non-professional actor and real-life singer Alaska) does indeed give the impression of antipathy rather than sadism, however much she trails Luci round on a dog collar. Alaska's limited acting skills thus deny us those touches of exaggeration which Pepi claims are necessary in film, if the cast is to convince the (male?) audience that the female desire represented on the screen is authentic.[35] The male, heterosexual viewer is thus deprived of those filmic signs which represent feminine *jouissance* to him. On the other hand, a relationship between two such mismatched characters is already wholly incongruous; the *frisson* of the film comes (as Alberto Fernández Torres suggests) from the combination of outrageous situations and resolutely naturalistic dialogue: the lesbian ménage between punk and housewife seems perfectly natural, even within the master and slave role-playing. But this perceived 'naturalness' raises the question of 'incidental homosexuality' that I mentioned in the introduction to this

[35] For the gender position of cinema audiences see Laura Mulvey's influential 'Visual Pleasure and Narrative Cinema', *Screen* 16/3 (1975); for a critique of sexual difference from a lesbian perspective, see Jackie Stacey, 'Desperately Seeking Difference', *Screen* 28/1 (1987), 48–61; and Teresa de Lauretis, *Technologies of Gender* (London, 1988).

chapter: if lesbian love is taken wholly for granted, then its specific relationship to social reality will be erased. There is only one point at which the affair is not taken for granted: when a 'flamenco rock' singer laughs on being told that Luci is Bom's girlfriend ('novia'). The main characters' reactions, however, show that this *faux pas* is clearly an aberration.

The relationship between the two women remains, none the less, the most sympathetic element in the film. Luci quite literally lets down her hair and gains in self-confidence, until she is tempted back to her husband by his superior expertise in sadism. And one formal technique in *Pepi, Luci* noted by John Hopewell (the absence of establishing shots) also tends to work against the ironic, dissociative devices and draw attention towards the characters and away from the highly coloured environment they inhabit. There seems little doubt that the audience is encouraged to identify with Pepi, Luci, and Bom in a way they are not with the men in the film, who are generally presented as sadistic or voyeuristic caricatures.

Without denying the comic tone of the film, it is worth considering what some lesbians have said about sadomasochism and role-playing, which have in recent years been the subject of intense debate.[36] Thus Margaret Hunt has recently suggested that in its attempt to root out the 'victimization' thought to be inherent in S/M, revolutionary feminism has de-eroticized women's liberation; moreover, it is not possible to make a clean, binary divide between lesbians who practice S/M and those who do not (p. 40). Cherry Smyth appraises butch/top and femme/bottom sex in lesbian pornography: even with a dildo, this practice need not 'replicate static and predictable male–female interaction'; rather it 'signifies the lack of fixity of gender . . .[the] potential split between the sexual object and the sexual aim, between subject and object of desire' (p. 156). Diane Hamer cites Parveen Adams's argument that S/M denotes 'an erotic plasticity and movement . . . a play with identity and a play with genitality'; as in butch/femme relations, 'lesbian desire turns on a relationship to difference [in which] different positions are taken up in relation to another's desire; and while the positions may be fixed . . . , the individuals who occupy them are not

---

[36] See Ch. 3 for a fuller account of this debate and for full refs. to these essays in the special issue of *FR*: 'Perverse Politics: Lesbian Issues', 34 (1990).

necessarily fixed.' (pp. 148–9). All of these women stress the fluidity of sadomasochistic role-playing, the way in which it offers a plurality of positions from which pleasure can be taken.

Clearly such views are controversial amongst lesbian women. And they are made in the context of a debate around pornography produced by and for women. But I would suggest that the central relationship in *Pepi, Luci* can also be read not as a mere reproduction (repetition) of heterosexual power structures, but rather as a liberating adoption of erotic roles, which are at once constrictive and mobile. The extreme divergence between the two partners (in age, class, and profession) suggests in parodic form those differences between lesbians which many women now seek to embrace;[37] and the fluidity of the lovers' roles (Luci abandons Bom when the latter becomes too kind to her) suggests that critique of homosexual identity which Richard Dyer associates with underground film-makers such as Warhol. When all social and erotic life is surface or role-playing, then there can be no stable position from which to affirm one's sense of self. Lesbian (or gay) identity thus becomes a 'fiction', albeit a necessary one (Dyer, p. 285). This does not, however, mean that we (men) can allow ourselves pleasure in scenes such as that in which an ecstatic Luci is beaten half to death by her jealous husband. Her confession to Bom from the hospital bed ('I'm much more of a bitch than you thought I was'), delivered with quiet sobriety, also remains disturbing. The representation of role-playing (in this case, bottom or femme) does not dissolve ethical dilemmas. Rather it requires the viewer to meditate on the power structures inherent in all sexual relations.

Towards the end of the film, Pepi invites the lovelorn Bom back to her flat for a meal. We first see the two women from outside, framed in separate window panes. The camera then moves inside the kitchen for a sequence of not-quite-symmetrical reverse angle shots (perhaps determined by the limited space of the location). Once more, the sequence has an air of improvization, which is not in fact the case: the dialogue figures in the original script. Bom is lamenting that she will never find a woman as good in bed as Luci. Pepi reassures her; and goes on

---

[37] For the erotic and deconstructive potential of differences between women, see Judith Butler's account of butch/femme identities in *Gender Trouble*, 122–4; cf. Sue-Ellen Case, 'Towards a Butch–Femme aesthetic', *Discourse* 11/1 (Fall–Winter 1988–9), 55–73.

to talk once more about the film she is planning to make: in one ending Luci and Bom get married in white and as a wedding present Pepi gives them the child she conceived after being raped by the policeman. This is appropriate, now that the two women have formed a home. But Bom has another ending: she and Pepi will settle down together as lovers. To the sound of a romantic tune, the camera cuts to an extreme close-up of the dish on the stove (salt cod or *bacalao*), an image which, according to the script (p. 88), takes on an 'ambiguous character'.

This is the only sequence in the film in which the extradiegetic ('incidental') music serves to reinforce the image, rather than to undermine or subvert it. It is a highly engaging scene in which both the ever-animated Maura and the normally stolid Alaska smile and gaze at each other with what seems to be genuine affection. And it is the scene on which the film ended in the original script: with a freeze frame 'like a hake'. I would suggest that such scenes of domestic, female intimacy (which recur throughout Almodóvar's œuvre) are more significant than they might appear. They imply not only a sense of continuing community amongst women from which men are inevitably and unthinkingly excluded but also a possibility for new kinds of female relationship when the twin pleasures of cinematic narrative and lesbian role-playing coincide. It is a conjunction that will be explored at greater length in *Entre tinieblas*.

3. *ENTRE TINIEBLAS*: WOMEN IN CHAINS

The scene is the dressing-room in a night club: 'like all dressing rooms it is reminiscent of a chapel' (script,[38] p. 3). Yolanda (Cristina S. Pascual: 'pretty worn out in spite of her youth', p. 2) is looking at herself in the mirror. Suddenly her reflection is joined by two nuns requesting an autograph. Yolanda turns to face them and the Mother Superior (Julieta Serrano) moves into shot on the right. She looks up at a photograph of two people on the wall. In extreme close-up, Yolanda's red-nailed hand cuts out her boyfriend from the photograph and signs her own image for the Mother Superior. There follows a medium shot of the three women together: the Mother Superior standing in the top left of the frame; Sor Estiércol ('Manure', Marisa Paredes) in

[38] 'Entre tinieblas: guión original de Pedro Almodóvar' (Madrid, 1982).

the top right; Yolanda sitting centre bottom between the two nuns, who look at one another over her head with enigmatic complicity. A poster of Mick Jagger is prominent behind them. The Mother Superior gives Yolanda the address of their order ('The Humble Redeemers') insisting she get in contact if ever she is in trouble.

This early sequence from *Entre tinieblas* is emblematic for a number of reasons. First, it suggests that this will be a film in which men play no part: Yolanda's boyfriend is quite literally cut out of the picture, and, indeed, is shortly to die of an overdose. Second, it suggests erotic exchange within a world of women: Yolanda offers her signature and is given in turn the chance of a refuge she will shortly take up; there will also be rivalry amongst the nuns for her affection. Finally, it points to the role of mirroring or reproduction in the film: although Almodóvar insists on the differences between women (between a singer and a nun), the narrative will suggest a merging between the two: the Mother Superior is so fascinated by fallen women that she herself becomes indistinguishable from them, exclaiming at one point 'I am the same as them.'

Entre tinieblas (Almodóvar's third feature) has higher production values than *Pepi, Luci,* and at least one critic (J. Batlle Caminal in *El país,* 31 October 1983) has commented on the technical accomplishment of its cinematography. Indeed the very first scenes (which we see before the autograph scene above, although they occur chronologically later) reveal a newly mobile frame and stylish *mise en scène.* Thus the film begins with the camera tracking Yolanda as she walks down the Madrid street where she lives; and then cuts to a tilt down the face of her building, before following her up the stairs to her flat. This location is shot from low angles and in muted blues and greys which contrast with Yolanda's blood-red trousers (a chromatic association maintained throughout the film). When Yolanda's boyfriend dies suddenly (the event that precipitates her flight to the convent) an extreme close-up of his head lying on the floor is framed so as to show her face reflected in a mirrored surface at the other side of the room. In *Entre tinieblas,* the aesthetic quality of the image, in particular the careful use of framing, will have a weight of significance which will often transcend the anecdotal subject matter. I shall argue that one particular visual technique (the use of frontality, or placing of the camera at an angle of ninety degrees to the action) has a particular effect on our identification with the characters, who are (superficially at least) as implausible as any in Almodóvar's œuvre.

Yolanda, then, suspected of murdering her junkie boyfriend, is forced to flee to the convent. And her arrival is presented as an Annunciation, eloquently exploiting the expressive potential of light: as the nuns prepare for mass in an extreme long shot of the darkened chapel, the doors behind them are flung open to reveal Yolanda, framed by a halo of brilliant light. In a rare crane shot, the camera rises as the Mother Superior advances up a path of light to welcome the lost sheep to the convent. The eloquence of the image is thus reinforced by reference to Christian iconography: Yolanda is blonde like an angel. However at this point in the film it is not yet clear whether such references are to be taken parodically, as a subversion of Catholic dogma, or seriously, as a secularization of divine love.

The problem recurs in a subsequent sequence in which Yolanda takes her first meal in the convent, dressed incongruously in the strapless red lurex dress in which she performs in the nightclub. Here the set-up is reminiscent of the Last Supper, with the five nuns and Yolanda ranged on one side of extended tables as they eat (Plate 4). But already there have been touches of unmotivated 'crazy comedy' similar to those in *Pepi, Luci*. We have learned that Sor Perdida ('Sister Sinner': Carmen Maura) has a cleaning fetish and a tiger called Niño ('Baby'); that Sor Estiércol ('Sister Manure': Marisa Paredes) is prone to LSD-inspired visisons; Sor Rata ('Sister Rat': Chus Lampreave) will prove to be the best-selling author of sleazy novels (Plate 3). But as always in Almodóvar, these eccentricities are quite taken for granted: when Yolanda recoils on catching a glimpse of the tiger, Sor Rata explains: 'It's logical for her to be frightened; it's the first time she's seen a tiger in a convent.' The humour relies (as so often in *Pepi, Luci*) on the contrast between that which is natural to the narrative's insiders and unnatural to the voyeur or observer figure who stands in for (represents) the spectator on the scene of perversity. In spite of the 'crazy comedy', then, (of the intermittent disruption of the codes denoting filmic verisimilitude) performances remain restrained. For example, the benevolent and sentimental Sor Perdida (Maura) would not seem out of place in *The Sound of Music* (were it not for her cleaning fetish and menagerie). Almodóvar thus rejects the easy anti-clerical option of a Buñuel, and is far indeed from the (heteroerotic) convent fantasies of a Borowczyc.

On its release, critics gave widely different accounts of *Entre tinieblas*. These variations arose from their perception of the film's register; of its relation to established genres; and of its direction of sympathy or identification towards the central character, Julieta Serrano's amorous Mother Superior. As we shall see, the question of their response to the lesbian theme of the narrative (which generally goes unmentioned) is vital here. There seems little doubt that the film was scandalous to many: there was a bomb scare at the Madrid opening[39] and the Italian press was hostile when it was shown (out of competition) at the Venice festival.[40] More characteristic of what was to come was the press coverage of the Barcelona première, which featured pictures of gay men in the audience who came dressed as nuns (*Correo catalán* 12 October 1983). The film was thus a site of conflicting ideological interpretation even before it was seen: between traditionalists and 'progres', heterosexual and homosexual audiences. Thus J. A. Mahieu wrote in *Fotogramas* (15 October 1983) that the Mother Superior represented 'the contradictions, fanaticisms, and repressions of traditional Spanish religious culture'; but claimed that the director observed her with 'an amused, distanced look'. However Francisco Marinero in *Diario 16* (8 October 1983) wrote that the film was characterized by 'crazy humour' ('humor disparatado') which is treated 'curiously enough . . . almost seriously'. Angeles Maso in *La vanguardia* (23 October 1983) singled out Julieta Serrano's Mother Superior as the one character not presented 'in a parodic context', and claimed that Almodóvar's 'innocent' fantasies were directed to the new Spanish consumer society. Perhaps the most interesting account in the dailies was from José Luis Guarner in *El periódico* (28 October 1983). Guarner claimed that the film (an impossible hybrid of a Mexican novelette, a Douglas Sirk melodrama, and an underground comic) is neither scandalous nor anti-clerical. Rather it reveals a certain affection for its characters and for the religious symbols it treats with respectful irony, 'as if trying to recuperate them through a happy, pagan sensuality.'

---

[39] See the review by Francisco Marinero in *Diario 16* (8 Oct. 1983).
[40] See Miguel Angel Trenas, 'Con Pedro Almodóvar llegó el escándalo', *La vanguardia* (29 Oct. 1983).

None of these reviewers uses the word 'lesbian'. One who does however is José Luis Téllez in *Contracampo*, 36 (Summer 1984). Téllez does not like the film: its generic mixture leaves it paralysed between comedy and tragedy (p.108). The spiralling implausibility of the plot (the Mother Superior is not only a lesbian, but also a drug addict and a blackmailer) renders audience identification impossible. Almodóvar is afraid to commit himself and thus produces a text emptied of all meaning, a 'simulacrum' (p. 109). Téllez makes one exception here: the scenes in which Yolanda confronts the Mother Superior deserve to be 'rescued in [the viewer's] memory' (p.110): here a certain distance between event and representation ('acontecimiento', 'relato') leads to a pertinent tension which is later frittered away in farcical mayhem.

Téllez's point is slightly obscure: his position is not that of the plain man arguing for naturalistic cinema; rather he demands a cinema which uses identification to provoke thought in its audience and to prevent films from being consumed like any other capitalist commodity. But what is interesting for our purpose is that Téllez locates the fruitful tension between image and referent (representation and object) in the scenes of lesbian desire. We shall now look at the most lyrical of those scenes, before attempting to relate *Entre tinieblas*'s challenging images of lesbianism to Richard Dyer's analysis of 'confrontational politics' in lesbian and gay film outside Spain.

Yolanda has been staying in the convent for some time. She enters the Mother Superior's office dressed in a red blouse, with the top buttons provocatively undone. Almodóvar cuts back and forth between Yolanda and the Mother Superior: the former walks across the room, her face marked by the criss-cross shadows cast by the lattice windows; the latter remains seated at her desk. Both are miming alternately the words to a bolero sung by Lucho Gatica: it tells of a love which is torture ('martirio'), a love which would better be forgot. As the sequence continues, the reverse angles become more frontal, until both actors are singing direct to camera (direct to the other woman). In this highly stylized and emotionally charged sequence the audience is addressed directly as a participant in lesbian seduction.

Yolanda sits next to the Mother Superior, who says that she adores music like the bolero which speaks of human feelings. Yolanda replies that this music tells the truth about life: everyone knows what love and disappointment are like. The Mother Superior compliments Yolanda on her appearance, elegantly wasted by drugs: there is a great beauty in physical deterioration. Yolanda looks at the wall behind the Mother Superior on which female pin-ups are displayed as if in an altar piece: Marilyn Monroe is prominent amongst the images.[41] The Mother Superior explains that she loves great sinners, for it is in imperfect creatures that God's greatness is to be found: Jesus died on the cross not to save the holy, but to redeem sinners. Julieta Serrano speaks her lines with quiet seriousness, entirely lacking in irony.

What we find in this sequence is the lesbian mirroring I first noted in the dressing-room sequence. The camera position and editing suggest a direct confrontation between the two actors in which their very different images (scarlet woman and black-garbed nun) are reflected symmetrically in one another. Indeed the last words of the bolero are 'one facing the other, that is all there is' ('frente a frente, nada más'). But this is no facile synthesis or narcissism. Rather the erotic charge of the scene derives from the continuing differences (of age, profession, and appearance) between the two women.

Moreover, the sequence suggests a lesbian appropriation of ready-made (heterosexual) images found in popular culture: thus each woman in turn mouths to the other words originally sung by a man to a woman. Popular music may voice universal feelings, as Yolanda suggests, but its use in this context marks a rare and specifically lesbian redirection of imagery generally naturalized as heterosexual.[42] If, in the title of the song, the two lovers are 'chained' together ('Encadenados/as'), then the nature of that amorous bond is quite specific to this lesbian narrative. Yolanda remains the recipient of the Mother Superior's advances only because she is obliged to remain in the convent as a refuge from the police.

The altar-like disposition of the images on the office wall is another example of the lesbian rearticulation of dominant (hetero-

---

[41] Cf. the use of *mise en scène* with de la Iglesia, once more: where the Monroe poster in *El pico* is merely the sign of a certain youth culture, here it comments ironically on the lesbian theme of the film. Recent French reviews also ignore the lesbian theme and attack the intermittence and artifice of the film: Jacques Valot, *RC* 445 (1989), 28–9; Paul Louis Thirard, *Positif* 336 (1989), 50–1.

[42] For the redeployment of heterosexual popular culture by lesbians and gay men, see Andrew Ross, *No Respect*, 157.

sexist) culture. The Mother Superior's praise of great female
sinners must ring ironically in the ears of viewers aware of her
passion for Yolanda: the image of Monroe, previously caught in
the unproblematic gaze of the heterosexual man, is here redupli-
cated, redirected, exposed to the unaccustomed look of the lesbian
woman. Like the S/M role-playing of *Pepi, Luci*, the popular and
religious iconography of *Entre tinieblas* forms a medium in which
women can act out their fantasies to and for one another.

In spite of the formal mirroring of the bolero scene, then, the
relationship between Yolanda and the Mother Superior is asymmetrical in two ways: the younger woman is dependent on the
older one, who could give her up to the police; the older is
dependent on the younger for the reciprocation of her love. This
desequilibrium is reinforced in a scene where the two women
confront one another once more, this time in the garden: Yolanda
uses the formal address 'usted'; the Mother Superior, the
informal 'tú'. But it is Yolanda who ends the discussion by
saying she is only using her lover as a tool ('instrumento') to get
what she wants.

The situation is repeated a little later when Merche (Cecilia
Roth), the youthful ex-lover of the Mother Superior, arrives at
the convent on the run from the police. When Merche says she
loves the Mother Superior, the latter exclaims 'You don't love
me; you need me.' It is perhaps not over-serious to see this scene
as another pointer to an important theme in the film: the
instrumental use of human beings in affective and sexual relations, a tendency from which lesbian relationships are not
exempt. The Mother Superior gravely replaces the shoes on
Merche's feet as she is led away by the police.

Entre tinieblas is a separatist narrative in which men have no
place: the convent is funded by a Marquesa whose husband has
died; Sor Rata has a venomous sister outside the convent (Eva
Siva, in a very different role from the submissive Luci), but no
visible male relations. The only significant male role is that of
the chaplain, who reveals an unexpected knowledge of and
interest in Cecil Beaton's costumes for *My Fair Lady*.[43] In addition
to the separatist echoes, the film also coincides with strains in

---

[43] It is typical of Almodóvar's hostility to stereotype that this character (played by
the hirsute Manuel Zarzo) proves to be heterosexual and marries Sor Víbora (Lina
Canalejas) at the end of the film.

cultural feminism: the investigation of traditional material (such as the religious) historically gendered as feminine (see Dyer, pp. 178–9). If we seek a lesbian/gay context for *Entre tinieblas*'s fearless provocations, however, we are more likely to find it in the confrontational cinema of the 1970s. In Richard Dyer's account, the aim of confrontational politics was to 'zap' the (heterosexual) public, to shock it into raised consciousness.[44] For Dyer, the central contradiction of confrontational politics was an unresolved conflict between vanguardism and libertarianism: the first involved taking the lead in telling people the truth about lesbian and gay life; the second involved refusing to have a position, and letting people think what they wished (p. 222). I would suggest that this is also a problem with Almodóvar's representation of lesbianism in *Entre tinieblas*: on the one hand, the logic of the narrative requires that heterosexual audiences accept the representativeness of homosexual desire (there is no romance between women and men with which they can identify); on the other hand, the film refuses to offer an unambiguous direction of sympathy towards Julieta Serrano's luminous (but also obsessive and deluded) Mother Superior. When she and Yolanda decide to withdraw from heroin together, they are shown in a striking image which recalls the shot before the cooking scene in *Pepi, Luci*: the women are seen from outside the building, each framed by a different window. They are at once together (in the same cinematic frame, in the same room) and apart (separated by the composition within the frame). It is a fitting image of the intermittent identification with and withdrawal from the lesbian woman which (as critics testify) must problematize audience response to the film. Confronted by a passionate but destructive lesbian affair, with no explicit prompting from the film as to which position they are to adopt, spectators may well be bemused.

At the end of the film, the nuns give a party for the Mother Superior. The *mise en scène* is gaudy: golden leaves and multi-coloured flowers strung on cellophane. Yolanda, dressed in a metallic cloak and matching gown, delivers a song direct to camera (direct to the Mother Superior watching in the centre of

---

[44] For confrontational politics in the UK, see Jeffrey Weeks, *Coming Out: Homosexual Politics in Britain from the Nineteenth Century to the Present* (London, 1977), 185–206. There is no comparable study for Spain.

the front row). It is called 'I left because I left' and speaks of a 'forbidden love'. Once more the camera positions and editing reinforce the sense of mirroring between the two women (of reflection and difference). After the party Yolanda does indeed leave, to form a spontaneous new grouping of women with the Marquesa and Sor Rata, a further example of Almodóvar's many same-sex 'pretended families'. When the Mother Superior discovers she has gone, she lets out what the script calls a 'cry of impotence, [a] terrible lament [which] pierces the convent walls'. (p. 64). As the camera tracks back to leave her once more framed within a window, the bolero she had mimed with Yolanda plays one final time on the soundtrack.

It is perhaps significant that in the original script there is a coda in which the Mother Superior is sent to prison for drug trafficking and Yolanda joins up with the Marquesa's grandson who (for reasons too complex to explain here) is Tarzan. Almodóvar chose rather to end his film with the unambiguously tragic image of the abandoned lesbian lover, even though this meant leaving diverse narrative strands unresolved. Attention is thus directed emphatically to this single focus of the drama, which must be taken as pre-eminent. If *Pepi, Luci* is a lesbian comedy (lurching between 'crazy' gags and social humour); *Entre tinieblas* is a lesbian tragedy, but one whose pathos is compromised by the film's oscillating register and stylized cinematic form. As Richard Dyer says, like much gay film-making it has the capacity to be very serious about something while treating it as if it were trivial (p. 144). The credits roll on the freeze-frame of Julieta Serrano behind the window: the shadows of palm fronds (hardly typical of Madrid) are cast on the wall, matching the tropical sound of Lucho Gatica's melancholy bolero. Lesbian desire is here aestheticized and distanced, but not ironized or belittled. It is a tricky sleight of hand that Almodóvar will also attempt to achieve in the all-male romance of *La ley del deseo*.

4. *LA LEY DEL DESEO*: CROSSING THE LINE

A long shot of an untidy bedroom. A young man moves into frame from the left. The script[45] says he is 'athletic and street-

---

[45] 'La ley del deseo: guión' (Madrid, 1987). See also José Arroyo, 'Law and Desire', *Descant* 20/1–2 (1989), 53–70. For another reading of this opening sequence,

wise' (p. 1). He turns out of the shadow into the light to face the camera. As the camera tracks forward, a voice off screen tells him to start undressing. When he looks at the camera the voice commands 'Don't look at me.' The man, now wearing only underpants, starts walking to the right; and in a disorienting cut on action, appears on the right of the screen in the next shot, rather than the left as we would expect. This is because it is not him but his image reflected in a mirror. He kisses his reflection and rubs his groin against the mirror.

Returning to the bed he caresses himself, removes his under-pants, and (instructed by the voice once more) begins to masturbate. This scene of desire is now crosscut with close-ups of two older bald and bespectacled men in a location which has not been established. Their voices become progressively more excited, as the young man reaches (or pretends to reach?) orgasm. An overhead shot of the two older men reveals they are reading their lines from a script into a microphone. As the young man lies on the bed, a figure whose face is not seen places a wad of money on the bedside table. The young man counts it with satisfaction.

This opening sequence of *Le ley del deseo* is not simply a scandalous provocation. It also suggests a number of themes which will be developed throughout the film. The first is the question of power in the erotic scene: the voice instructs the young man to perform acts for the camera that are generally considered to be private. The second is solitude and narcissism: the young man is instructed to act as if he is on his own; the older men (the 'Voices') are in a separate, undisclosed location. As in *Entre tinieblas*, the role of the mirror is emblematic here, suggesting as it does both reflection and alienation, the represen-tation of the self to and for the other (the spectators within the film, the audience in the cinema). There is thus a reflexive commentary on film itself in this sequence: a blurring between film as the material trace of bodily presence (physical activity) and film as the formal construction of visual narrative (the processes of scripting and sound recording which are themselves represented within the frame).

---

see Christopher Whyte, 'Pedro Almodóvar; Or, Camp and the Limits of Love', unpub. paper read at the Conference on 'Questions of Homosexuality' at the Institute of Romance Studies in the University of London (June 1991).

As the sequence ends and moody saxophone music begins, a series of quick cuts establishes that what we have seen is the final sequence of a film-within-a-film, made by director Pablo (Eusebio Poncela). His sister Tina (Carmen Maura at her most glamorous) emerges from the première to congratulate her brother on his success. Antonio (Antonio Banderas), who is to be Pablo's obsessive lover, moves into the same shot. Over a freeze-frame of the three, the title of the film is written in hot pink. We next follow Antonio ('age twenty, looks like an Andalusian *señorito*', p. 10) to the toilet. As he unzips his flies the camera tilts up to a close up of his face, cutting to an extreme close up of his lips. He masturbates (out of frame) whispering the words the youth was told to repeat by the Voice in the film: 'Fuck me' ('Fóllame'). Through purely (cinemato)graphic means, the sequence establishes another theme of the film: art as a potent source of fantasy and fetish. Extreme close ups of men's lips (sometimes framed by blood) will recur on several occasions.

The start of the film works both to place homosexual desire within a hermetic, aestheticized space (the film-within-a-film, the fetishistic close-up) and to effect an analysis of that desire and its place within the cinematic apparatus. As we shall see, although critics have often claimed (with Almodóvar himself) that homosexuality is incidental to this tragic *amour fou*, the narrative does not avoid the confrontation between Pablo's sympathetic Madrid milieu and less tolerant environments, particularly outside the capital. This intermittent concern for socialization (for the relation between the gay protagonists and straight society) will come into conflict with two other features of *La ley del deseo*: its critique of representation (of cinema, writing, and photography) and its appeal to melodrama (to the expressive potential of music, *mise en scène*, and compulsive repetition).

As the first (and only) film by Almodóvar in which male homosexuality is consistently centre-frame, *La ley del deseo* has provoked particular controversy. In interviews given during the shooting of the film and after its release, the director constantly repeats that it is a film not about homosexuality, but about love in general, about the couple, even about the family. Thus the relationship between main character Pablo and his first lover Juan (the moody Miguel Molina) is described as 'fraternal'; and that between Juan and his second lover Antonio (the obsessive Antonio Banderas) as 'maternal': Antonio wants to care for Pablo as if he were his child. On the other hand, Almodóvar is anxious to depict the specificity of homosexual relations which need not rely on the heterosexual precedent of family life; and to show that gay men are 'normal', not 'zombies'.[46] He thus repeats the paradox of confrontational politics we saw in relation to *Entre tinieblas*, shifting between libertarian and vanguardistic viewpoints (letting the audience decide for itself what homosexuality is and directing the audience towards a correct awareness of what it really is).

It is ironic that of the reviewers it is only Pedro Crespo in the conservative *ABC* (8 February 1987) who raises the question of the sexual preference of the film's audience.[47] In an insinuating litotes (in the form of a double negative) he claims that the film is 'not without interest' for viewers who are not directly concerned by homosexuality; but for those who are, it has the bonus of handsome actors Banderas and Molina. Crespo thus foregrounds (albeit homophobically) the factor of exhibition that Almodóvar chooses not to acknowledge in his explicit statements about his films: sexual-object choice (of the characters within the film, of the audience outside it) can never be indifferent, must always play its part in the representation of and response to cinematic fantasy.

Almodóvar's assimilation of homosexual relations to the family need not necessarily be negative. For one pleasure of *La ley del deseo* is the unselfconscious way in which it captures the everyday domesticity of gay ménages rarely shown on screen: witness the scenes in which Pablo and Juan chastely but playfully prepare for bed; in which Pablo and Antonio shower together; or in which lesbian Tina drinks milk in bed with her lover's daughter Ada (Manuela Velasco). Here the naturalistic presentation serves a political point: calling attention to the daily life of

[46] See the interviews with Isabel Vallina, 'Homosexuales en cartel', *Interviú* (29 Oct. 1986); Rafa Fernández, 'Pedro Almodóvar: "*La ley del deseo* no es una película de homosexuales"', *Diario 16* (18 Jan. 1987); and Txerra Cirbián, 'Almodóvar: "*La ley del deseo* es mi película más madura"', interview, *El periódico* (19 Feb. 1987). A homophobic location report by Carlos Fernando claims that men kissing men is against 'natural law', but good for box office: 'Pedro Almodóvar lleva a cabo su antigua aspiración de hacer un film de hermanos', *Diario 16* (1 Sept. 1986).

[47] The review by Angel Fernández Santos in *El país* ('La ley de exceso') attacks the film's uneven quality (11 Feb. 1987).

'pretended families' who do not experience their position as marginal. Indeed as the narrative develops (in an inversion typical of Almodóvar) it is the heterosexual family that is revealed as the locus of perversion: Tina is a transsexual who was encouraged to change her gender by the incestuous father who was later to abandon her. As the film about 'hermanos' (Pablo and Tina were once 'brothers' and are now 'brother and sister'), *La ley del deseo* redefines the couple as a chaste fraternal relation, a disinterested 'horizontal' love which transcends the patriarchal ravages of 'vertical' filiation.

(Homo)sexual relations, on the other hand, are never innocent of power. And if we look more closely at one important sequence we shall see how power relations are inscribed at the formal (cinematographic) level of the text. The obsessive Antonio has pursued the egotistic Pablo, who has finally brought him back to his flat. The camera tracks left to right over their naked bodies before coming to rest on a close-up of their heads as they embrace. Pablo is on top. At this passionate moment, Antonio starts to question Pablo about his 'promiscuity' and the danger it raises of sexually transmitted disease.[48] As they disentangle themselves there is a cut to an overhead shot of them lying supine on the bed. The next shot is a close-up of their heads once more, but from the opposite side to the first shot, and with Antonio now on top of Pablo. The camera has thus 'crossed the line': the 180 degrees axis of action, a relatively rare technique and one experienced as disorienting within Hollywood-style continuity editing. It seems clear, however, that the effect is calculated. Through its formal mirroring of shot and frame (its repetition and inversion) the cinematography suggests the instability and reciprocity of homosexual relations, in which either partner may choose to play the dominant role. As Antonio submits with some anxiety to anal penetration (once more in an overhead shot) the logic of the editing has suggested that his role in this relationship is by no means 'passive', that he will come to dominate the self-possessed Pablo.

It would be a mistake to read too much into details of camera position. But there is no doubt that the meaning of *La ley del deseo* lies as much in its highly stylized approach to cinematic form as

---

[48] In the *Advocate* interview (n. 9 above), Almodóvar comments with reference to this sequence on the lack of awareness of AIDS and safer sex in Spain.

in its intricately complicated plot. This stylization is particularly prominent in scenes which call into question the various processes of representation itself. Thus Pablo is a writer and filmmaker by profession; and he attempts to 'script' his own love life, writing a letter to his first lover Juan which he asks Juan to return to him after signing it himself: it is the perfect letter he would wish to receive from the lover of his fantasies. As he types, the voices of the two men reading the words on the page come together and merge on the soundtrack, an auditory equivalent of Pablo's egotism. His correspondence is a circulation of the same, a narcissistic mirroring of the self. In a shock cut, Almodóvar gives us a shot of Pablo's face from within the typewriter. In a later sequence, Pablo types rhythmically in time to a song ('Lo dudo' by los Panchos) which will be repeated at vital points in the story. I argue below that music and rhythm play an essential role in the melodramatic texture of film.

Another highly stylized sequence also blurs the boundary between fiction and the sentimental narrative of the self. Tina is an actress and she has been offered the role of the abandoned lover in Pablo's theatrical production of Cocteau's *La Voix humaine*. In a sequence which (characteristically) has no establishing shot to tell the audience the location, the camera tracks slowly from left to right, as in the foreground the child Ada is pulled in and out of frame on a dolly, miming to Jacques Brel's 'Ne me quitte pas'. In the background Carmen Maura's Tina wreaks havoc on the furniture. As the script suggests (p. 55) the effect is to disorient the viewer, who will at first believe that the stage set is real. But the passionate performance by actress Tina is theatrically combined with off-stage romance: waiting in the wings is her lesbian lover and natural mother of the child (played by real-life transsexual Bibí Andersen) who has returned from abroad in an attempt to retrieve Ada.[49] As the dolly rolls once more across the stage and the camera tracks with it from right to left (in a mirror image of the previous shot) Ada cries (real?) tears and struggles to mime the words of the song once more. Life and art are fatally confused for both character and audience.

[49] For Andersen's successful career as media celebrity, see Eduardo Calvo García, 'Bibí: el sexo de los ángeles', *La calle*, 201 (27 Jan.–2 Feb. 1982), 26–8. Transsexualism seems to relate to the unpredictability and virtuality of Almodóvar's characters, who change gender as easily as they change personality; it is not, however, examined as a specific sexual identity.

Indeed Pablo attacks his sister for overacting that night: real life is just too real for the theatre.

The third model of representation in the film (after writing and theatre) is the photograph. In scenes where the snapshot takes on a symbolic importance it also holds in *Entre tinieblas*, Pablo tears up the surviving pictures of himself and Tina as children (when both were boys); and Tina finally confronts him with one she has retained. Family history is thus constructed and conserved in the narrative of the photo album; but it is also the site of struggle, of variant interpretations and potential falsifications: the images do not reveal the true story of Tina's life, a story which she fears has been appropriated in the script that Pablo is writing.

Fact and fiction thus merge and fuse in the highly coloured biographies of Almodóvar's eccentric characters. However, such role-playing is not purely gratuitous, however much it responds to personal fantasy. For example, the closeted Antonio asks his lover Pablo to sign his letters to him with a woman's name, in case his mother comes across them. Outside the *demi-monde* of the capital, gay men must adopt fictional disguise. But in a typical twist, the imaginary woman who signs Pablo's letters ('Laura P.') takes on an active role in the plot: after the jealous Antonio has murdered his rival Juan, the police at first see the letters from 'Laura' as a missing link between the three men.

At times, then, the film acknowledges the conflict between private, homosexual life and the public, heterosexual sphere. Thus when Antonio is at home in Andalucía he is spied on by his castrating mother. A publicity still shows his troubled face behind the grille or *reja* of the family home: a man behind bars (Plate 5). And when the police investigate the murder of Pablo's first lover Juan (both in Andalucía and Madrid) there is open conflict between gay milieu and the forces of power. However, it is significant that even here there is no simple opposition between good characters and bad: one of the Civil Guards is more sympathetic than the other; one of the Madrid policemen more tolerant, corrupt, and lazy than his humourless and homophobic partner. Perhaps the most comic moment in the film comes when Carmen Maura, accused of 'not being a real woman', floors the second policeman with a defiantly unladylike punch. Here the genuine question of police maltreatment of sexual minorities is exorcised in parodic form: the humour prevents the audience from confronting the problem even as the wounded policeman exclaims that these 'queers' ('maricones') will pay for what they have done to him.

Driving back to Madrid and pursued by the police, Pablo crashes his car and loses his memory. In an effort to shock him into regaining it, Carmen Maura's Tina tells for the first time the full story of her love affair with their father and the sex change he insisted s/he have. I would suggest that this climactic scene (which Maura plays entirely straight) can be read as a parody of the affirmation politics which Richard Dyer has analysed in lesbian and gay cinema of the Seventies. For Dyer affirmation politics means consciousness-raising, coming out, and the creation of positive images (p. 231). In the first case, confession leads to 'breaking through the façade', to the discovery of 'a true, authentic self and identity' and a revelation of 'the truth about the past from the vantage-point of the raised consciousness of the present'. In such a mode, the individual voice is seen as a 'source of knowledge and vehicle of truth' (p. 243). The hidden agenda of consciousness-raising, however, is that its autobiographical narratives are always the same, invariably repeated: 'conflict, contradiction, and difficulty are erased' (p. 246). This 'quest for sameness' also occurs in 'coming out', in which the assertion of a true self to others constitutes an unchanging 'narrative structure par exellence' (p. 252). Finally, the question of 'positive images' is more complex than it might first appear. For there can be no agreement as to whether 'positive' means 'the degree to which [gay life] is like straight life or the degree to which it differs from it' (p. 264). In summary, then, 'affirmation cinema presented the question of representation, as of identity, as unproblematic' (p. 270).

Clearly Almodóvar's relatively big-budget melodrama is quite different from the independently produced documentaries of the gay movement which Dyer is discussing here. But it draws none the less on similar structures. Thus the glamorous Tina tearfully confesses the 'true story' of her life. It is an act of both consciousness-raising and coming out (as a transsexual and a lesbian): she hopes both to 'break through the façade' of her own unhappiness and to dispel her brother's amnesia. Her bizarre autobiography (however different from the more everyday stories of lesbian and gay activists) proclaims the discovery of an authentic identity which can reappraise the past from the new-found perspective of the present. It also relies on the privilege of the speaking voice as incarnation of personal truth, a privilege to which the audience will tend to defer in spite of the improbability of the narrative it tells.

On the other hand, Tina's parodically heightened story can hardly serve as 'representative' of lesbian experience; and the image she presents is hardly positive. Indeed the audience's knowledge that she is played by Maura (a biological woman, and heterosexual to boot) gives an added level of irony to this baring of the soul. At the end of the sequence the two siblings embrace tearfully: the magic of affirmation has done its work. But for the audience, identity and representation have been thoroughly denaturalized: the quest for the same (for the essential self thought to be located in sexuality) has been contaminated by melodrama.

The power of the film lies in its oblique engagement with a genre gendered as feminine, namely melodrama. Tania Modleski has given an account of filmic melodrama which attempts to read women back into the frame (and into the audience).[50] Although she is dealing with Max Ophuls's *Letter from an Unknown Woman* (1948), many of the points she makes are relevant to *La ley del deseo*, in which (as we have seen) letters also play a prominent role in the plot. Modleski begins by citing Cixous on the connection between hysteria and silence: the great (female) victims of melodrama have been unable to voice their condition. Citing Geoffrey Nowell-Smith,[51] she argues that in the family romance of melodrama (in which the child must submit to the symbolic law of the Father), 'what is repressed at the level of the story often returns through the music or the mise en scène.' (p. 327) Peter Brooks has defined melodrama as the genre which 'works to overcome all repression in order to achieve full expressivity'.[52] For Modleski it is the genre in which female character and spectator alike are condemned to muteness. But if we examine melodrama in terms of 'spatial and musical categor-ies' rather than 'intellectual or literary ones', then music and

---

[50] See n. 21 above. For another approach to gender and melodrama, see Laura Mulvey, 'Afterthoughts on "Visual Pleasure and Narrative Cinema"', in E. Ann Kaplan (ed.), *Psychoanalysis and Cinema* (London, 1990), 24–35.

[51] 'Minelli and Melodrama', in *Home*, ed. Christine Gledhill, 70–4.

[52] Peter Brooks, *The Melodramatic Imagination* (New Haven, Conn., 1976), 41.

rhythm may take on new meanings opposed to the (social, explicit) male Word (p. 329).

Modleski examines Ophuls's *Letter* for its use of repetition: 'Unlike most Hollywood narratives, which give the impression of a progressive movement towards an end that is significantly different from the beginning, much melodrama gives the impression of ceaseless returning to a prior state' (p. 330). She identifies this narrative structure with Kristeva's 'women's time'; here repetition in a space outside history is opposed to (male) 'time as project, teleology . . . the time of history'. As in Lacan, entrance into the symbolic order (into language and history) is bought only at the cost of death (the acceptance of castration): the male protagonist in *Letter* can only achieve selfhood when the woman who has loved him is no longer accessible: he assumes 'a certain relation to desire: one based on an expectation destined to remain eternally unfulfilled' (p. 331). Modleski goes on to question the binaries of 'men's time and women's time', history and repetition. It may be that what appeals to men in melodrama is a 'vicarious, hysterical, experience of femininity which can be more definitively laid to rest for having been "worked through"'(p. 332).

It is not Modleski's brief to examine the figure of the gay man in melodrama; nor does she differentiate amongst the 'male critics' said to derive (vicarious) pleasure from the picture.[53] But her account of *Letter* does correspond at many points to the homosexual melodrama of *La ley del deseo*. Thus Pablo's tragedy is muteness. Condemned (like the man in *Letter*) to the repetition of identical amorous adventures, he fails to note the specificity (the otherness) of his lovers, and can only realize his desire for them when both are dead. Ironically he attempts to speak for the other characters ('directing' them and literally writing their lines) but he cannot speak of or for his desire until it is too late. Instead of proceeding teleologically towards a definitive end, the narrative obsessively repeats certain scenes (Pablo failing to respond to the demands of his lovers) and constantly returns to the ahistorical, abstracted scene of writing: in his screenplay

---

[53] Cf. Joseph A. Boone on some feminists' lack of attention to the sexual preference of male critics: 'Of Me(n) and Feminism: Who(se) is the Sex that Writes?', in *Engendering Men*, ed. Joseph A. Boone and Michael Cadden (New York, 1990), 11–25 (p. 23); and Craig Owens, 'Outlaws: Gay Men in Feminism', in *Men in Feminism*, ed. Alice Jardine and Paul Smith (New York, 1987), 219–32.

Pablo (like the pre-Oedipal child) can express his fantasies
without confronting paternal authority. The narrative of this
confrontation (with the police, with Antonio's family) is, as we
have seen, fragmentary: Pablo does not assume his castration
until the very end of the film. Where Tina's story is one of
progressive self-realization (of the achievement of a true identity,
however parodic), Pablo remains the same, self-absorbed and
narcissistic. The cyclical structures of 'women's time' are thus
not confined to biological females. Modleski cites Stephen
Heath[54] in this context: 'Repetition is the return to the same in
order to abolish the difficult time of desire, and the resurgence in
that moment of inescapable difference' (p. 336). It is an experience which may be common to subjects of both genders and all
sexual preferences, but one which will inevitably be inflected by
their differing relations to symbolic law.

One feature mentioned by Modleski to which I have yet to
refer is the use of music and rhythm. And if we look at the final
sequence of the film we can try to examine how this works.
Antonio, now clearly insane, is holding Pablo captive in Tina's
flat while the police lie in wait outside. The flat is luridly
decorated with a 'Cruz de Mayo', an altarpiece bright with
secular and religious ornaments. As los Panchos sing 'Lo dudo'
once more, Antonio tenderly undresses Pablo (an inversion of
the opening scene, in which it was the film director who made
another man strip). In an overhead shot reminiscent of the first
time the two men make love, we see them kiss: Antonio claims
that he knew from the beginning that Pablo was the one man for
him; they can now forget about everything beyond each other
for the hour they have been allowed by the police. Eusebio
Poncela eloquently suggests (without dialogue) Pablo's changing
emotions: from fear and disgust to a new-found love. But Antonio
has decided to take his life; and as the Cruz de Mayo bursts into
flames, Pablo cradles Antonio's near-naked corpse in his arms,
in a visual echo of a *pietà* (script, p. 221). Although the camera
angle does not change, there are a series of dissolves during this
final shot, suggesting a fluidly merging and abstracted sense of
time.

The role of music is vital in this sequence, and not just in
establishing a mood. The old-fashioned and sentimental Mexi-

---

[54] *Questions of Cinema* (London, 1981), 156.

can ballad makes an eloquent commentary on the action. It begins with the cooing repetition: 'Lo dudo, lo dudo, lo dudo'. The singer doubts that his lover will love him as he does her; but he also doubts that she will find a love purer than his. As in *Entre tinieblas*, we have here a homosexual redirection of a song assumed to be intended for a heterosexual partner. But the insistent reiteration of the lyric (combined of course with the gentle rhythm of the music) suggests an affective space outside history in which desire is given up to endless repetition. I would suggest that in the unapologetic sentimentality of the song (as in others used on the soundtrack) and in the extravagance of the *mise en scène* (the flaming altar) we find a return of that which is repressed in the film's narrative. Insistent on showing us the 'normality' and 'naturalness' of his sometimes extravagant but never effeminate or affected characters, Almodóvar allows a taboo exoticism and otherness to return on the soundtrack and in the art direction. This is not to say that feminization is the 'truth' of homosexuality that must struggle to express itself whatever the cost. Rather it is to suggest that by placing itself on the side of the 'woman' (on the side of love, loss, and timeless-ness) Almodóvar's cinema of gay male desire 'crosses the line' between male and female narrative, makes possible a certain pleasure in the place gendered as female, a pleasure which should not be dismissed as vicarious.

5. MORAL MELODRAMA

In 1988 *Cambio 16* chose Pedro Almodóvar as their Man of the Year, ahead of competitors Yasser Arafat and Jacques Delors. It was a key moment for the man whose cinema had come to represent Spain abroad and to exemplify the historical moment of the post-transition and *desencanto*. Homosexuality was clearly compatible with this representative function; as in the films themselves, it was wholly 'taken for granted'. Foreigners could be less pliant, accusing the director of using 'homosexual imagery' in the heterosexual love story *¡Atame!* (1990), in which Antonio Banderas once more plays an obsessive and violent lover.[55]

I take it for granted that to raise the question of homosexual

---

[55] See the 'Coda' to this chapter.

desire in these films is not to invoke the shibboleth of 'intrinsically' homosexual imagery. Indeed the overt depiction of gay life
is often lacking from the films. As Dominique Fernandez notes,
in *La ley del deseo* the action never takes place in exclusively gay
locations:[56] the bars and discotheques are clearly 'mixed'. The
problem with this opening out of homosexuality into heterosexual milieux is that it represses the specificity of lesbian and gay
experience: *pace* David Leavitt, if homosexuality were as socially
acceptable as Almodóvar's films suggest, then the exclusively
lesbian or gay establishments in Madrid (unshown in the films)
would be unnecessary. Moreover, the films show little interaction
between lesbian and gay characters and the institutions which
shape their lives: the family, the workplace, the legal and medical
establishments. They tend to take place in a utopian, asocial
space: the post-punk *movida*, the convent, the *demi-monde* of
cinema and theatre. But once again this space is not exclusively
homosexual: its most extreme version is the flat in *¡Atame!* where
the crazed Antonio Banderas keeps Victoria Abril tied to a bed.
The problem for the critic, then, is to respect Almodóvar's
concern for the generalities of sex and love, without reinforcing
his repression of the specificity of homosexual desire.

These films are characterized by intermittence. *Pepi, Luci*
swings wildly between crazy farce and social comedy; *Entre
tinieblas* oscillates between decorative stylization and naked sen-
timent; *La ley del deseo* criss-crosses the border between social
realism and melodrama. The question is whether, in this insistent, rhythmic discontinuity, homosexuality as a discrete
phenomenon dissolves entirely into difference: certainly it is
presented within the films as just another item on the libidinal
menu. In one of the very few Spanish accounts of homosexuality
in the cinema, Francisco Ors makes a number of points which
may help us out of this impasse.[57] He begins by suggesting that
homosexuality is not to be limited to genital sex; rather it is a
broader matter of taste and ethos. Citing the example of von
Sternberg and Dietrich, he claims that gay cinema is hostile to
realism as the reproduction of the real. Rather it insists on the
transformation of the concrete, on the metamorphosis of the

---

[56] *Le Rapt de Ganymède* (Paris, 1989), 330. This book is a collection of essays on gay
literature and culture.

[57] 'Sternberg en la cumbre del esplendor homosexual de Hollywood', *Contracampo*
22 (1981), 11–16.

body. Thus Dietrich's 'natural' face was quite literally rearranged by Hollywood technicians, lit and photographed to produce an effect of improbable beauty. The homosexual mode would thus be a revolt against the real (which condemns us to marginality), and an embrace of that anti-naturalism which stands as an icon of utopian change.

Ors's thesis, which unfortunately remains undeveloped, suggests a homosexual culture which is a position, rather than an identity, a position which exists only in relation to dominant (naturalistic) forms of representation. In the light of his argument we can read Almodóvar's oscillation between naturalistic and non-naturalistic modes in a specifically gay context as an investigation of the oblique relation between homosexual subjects and that majority culture from which we are in part excluded. It is significant that Ors cites the body of the star (of Dietrich) as the medium for this investigation. For in the case of Almodóvar, also, the narrative of discontinuity and transformation is effected in the actress. Thus Carmen Maura undergoes a bewildering series of transformations: from lewd nymphette, to sentimental nun, to ostentatiously feminine transsexual. These metamorphoses could be read (following Ors) as an insistence on cinema's capacity to transform the real, to accede to (homosexual) fantasy. The role of the star would thus be to embody those contradictions (between private and public, individual and social) which cannot be addressed directly within the filmic narrative itself.[58]

We have seen that one particular problem with Almodóvar's cinema is its intermittent tone: critics differ widely as to what extent a film such as *Entre tinieblas* is to be taken seriously. But this problem is also inflected by the question of homosexuality. It seems likely that (male, heterosexual) critics chose to read *Entre tinieblas* as a farce because they do not believe that lesbian love can be more than just another shock tactic in Almodóvar's repertoire of incendiary provocations. They thus chose to disregard the codes of performance, music, and *mise en scène* that quite clearly frame the love scenes as amorous encounters. Almodóvar questions this fiction of a homogeneous, heterosexual audience

---

[58] Here I follow Richard Dyer's argument in *Heavenly Bodies* (London, 1986). See also the more recent collection by Christine Gledhill (ed.), *Film Stars: System, Meaning, and Desire* (London, 1991).

by confronting the spectator with techniques infrequent in
commercial cinema: the reproduction and subversion of pornographic images; the direct address to camera, which makes us
the countershot of the lesbian look; the internalization of that
voyeurism (scopophilia) which is at the heart of cinematic
pleasure. Such techniques are not merely formal; rather they
attack the naturalized construction of the 'general public' which
Hollywood takes for granted.

We find no 'Good Homosexuals' in Almodóvar. Unlike Eloy
de la Iglesia in the previous decade, he is not concerned with
affirming the dignity of a homosexual identity which had been
deprived of access to the cinema. Nor are his images compatible
with any recognizable political programme. I would argue that
if we can read his cinema as 'postmodern' it is not in the common
sense in which the term is used (particularly in Spain), as a label
for a particular style. Rather it is because these films tend to
unsettle traditional notions of epistemology and ontology (of
knowledge and identity).[59] Thus many of the films lack the
identification figures who would normally be endowed with the
authority of truth: either there is no central figure and we must
choose one from amongst a gallery (*Pepi, Luci*; *Entre tinieblas*) or
the protagonist is deluded, narcissistic, and unreliable (Pablo in
La ley del deseo). Likewise the collage effect of the films (the
insertion of parody adverts or video clips) tends to call into
question any single authoritative register as origin of truth, voice
of the real. In a rather similar way, identity becomes provisional,
discontinuous. Characters often have no origin (where is the
teenage Bom's family?) or reveal extraordinary and unmotivated
dimensions (the millionaire Marquesa in *Entre tinieblas* is also a
beautician; the singer Yolanda is also a botanist 'specializing in
hybrids'). These are not simply 'crazy' gags; they are also
pointers to the virtuality of the character (in cinema, in life) who
is subject to constant change and redirection. As a 'specialist in
hybrids' himself, Almodóvar does not allow us the reassurance
of a single genre and a unified sense of self.

In scenes where characters are indeed given a sense of origin,
it is generally parodic: exemplary here is transsexual Tina's
tearful confession in *La ley del deseo* of the (literal) castration

---

[59] This 'weakening' of ontology and epistemology is the definition of postmodernism given by Vattimo (see n. 14 above).

demanded by a tyrannical father: in this parodic formulation, the Oedipal narrative is stripped of its primary prestige, is reduced to just another story to be reproduced and redirected at will. The important verb in this process of reproduction and redirection is 'to mime'. Bom and her friends mime to zarzuela as they beat up the policeman's twin brother; Yolanda and the Mother Superior mime to a bolero as they amorously confront one another in the office; Antonio mimes to Los Panchos as he prepares for his final night of love with Pablo. Miming suggests the (postmodern) reproduction of found material, the acknowledgement that we cannot go forward without working through the past. But it also has a specifically homosexual inflection: for lesbians and gay men, obliquely placed in relation to a dominant culture which does not speak to our experience, miming is a constant feature of our life in a hostile environment, and of our resistance to that environment.[60]

I would suggest, finally, that the (much disputed) genre of Almodóvar's film is the 'moral melodrama'. Thus on the one hand (in the words of Marsha Kinder) pleasure could be seen in the Eighties as 'the new Spanish morality', an implicit challenge to the dour repressions of forty years of dictatorship.[61] And on the other, the spiralling excesses of Almodóvar's cinema suggest (in Peter Brooks's words) the 'melodramatic imagination [as] the postulation of a signified in excess of the possibilities of the signifier' (p. 199). As moral melodrama (as a postmodern ethics)[62] Pedro Almodóvar's cinema of desire both holds fast to the old certainties of love and identity, and obsessively calls those certainties into question. It is a process and a product from which a (broadly defined) homosexual desire is inseparable.

---

[60] The 'mimed' identity I propose here coincides with Judith Butler's proposal in *Gender Trouble* that sex and gender be read as 'performatives' with no ontological reality beyond the gestures that call them into being: cf. Butler's essay on Douglas Sirk (a director much loved by Almodóvar): 'Lana's "Imitation": Melodramatic Repetition and the Gender Performative', *Genders* 9 (1990), 1–18.

[61] 'Pleasure and the New Spanish Morality: A Conversation with Pedro Almodóvar', *FQ* (Fall 1987), 33–4.

[62] See Seán Hand, 'Reading, "Post-modern", Ethics' [*sic*], *TP* 13 (1990), 267–84 for a defence of the postmodern as an engagement with temporality and politics which cites Derrida, Levinas, and Vattimo.

Coda: ¡Atame! ('Tie Me Up! Tie Me Down!', 1990)

Almodóvar's first film of the 1990s raises thorny questions we have already examined in his films of the previous decade, including sado-masochism and pornography. However, the libidinal power structures we saw in *Pepi, Luci* and *Entre tinieblas* are now transposed into a heterosexual framework. *¡Atame!*'s plot is uncharacteristically simple: on his release from a psychiatric prison, Ricky (Antonio Banderas) kidnaps the junkie porn star Marina (Victoria Abril) and ties her to the bed; inevitably, she falls in love with him, proving (Almodóvar suggests) that we must accept the 'bonds' or 'ties' of commitment or learn to live alone: ' "Tie me up" ', he says, 'equals "I love you" '.[1] *¡Atame!*'s reception in English-speaking countries was much more hostile than that of the earlier films. And one question I raise at the end of this Coda is that of national identities: to what extent should critics defer to the specificity of the Spanish context and to what extent should they judge Almodóvar's films by 'universal' (non-Hispanic) criteria? A second question is also relevant here: is it legitimate to invoke the figure of the director when considering the film? In many discussions of *¡Atame!* the homosexuality of the director is made to intrude into the cinematic space, at once determining and legitimizing the critic's response to a heterosexual love story. Personal identity, like national identity, can be invoked for both progressive and reactionary purposes. I reread these territorial questions (of the proper limits of national and subjective boundaries) in the light of Andrew Ross's recent historicizing account of camp.

The soundtrack of *¡Atame!* begins with a heartbeat. The

---

[1] See the anonymous interview with Almodóvar in the production notes for *¡Atame!*; and Andrés F. Rubio, ' " 'Atame' equivale a 'te quiero" ', dice Pedro Almodóvar de su última película', *El país internacional* (18 Dec. 1989). For desire in an earlier film, see Peter W. Evans, 'Almodóvar's *Matador*: Genre, Subjectivity, and Desire', forthcoming in *BHS*.

camera pulls back to reveal multiple reproductions of a kitschy postcard depicting the Sacred Heart of Christ. On his release Ricky, obsessed by the woman he has met only once, buys Marina a heart-shaped box of chocolates. It is the gift of love: the sign of absolute devotion. Throughout the film, blood-red will be prominent in the often lurid palette of the art design, from Ricky's shirt to Marina's telephone. What can we make of such images? The first point is that the conceptual and emotional work in this film is carried out by the image itself and not by the plot, which is flagrantly derivative. The slippage from heartbeat to Sacred Heart to chocolate box suggests, in purely graphic form, that physiology is inseparable from symbolization, that the body is always already bound up in the image repertoire of a culture that precedes and envelops it. The second point is that this image repertoire has no fixed value but is open to redirection, as when the divine is humanized, brought down to earth with a literal bump: Ricky shows not Christ-like gentleness to the woman he claims to love but floors her with a vicious head-butt. The third point is the new found prominence of *mise-en-scène*. As in Vattimo's prescription for postmodern art,[2] that which was once marginal (the neglected object of a distracted perception) is here moved into centre frame and offered up quite explicitly for the spectator's visual pleasure: in Marina's apartment even the sheets are by Sybilla, a well-known Madrid fashion designer.

But if commodities and surfaces move to the centre, what becomes of the characters? As in the earlier films, subjectivity here seems disturbingly 'weak' or 'light'. Thus the deranged Ricky appears to change character on donning a heavy-metal wig; and just as in *Entre tinieblas* the nightclub singer can also be a botanist, so in this film porn star Marina is also a veterinary surgeon, earnestly counselling a tinker on the best treatment for his horse's ailments. Victoria Abril has spoken in an interview of her attempt to give depth to the character: as Marina is often rendered speechless by a plaster across the mouth, the actress sought to make the audience 'hear' her think.[3] But in spite of Abril's animated and touching performance (quite different to the stolid and monotonous Banderas), it is by no means clear

---

[2] See Vattimo on 'The Death or Decline of Art', in *La fine della modernità* (Milan, 1987), 59–72 (esp. p. 69).

[3] See Philippe Vecchi, 'Accroche-moi', *Libération* (23–4 June 1990).

that the film requires this kind of emotional response of its audience. In *La ley del deseo*, we remember, Almodóvar sought to show that gay men were not 'zombies'. But in *¡Atame!* it is to George A. Romero's zombie epics that he makes reference: there is a poster for *Night of the Living Dead* in the studio and the film itself is later glimpsed on television. Some critics have seen *¡Atame!* as promoting (rather than documenting or analysing) a shallow and flashy consumerism in which people are mercilessly reified and commodities lovingly fetishized: for them, the care lavished on costume and decor tends to drain the central characters of genuine life and emotion.[4] As in Romero, it would seem that the zombies have taken over the shopping mall.

But this is to misread a film which clearly signposts its own reflexivity as a comment on the cinematic process. Thus Marina is filming a B-movie ('Midnight Phantom') with a director who constantly ogles her. And when she removes her underwear for a scene she tells him 'Don't look at me.' The lure of voyeurism is thus internalized in the narrative and readdressed to the audience in the cinema. What is more, the set on which the film is being made is the same as that used in Almodóvar's previous *Mujeres al borde*; only this time we get to see it from behind. Once more the illusion of film-making is at once broken and reaffirmed. Almodóvar lays bare the cinematic device, only to recuperate it at a higher level. Finally, there is the director, famous (like Almodóvar) for his work with actresses. Played by veteran Francisco Rabal, his name is Máximo Espejo ('consummate mirror'). Almodóvar has said that the director is a mirror to the actors, who must see their performance reflected in his eyes. But the grizzled and impotent Espejo, confined to a wheelchair, is also the vanishing point of the film, that place at which the young gay *auteur* and his older straight surrogate mirror each other in a knowing play of reflection. In all these cases, scopophilia leads to territorialization: the imposition of a hermetic empire of the visual, whose limits are those of the filmic apparatus (of the actor, set, and director) itself. It is no accident

---

[4] See e.g. Lawrence O'Toole, 'Almodóvar in Bondage', *SS* 59/4 (Autumn 1990), 270–3. Jacques Chevallier, on the other hand, argues that the film alternates between true emotion and critical or humorous distancing. See his review of *¡Atame!*, *RC* 461 (1990), 25.

that in the original germ of the script, the action took place entirely within the space of a film-set.[5]

This claustrophobic space is one of citation: Almodóvar genuflects here to Buñuel's masterpiece of inertia and confinement *El ángel exterminador* ('The Exterminating Angel', 1962). But it also suggests a new mode of cinematic consumption. In an essay on Almodóvar called 'L'Amour du cinéma' Jean Douchet[6] suggests that for younger audiences the relationship to cinema is now 'historical' (p. 52). In a phrase reminiscent of Terenci Moix, he writes that in a previous era the audience existed, was born ('est . . . naît') in the cinema. Now that immediate and unselfconscious experience has become one of memory, citation, and lost aura (p. 53). Almodóvar has the passion of or for cinema, the passion of the cinematic object that is recreated in his own image. His fans thus tend to say quite simply 'I love Almodóvar', without needing to qualify their statement. In spite of his love of the 'second degree', however, for Douchet Almodóvar reciprocates the cinematic passion of his young audience: in *¡Atame!* scepticism gives way to a new-found belief in love.

Lawrence O'Toole[7] has also suggested that the response to Almodóvar tends to be unconditional: in line with the 'excess' O'Toole claims is typical of the 'gay sensibility', it is not enough to like his films; one has to 'adore' them (p. 270). But unlike Douchet, O'Toole denies *¡Atame!* both irony and genuine emotion. Almodóvar is the unwitting victim of a Warholian aesthetic, 'imprisoned on the surface' and 'wearing his artifice on his sleeve' (pp. 271, 272). And if his films are about a certain attitude to the past, then this is a sign of witless superficiality, not (as I would suggest myself) of a sceptical awareness of the limits of representation.

What, then, if this cult of the surface is read as critique, as a means of investigating the questions of pornography, heterosexuality, and femininity? Let us take a particularly scandalous sequence as an example. In extreme close-up and from an overhead angle a toy diver comes into frame on the left; the camera follows it as it moves up between a woman's massively magnified thighs until it reaches the pubic area. There it continues gently to vibrate. Cut to Victoria Abril with a quietly

---

[5] See National Film Theatre, programme notes to *¡Atame!* (London, 1990).
[6] *CaC* 435 (1990), 52–3.   [7] See n. 4 above.

ecstatic expression on her face. While filming this sequence Almodóvar stressed to a French journalist who was visiting the set that the shot was not pornographic; rather it was a 'metaphor' for Marina's position at that point in the film: although she does not know it herself, she is awaiting the approach of the man whose surrogate is the mechanical toy.[8] Rather than displacing this scene into metaphor, however, we can ask what spectator positions it offers itself up to. As Andrew Ross reminds us, the ways in which pornography is actually consumed are very complex, depending both on distributional technologies and individual libidinal make-up (*No Respect*, 194). For Ross, graphic sexual images should not be reduced to mere symptoms of a 'fixed world of gendered power relations', an 'ahistorical patriarchy'; nor can they be read only in a strictly literalist way for their content, irrespective of the varied 'constructions of representation and fantasy in consumption' (p. 188). It is important here to note that at least one lesbian critic (Mandy Merck) has written in praise of this sequence:[9] we can no longer assume that only straight men derive pleasure from such images.

Moreover, we should pay attention here to the camera angle and not reduce the image to pure (unmediated) content. On the one hand, the overhead shot (repeated later when Marina is bound to the bed) is the consummate technique of visual command or scopophilia: the hidden voyeur looks down on the object of the gaze, exploiting that link between 'sex' and 'knowledge' which for Eve Sedgwick is central to our culture (*Closet*, 73). On the other hand, when the overhead shot is used as it is here without being preceded by a long (establishing) shot and in combination with an extreme close-up of unidentified body parts, it tends, initially at least, to disorient voyeurs, to disturb their fixed and dominant position. Like Jonathan Dollimore's 'proximate' other, it suggests a relation of troubling nearness in which the object may 'track back' into the subject, disrupting his or her clearly defined subjective territory. In other words, we should

---

[8] Ange-Dominique Bouzet, 'Tournage au bout de la crise de nerfs', *Libération* (9 Jan. 1990).

[9] Review of *¡Atame!*, *City Limits* (London) (5–12 July 1990). In 'La Prisonnière de l'amour', *Positif* 352 (1990), 54–5 Philippe Rouyer claims that the scene escapes pornography because of its humour and metaphorical meaning in the context of the film. On its release in the USA *¡Atame!* was initially given an X certificate, normally reserved for hard-core pornography. See Alberto Montagut, 'Batalla para evitar que *¡Atame!* sea declarada "porno"', *El país internacional* (16 Apr. 1990).

not sublate such sexually graphic material safely into symbolism (into a metaphor of the heroine's psychological situation at this point in the film); but neither should we be content to revel in the visual pleasure it will afford certain kinds of audience. Rather we should ask how the filmic grammar of the sequence (framing, editing, camera angle) serves both to incite desire and to preclude it, to lead the viewer on or in to a future image that would more closely 'fit' the expectations it has itself awoken. Ricky goes shopping for softer ropes and less painful plasters with which to bind and silence Marina: even in this grotesque parody of the domestic ménage there is room for a greater adequation between the material needs of the real and the more abstract demands of fantasy. Indeed, as the film quite clearly shows, it is in the space between these two poles that desire (narrative) opens up.

The deluded Ricky's treatment of Marina is thus a parody of heterosexual relations in the sane world. Returning from a shopping expedition, he calls out 'Honey, I'm home.' And once Marina is safely bound to the bed he quickly sets about mending domestic appliances or fixing breakfast. He had announced his intentions to the actress with the words: 'I'm 23 years old; I have 50 thousand pesetas, and I'm alone in the world. I'd like to be a good father to your children.' What is crazy here is not the paternal ambition, voiced by innumerable clean-cut movie heroes, but rather the context in which it is expressed. Heterosexuality is here stripped down to the bare minimum of physical reproduction, emptied of all wider social or affective resonance. When relations between men and women are hollowed out in this way (reduced to pure surface) then power imbalances are cruelly denaturalized. In one publicity still for the film (Plate 6) Antonio Banderas is shown in extreme close-up once more with head upright and eyes lowered; Victoria Abril stares out at the viewer, her head placed on one side. There could be no clearer image of the lack of reciprocity or 'fit' between the sexes within the film (and outside it).

Some women have accused Almodóvar of misogyny. Thus in her review of *Mujeres al borde* Jill Forbes[10] claims that the film is 'profoundly reactionary' in its representation of women humiliated by their dependence on men. But Forbes herself suggests

[10] *SS* 58/2 (Spring 1989), 135.

another reading of gender in Almodóvar: in *Mujeres* the very physical female protagonists circle around a man who is intangible, disembodied, filtered through technology. The (singularly unattractive) Iván speaks mainly through the answerphone and earns his living by dubbing foreign language films: in other words, he is a mere impersonation of masculinity. The women, on the other hand, ostensibly neurotic, are surprisingly strong: when Carmen Maura's Pepa finally catches up with 'Iván the terrible' she refuses even to speak to him after saving his life. I would suggest, then, that in *¡Atame!* also we should attempt to read gender relations as parody by paying attention to the codes of performance that 'frame' and inflect the narrative content.

In the production notes, Almodóvar himself (stung by Anglo-American criticism of the film's theme) appeals to personal ethos: how could anyone believe that he, of all people, was *machista?* This strategy of legitimation by reference to the director's identity is also used by critics with very different consequences: thus Mandy Merck rereads the film as an allegory of gay male love; and Bert Cardullo[11] attacks it for being of interest only to 'camp followers'. But even at the level of content, as the narrative develops it suggests a gender-separatist world in which woman is triumphant. Thus Marina (who appears to have no father or brother) is given a lovable mother (played by Almodóvar's own mother, Francisca Caballero) and a feisty sister (Loles León). In characteristic scenes, at once zany and intimate, Marina's mother is shown dancing and cooking with her granddaughter (reproducing the feminine function). At the end of the film, Ricky comes to live with this female community: but on their terms. Women thus move from the margin to the centre, stand alone as the norm of social and familial reproduction which proceeds independently of men. The latter are monstrous aberrations who disrupt violently (but momentarily) the female continuum: Marina survives both the voyeuristic fetishism of her director and the more physical abuse of her abductor. Emblematic here is the 'Midnight Phantom' of the film-within-a-film, a silent and fetishistically garbed assailant lassoed by Marina with the telephone flex. Men are also tied up in this film, imprisoned by the bonds of heterosexual masculinity.

---

[11] 'Lovers and Other Strangers', *HuR* 43/4 (Winter 1991), 645–53, is a diatribe against Almodóvar, Peter Greenaway, and AIDS drama *Longtime Companion*.

To insist on the triumph of the feminine in *¡Atame!* is not to deny its stress on the continuing vulnerability of women. But, in its emphasis on the virtuality of feminine identity (on the successive reincarnations of the Abril character) the film suggests a critique (rather than a celebration) of that potential for aggression to which women are subject under patriarchy. As Sedgwick writes: 'To conceive oneself as a woman at all must mean trying to conceive oneself, over and over, as if incarnated in ever more vulnerable situations and embodiments' (*Closet*, 62). The (cinematic) spectacle of the woman in peril thus rehearses (but need not reinforce) a feminine vulnerability which is not natural or eternal, but systematic and social.

The film ends with the three characters (Ricky, Marina, and her sister Lola) returning to Madrid: the women had gone to seek out Ricky in the ruins of the village in which he was born and to which he has retreated. The ruinous village suggests a certain loss of origin in contemporary Spain: there is now no alternative to the random atomism and anonymity of the city. In the final sequence the trio sing along to an anaemic Spanish version of the disco hit of the 1970s, 'I Will Survive'. They sing very badly. This is the happy ending which O'Toole claims is 'without irony'. I would suggest, rather, that this is once more an example of the double 'miming' we have seen elsewhere in Almodóvar's œuvre: just as the characters reproduce their feelings in the form of popular culture, so Almodóvar echoes that culture and subjects it to redirection. *¡Atame!* acknowledges the continuing survival of heterosexual narrative (boy meets girl) and heterosexual desire (boy wants girl) but both are repeated in a radically relativized and 'weakened' form. It suggests that there is no way forward (for the film-maker, for the gay man), no radical break with the past, which does not involve a working through that past to new and more fragile forms of art and identity.

This, very broadly, is the argument of Andrew Ross's 'The Uses of Camp'.[12] Ross suggests that camp is not (as is sometimes thought) the denial of history, but rather a certain staggering of history whereby 'the products of a much earlier mode of production . . . become available for redefinition according to contemporary codes of taste' (*No Respect*, 139). One example is the

[12] In *No Respect* (New York, 1989).

appearance in television soap operas of former movie stars from the classic era of Hollywood. This technological staggering is related to both class and sexuality: camp is determined by the waning of cultural power and the oblique relation of lesbian and gay audiences to dominant modes of cultural production (pp. 146, 157). As a 'rediscovery of history's waste'[13] (p. 151) camp hints at mortality, a *memento mori* to modes of taste that are no longer current (p. 152). And in its commitment to the imaginary identifications and symbolic constructions of gay identity it coincides with a certain feminism: that which reveals the 'cultural constitution of sexuality and gender identity . . . the non-essentialist masquerade of femininity'. The politics of camp (if such a thing exists) thus differs from that of the old liberation movements in its 'commitment to the mimicry of existing cultural forms and its refusal to advocate wholesale breaks with those same forms' (p. 161). It should be clear that this new definition of camp coincides with many aspects of Almodóvar's filmic practice.

Ross thus views camp (and the homosexual spectatorship with which it is associated) not as an essential entity but rather as a historically produced position inextricable from changes in reproductive technologies. And he suggests (like Almodóvar) that this position is founded on strategies of survival: rather than simply dismissing consumerism as inauthentic, we should acknowledge its role in the creation of a fragile and provisional gay male subject position. Camp is thus a 'commentary on survival in a world dominated by the tastes, interests, and definitions of others' (p. 144). This definition also holds good for the films of Almodóvar in which marginal characters survive (like the director himself) by plundering dominant codes, dominant narratives.

Ross is also aware that modes of cultural and subjective survival are inflected by nationality. For example, he notes how, since the waning of British imperial power, a Union Jack can be camp in the way that the Stars and Stripes cannot (p. 144). And he suggests at one point that it is 'Anglo-Saxon society' that has gendered as feminine the ornamentation and emotion that camp

---

[13] For a graphic illustration of Almodóvar's love of the detritus of consumerism, cf. the garbage truck on which he and the stars of *¡Atame!* arrived for the film's Madrid premiere: Ben Brantley, 'The Wild Man of La Mancha', *Sunday Times Magazine* (London) (18 June 1990).

has reappropriated for gay men (p. 158). This brings me to my final question: is it possible to identify a specifically Spanish inflection of the 'gay sensibility'? Or is the attempt to do so doomed to fall back into reified notions of national identity which are themselves incapable of addressing regional variations within the nation-state?

There is no doubt that radical differences exist between the national languages in which cinema is discussed: Spanish and French accounts of ¡Atame! simply do not mention the problem of sexual violence against women that dominated English-language debate.[14] Indeed, one French account takes Marina's drug addiction, not her bondage, as the fundamental metaphor of the film.[15] It is clear that the much greater awareness of 'radical' or 'revolutionary' feminist themes in Britain and the USA affected press reception in these countries. Moreover, foreign accounts have tended to rely on clichéd versions of Hispanicity: thus Frédéric Strauss claimed in Cahiers du cinema that ¡Atame! was linked to a typically Spanish tradition of melodrama (which he does not trouble to examine).[16] On the other hand, Isabel Cadalso's 'Pedro Almodóvar: A Spanish Perspective' relies equally on stereotypical notions of a 'Mediterranean spirit of freedom' and reduces Almodóvar's cinema to a banal plea for humanity and tolerance.[17]

Cadalso's response illustrates what John Hopewell has called the 'mythology' of Spanish cinema, which reads the history of the genre as a cumulative movement towards liberal tolerance, in which forty years of dictatorship are a tragic but incidental interruption. As Hopewell notes, such a reading not only neglects the genuine merits of some films made under Franco, it also judges complex cultural phenomena by the single criterion of 'progressive' political content (El cine, 410–11). Cadalso's analysis is thus incapable of distinguishing between the perverse passions of ¡Atame! and the dull didacticism of, say, Juan Antonio Bardem's Lorca, muerte de un poeta ('Lorca: Death of a Poet', 1987). Indeed

[14] See Jordi Vallvés, 'Pedro Almodóvar presentó ayer en Barcelona su último filme, ¡Atame!', Diario 16 (13 Jan. 1990); Frédéric Strauss, 'Festival de Berlin: Pedro Almodóvar', CaC 430 (1990), 6.
[15] See n. 3 above; Frédéric Strauss compares Marina's bondage to Almodóvar's 'bond' with the past, whose images he is condemned constantly to repeat. See his review of ¡Atame!, CaC 433 (1990), 88.
[16] See Strauss n. 14 above.   [17] Cineaste 18/1 (1990), 36–7.

Cadalso's description of the 'Mediterranean sensibility' is
remarkably similar to well-meaning accounts of the tragic poet:
Almodóvar's work is 'a cry for freedom, flexibility, and self-
liberation in a world where fascism—in the forms of religious
fanaticism, racism, chauvinism, sexism, homophobia, and intol-
erance in general—still appears all too frequently' (p. 37).

In 'The Politics of Passion: Pedro Almodóvar and the Camp
Aesthetic', Marcia Pally makes a similar anti-authoritarian
point, claiming that Almodóvar rejects 'creeds of decency'
whether they are 'priestly, feminist, fascist, or gay lib'.[18] Pally is
drawing on the *¡Atame!* production notes at this point (though
she does not acknowledge the debt) and her attitude is one
shared by many Spaniards. The problem is, however, one of
discrimination: it is simply not the case that fascism, feminism,
and anti-homophobia have the same effects in the world; and to
bracket them together as common enemies of liberal tolerance is
scarcely convincing. What we need is an alternative to both the
facile stereotype of an unchanging Mediterranean sensibility and
the falsely historicist platitude that reduces all contemporary art
to an allegory of political development. This alternative is what
I have called 'postmodern ethics'. It is no coincidence that
Gianni Vattimo has recently proposed Spain as the site of a
postmodern sensibility untainted by the dour Northern inherit-
ance of Protestantism and rationalism.[19] Vattimo's reading suggests neither that Spanish culture be floated free from its history,
nor that it be weighed down by literalist historical determinism.
Rather it points the way to new 'weak' allegories of nationality
which will remain open to a 'critical regionalism'.

I would suggest, finally, that this question of nationality
suggests a new approach to lesbian and gay cultures, a third way
between Sedgwick's 'minoritizing' and 'universalizing' dichotomy. For, as Almodóvar's success has shown, the so-called gay
sensibility has been generalized, disseminated throughout the
dominant culture. There is thus no future in attempting to
preserve a uniquely homosexual cultural territory, if ever one
existed. But if (as *¡Atame!* has also shown) we must resist both
the reductive literalism of content analysis and the facile consolations of allegory, then what is left? Perhaps our task is to work

---

[18] In the same issue of *Cineaste* as Cadalso, p. 31–5, 38–9.
[19] See my review of *¡Atame!* in *TLS* (20–6 July 1990).

through the 'remainder' of an outdated homosexual 'self' in the mode of homographesis: attempting to undo the violent metaphors on which lesbian and gay identities were based and make visible the metonymic relation between subjects and their sexual-object choice. And this is no mere textual matter; for the metaphorical identification of homosexuality, femininity, and sickness (repeated by at least one critic of *¡Atame!*) now has potentially fatal effects for all of us.[20] Andrew Ross proposes that AIDS is productive of new subject positions, new places from which to speak the self: 'The recent appearance of new kinds of identity—HIV positive and HIV negative—threatens to inaugurate a new level of policing *at the same time* as it provides resisting activists with especially legitimate grounds for getting their case heard' (p. 203). Ross proposes 'new and different social relations to the body . . . imagined without the guarantee of knowing in advance whether they are right or wrong' (p. 208). Even here, then, we can trace (as in the history of the Spanish gay movement) a certain productivity in law, a certain possibility of reversing the discourse of the other. If we take up Ross's challenge, we may yet come to understand Foucault's elusive suggestion that homosexuality is 'not a form of desire but something to be desired' (Boone and Cadden, *Engendering Men*, 172).

It may be that the national and sexual fictions known as 'Spain' and 'homosexuality' have something in common: both are dangerously close to the same (to 'our culture'); and both threaten to 'track back' from their position of proximity into that same: redrawing the geographical boundaries, retracing the libidinal margins. The rich and varied fictions of lesbian and gay identities in Spanish writing and film thus point to a double repression which returns with a double force. A newly self-confident Spain increases its cultural participation in the Europe from which it was once exiled; Spanish (Basque, Catalan) lesbian and gays continue to express themselves in text and cinema. We cannot know in advance where such new and different relations to the body and to pleasure will lead.

---

[20] The critic is Bert Cardullo, who also writes that he will not support research seeking a cure for a disease which 'promiscuous homosexuals' have brought on themselves.

Glossary of Film Terms

I have referred to the third edition of the indispensable *Film Art: An Introduction* by David Bordwell and Kristin Thompson (New York, 1990). Their glossary (pp. 408–12) gives fuller definitions of many of the terms below.

camera angle: The position of the camera on a vertical continuum relative to the object being shot.

close-up: A shot in which a smallish object (e.g. the human head) fits easily within the frame.

continuity editing: The conventions through which the impression of an unbroken continuum of space and time is suggested in Hollywood cinema.

crane shot: A shot in which the camera rises above the ground on a mobile support.

cross-cutting: Swiftly cutting backwards and forwards between more than one scene.

crossing the line: breaking the 180° rule typical of continuity editing (see *180° rule*).

cutaway: A sudden shift to another scene of action.

dissolve: The slow fading of one shot into another.

dolly: A trolly on which the camera is pulled along the ground.

establishing shot: A long shot, often the first in a sequence, which establishes the positions of elements relative to each other.

external diegetic sound: Sound which comes from out of frame, but within the story space (unlike incidental music, which is non-diegetic).

extreme close-up: A shot in which a small object (e.g. a part of the body) fits easily within the frame.

framing: The size and position of objects relative to the edges of the screen.

frontality: The placing of the camera at a 90° angle to the action.

graphic match: A visual rhyme between two successive shots.

long shot: A shot in which a large object (e.g. a complete human figure) fits easily within the frame.

long take: A shot that is allowed to continue for longer than usual without editing.

match on action: A cut between two shots of the same action from different positions, giving an impression of seamless simultaneity.

medium long shot: A shot in which a largish object (e.g. the human figure from lower leg up) fits easily within the frame.

medium shot: A shot in which a medium-size object (e.g. the top half of a human figure) fits easily within the frame.

mise en scène: Everything found within the frame, including set decoration, costume, and styles of performance.

180° rule: The convention that the camera can be placed in any position as long as it remains on one side of the action.

overhead shot: A shot looking down vertically on the action from above.

pan: A movement in which the camera turns to right or left on a horizontal axis.

plan américain: same as *medium long shot* (q.v.).

POV: A shot which is understood to be from a character's point of view.

racking focus: A shift in focus between planes at different distances from the camera within the same shot.

reverse angle: Two successive shots from equal and opposite angles, typically of characters during conversation.

sequence shot: A relatively long and complete scene shot in one take without editing.

shock cut: The immediate juxtaposition of two incongruous shots (e.g. from a sex scene to a religious icon).

shot/countershot: same as *reverse angle* (q.v.).

suture: The 'sewing' together of imaginary and symbolic in Hollywood cinema carried out by continuity editing. It serves to ensure the sense of a unified narrative and subject position.

tilt: A movement by which the camera moves up or down while its support remains fixed.

tracking shot: A shot in which the camera is pushed horizontally along the ground on a dolly.

two shot: A shot in which two actors appear within the frame.

Bibliography

I. GENERAL AND THEORETICAL

Adams, Parveen, 'Of Female Bondage', in *Between Feminism and Psycho-analysis*, ed. Teresa Brennan (New York, 1989), 247–65.

Allen, Paula Gunn, 'Lesbians in American Indian Cultures', in *Hidden from History: Reclaiming the Gay and Lesbian Past*, edd. Martin Duberman, Martha Vicinus, and George Chauncey, Jr. (New York, 1990), 106–17.

Baudrillard, Jean, 'Simulacra and Simulations', in *Selected Writings*, ed. Mark Poster (Cambridge, 1988), 166–84.

Benstock, Shari, 'Expatriate Sapphic Modernism: Entering Literary History', in Karla Jay and Joanne Glasgow (eds.), *Lesbian Texts and Contexts: Radical Revisions* (New York, 1990), 183–203.

Bersani, Leo, 'Representation and its Discontents', *Raritan* 1 (1981), 3–17.

—— 'Is the Rectum a Grave?', *October* 43 (1987), 197–222.

Boone, Joseph A., 'Of Me(n) and Feminism: Who(se) is the Sex that Writes', in *Engendering Men: The Question of Male Feminist Criticism*, ed. Joseph A. Boone and Michael Cadden (New York, 1990), 11–25.

Brooks, Peter, *The Melodramatic Imagination* (New Haven, Conn., 1976).

Butler, Judith, *Female Trouble: Feminism and the Subversion of Identity* (New York, 1990).

—— 'Lana's "Imitation": Melodramatic Repetition and the Gender Performative', *Genders* 9 (1990), 1–18.

Butters, Ronald R., John M. Clum, and Michael Moon (eds.), *Displacing Homophobia: Gay Male Perspectives in Literature and Culture*, (Durham, NC, 1989).

Caplan, Pat, *The Cultural Construction of Sexuality* (New York, 1987).

Case, Sue-Ellen, 'Towards a Butch-Femme Aesthetic', *Discourse* 11/1 (Fall–Winter 1988–9), 55–73.

Castle, Terry, 'Sylvia Townsend Warner and the Counterplot of Lesbian Fiction', *TP* 4 (1990), 123–35.

Cohen, Ed, 'Writing Gone Wilde: Homoerotic Desire in the Closet of Representation', *PMLA* 102 (1987), 802–13.

Collecott, Diana, 'What Is Not Said: a Study in Textual Inversion', *TP* 4 (1990), 236–58.

Curb, Rosemary, 'Core of the Apple: Mother–Daughter Fusion/Separation in Three Recent Lesbian Plays', in *Lesbian Texts and Contexts:*

Radical Revisions, ed. Karla Jay and Joanne Glasgow (New York, 1990), 355–76.

de Lauretis, Teresa, 'Sexual Indifference and Lesbian Representation', *TJ* 40 (May 1988), 155–77.

—— *Technologies of Gender* (London, 1988).

Dellamora, Richard, *Masculine Desire: The Sexual Politics of Victorian Aestheticism* (Chapel Hill, NC, 1990).

Dollimore, Jonathan, 'Different Desires: Subjectivity and Transgression in Wilde and Gide', *TP* 1 (1987), 48–67.

—— *Sexual Dissidence: Augustine to Wilde, Freud to Foucault* (Oxford, 1991).

Duberman, Martin, Martha Vicinus, and George Chauncey, Jr. (eds.), *Hidden from History: Reclaiming the Gay and Lesbian Past* (New York, 1990).

Dunn, Sara, 'Voyages of the Valkyries: Recent Lesbian Pornographic Writing', *FR* 34 (1990), 161–70.

Dyer, Richard (ed.), *Gays and Film* (London, 1977).

—— *Heavenly Bodies* (London, 1986).

—— *Now You See It: Studies on Lesbian and Gay Film* (London, 1990).

Edelman, Lee, 'Homographesis', *YJC* 3 (1989), 189–207.

—— 'Redeeming the Phallus: Wallace Stevens, Frank Lentricchia, and the Politics of (Hetero)Sexuality', in *Engendering Men: The Question of Male Feminist Criticism*, edd. Joseph A. Boone and Michael Cadden (New York, 1990), 36–52.

Elsaesser, Thomas, 'Tales of Sound and Fury: Observations on the Family Melodrama', in *Home Is Where the Heart Is: Studies in Melodrama and the Woman's Film*, ed. Christine Gledhill (London, 1990), 43–69.

Farwell, Marilyn R., 'Heterosexual Plots and Lesbian Subtexts: Toward a Theory of Lesbian Narrative Space', in Karla Jay and Joanne Glasgow (eds.), *Lesbian Texts and Contexts: Radical Revisions* (New York, 1990), 91–103.

Feldstein, Richard and Judith Roof (eds.), *Feminism and Psychoanalysis* (Ithaca, NY, 1989).

Fernandez, Dominique, *Le Rapt de Ganymède* (Paris, 1989).

Finkielkraut, Alain, *La Sagesse de l'amour* (Paris, 1984).

Fischer, Lucy, *Shot/Countershot: Film Tradition and Women's Cinema* (London, 1989).

Freedman, Estelle B., Barbara C. Gelpi, Susan L. Johnson, and Kathleen M. Weston (eds.), *The Lesbian Issue: Essays from 'Signs'*, (Chicago, 1985).

Fuss, Diana, *Essentially Speaking: Feminism, Nature, and Difference* (New York and London, (1991).

Garber, Eric, 'A Spectacle in Colour: The Lesbian and Gay Subculture of Jazz Age Harlem', in *Hidden from History: Reclaiming the Gay and*

Lesbian Past, ed. Martin Duberman, Martha Vicinus, and George Chauncey, Jr. (New York, 1990), 318–31.

Garner, Shirley Nelson, 'Feminism, Psychoanalysis, and the Heterosexual Imperative', in *Feminism and Psychoanalysis*, ed. Richard Feldstein and Judith Roof (Ithaca, NY, 1989), 164–81.

Garsi, Jean-François (ed.), *Cinémas homosexuels* (Paris, 1983).

Gledhill, Christine (ed.), *Home Is Where the Heart Is: Studies in Melodrama and the Woman's Film*, (London, 1990).

—— *Film Stars: System, Meaning, and Desire* (London, 1991).

Hall Carpenter Archives, the, *Inventing Ourselves: Lesbian Life Stories* (New York, 1989).

—— *Walking after Midnight: Gay Men's Life Stories* (New York, 1989).

Halperin, David, *One Hundred Years of Homosexuality* (New York, 1990).

Hamer, Diane, 'Significant Others: Lesbianism and Psychoanalytic Theory', *FR* 34 (1990), 134–51.

Hand, Seán, 'Reading, "Post-modern", Ethics', *TP* 13 (1990), 267–84.

Heath, Stephen, 'Film Performance', in *Cinetracts* 12 (1977).

—— *Questions of Cinema* (London, 1981).

Hocquenghem, Guy, *L'Après-mai des faunes: Volutions*, introd. by Gilles Deleuze (Paris, 1974).

—— *La Dérive homosexuelle* (Paris, 1977).

—— *Homosexual Desire*, introd. by Jeffrey Weeks (London, 1978).

—— *La Beauté du métis* (Paris, 1979).

Hunt, Margaret, 'The De-eroticization of Women's Liberation: Social Purity Movement and the Revolutionary Feminism of Sheila Jeffreys', *FR* 34 (1990), 23–46.

Irigaray, Luce, *Ce sexe qui n'en est pas un* (Paris, 1977).

Jameson, Frederick, *Marxism and Form* (Princeton, NJ, 1971).

Jay, Karla, and Joanne Glasgow (eds.), *Lesbian Texts and Contexts: Radical Revisions* (New York, 1990).

Kitzinger, Celia, *The Social Construction of Lesbianism* (London, 1987).

Klein, Yvonne M., 'Myth and Community in Recent Lesbian Autobiographical Fiction', in *Lesbian Texts and Contexts*, ed. Karla Jay and Joanne Glasgow (New York, 1990), 330–8.

Koestenbaum, Wayne, *Double Talk: The Erotics of Male Literary Collaboration* (New York, 1989).

—— 'Wilde's Hard Labour and the Birth of Gay Reading', in *Engendering Men: The Question of Male Feminist Criticism*, ed. Joseph A. Boone, and Michael Cadden (New York and London, 1990), 176–89.

Kristeva, Julia, 'Women's Time' in *Signs* 7/1 (1981), 13–35.

—— *Histoires d'amour* (Paris, 1983).

Kuhn, Annette, 'Women's Genres: Melodrama, Soap Opera, and

Theory', in *Home Is Where the Heart Is: Studies in Melodrama and the Woman's Film*, ed. Christine Gledhill (London, 1990), 339–49.

Lancini, Fiorenzo, and Paolo Sangalli, *La gaia musa* (Milan, 1981).

Laplanche, Jean, and J. B. Pontalis, *The Language of Psychoanalysis* (London, 1983).

Lejeune, Philippe, *Le Pacte autobiographique* (Paris, 1975).

Marshall, Bill, 'Gays and Marxism', in *Coming On Strong: Gay Politics and Culture*, ed. Simon Shepherd and Mick Wallis (London, 1989), 258–74.

—— 'The Autobiographies of Daniel Guérin and Yves Navarre', unpub. paper read at the Conference on 'Questions of Homosexuality' at the Institute of Romance Studies in the University of London (June 1991).

Martin, Biddy, 'Lesbian Identity and Autobiographical Difference(s)', in *Life/Lines*, ed. Bella Brodski and Celeste Schenck (Ithaca, NY, 1988), 77–103.

Meese, Elizabeth, 'Theorizing Lesbian: Writing—A Love Letter', in Karla Jay and Joanne Glasgow (eds), *Lesbian Texts and Contexts: Radical Revisions* (New York, 1990), 70–88.

Mercer, Kobena and Isaac Julien, 'Race, Sexual Politics, and Black Masculinity: A Dossier', in *Male Order: Unwrapping Masculinity*, ed. Rowena Chapman and Jonathan Rutherford (London, 1988), 97–164.

Mieli, Mario, *Elementos de crítica homosexual* (Barcelona, 1979).

Modleski, Tania, 'Time and Desire in the Woman's Film', *Home Is Where the Heart Is: Studies in Melodrama and the Woman's Film*, ed. Christine Gledhill (London, 1990), 326–38.

Moraga, Cherríe and Gloria Anzaldúa, *This Bridge Called My Back* (New York, 1983).

Mulvey, Laura, 'Visual Pleasure and Narrative Cinema', *Screen* 16/3 (1975).

—— 'Afterthoughts on "Visual Pleasure and Narrative Cinema"', in E. Ann Kaplan (ed.), *Psychoanalysis and Cinema* (London, 1990), 24–35.

Neale, Steve, *Genre* (London, 1987).

Nicolas, Jean, *La cuestión homosexual* (Barcelona, 1978).

Norris, Christopher, 'Lost in the Fun-House: Baudrillard and the Politics of Postmodernism', *TP* 3 (1989), 360–88.

Nowell-Smith, Geoffrey, 'Minelli and Melodrama', in *Home Is Where the Heart Is: Studies in Melodrama and the Woman's Film*, ed. Christine Gledhill (London, 1990), 70–4.

Owens, Craig, 'Outlaws: Gay Men in Feminism', in *Men in Feminism*, ed. Alice Jardine and Paul Smith (New York, 1987), 219–32.

Philbert, Bertrand, *L'Homosexualité à l'écran* (Paris, 1984).

Porter, Kevin, and Jeffrey Weeks (eds), *Between the Acts: Lives of Homosexual Men 1885–1967* (New York, 1991).

Pratt, Murray J., 'Reading AIDS: Questions of Identity in Guibert's Autobiographies', unpub. paper read at the Conference on 'Questions of Homosexuality' at the Institute of Romance Studies in the University of London (June 1991).

Proust, Marcel, *À la recherche du temps perdu, II: Le Côté de Guermantes* (Paris, 1954).

Rose, Jacqueline, *The Haunting of Sylvia Plath* (London, 1991).

Ross, Andrew, *No Respect: Intellectuals and Popular Culture* (New York, 1989).

—— 'Cowboys, Cadillacs, and Cosmonauts: Families, Film Genres, and Technocultures', in James A. Boone and Michael Cadden (eds.), *Engendering Men* (New York, 1990), 87–101.

Russo, Vito, *The Celluloid Closet: Homosexuality and the Movies* (New York, 1981).

Ryan, Joanna, 'Psychoanalysis and Women Loving Women', in *Sex and Love: New Thoughts on Old Contradictions*, ed. Sue Cartledge and Joanna Ryan (London, 1983), 196–209.

SAMOIS, *Coming to Power: Writings and Graphics on Lesbian S/M* (Boston, 1982).

Sedgwick, Eve Kosofsky, *Between Men: English Literature and Male Homosocial Desire* (New York, 1985).

—— 'Across Gender, Across Sexuality: Willa Cather and Others', in *Displacing Homophobia: Gay Male Perspectives in Literature and Culture*, ed. Ronald R. Butters, John M. Clum, and Michael Moon (Durham, NC, 1989), 53–72.

—— *Epistemology of the Closet* (New York, 1991).

—— and Michael Moon, 'Divinity: A Dossier', *Discourse* (Winter 1991) (forthcoming).

Shaktini, Namasker, 'Displacing the Phallic Subject: Wittig's Lesbian Writing', in *The Lesbian Issue: Essays from 'Signs'*, ed. Estelle B. Freedman, Barbara C. Gelpi, Susan L. Johnson, and Kathleen M. Weston (Chicago, 1985), 137–52.

—— 'A Revolutionary Signifier: *The Lesbian Body*', in *Lesbian Texts and Contexts: Radical Revisions*, ed. Karla Jay and Joanne Glasgow (New York, 1990), 291–303.

Sinfield, Alan, 'Who Was Afraid of Joe Orton?', *TP* 4 (1990), 259–77.

—— review of Eve Kosofsky Sedgwick, *Epistemology of the Closet*, *GLAN* 1 (April 1991), 8–10.

Smith, Barbara, *Home Girls: A Black Feminist Anthology* (New York, 1983).

Smyth, Cherry, 'The Pleasure Threshold: Looking at Lesbian Pornography on Film', *FR* 34 (1990), 152–9.

Sontag, Susan, 'Notes on Camp', in *Against Interpretation* (London, 1967), 275–92.

Special Issue on Autobiography, *CC* 12 (1990).

Special Issue on Autobiography, *FMLS* 26/3 (1990).

Stacey, Jackie, 'Desperately Seeking Difference', *Screen* 28/1 (1987), 48–61.

Stanley, Liz, *The Auto/Biographical I: Theory and Practice of Feminist Auto/Biography* (Ann Arbor, Mich., forthcoming (1992)).

Tambling, Jeremy, *Confessions: Sin, Sexuality, the Subject* (Manchester, 1990).

Vattimo, Gianni, *La Fine della modernità: nichilismo ed ermeneutica nella cultura postmoderna* (Milan, 1987).

Warner, Michael, 'Homo-Narcissism; or Heterosexuality', in *Engendering Men: The Question of Male Feminist Criticism*, ed. Joseph A. Boone, and Michael Cadden (New York, 1990), 190–206.

Weeks, Jeffrey, *Coming Out: Homosexual Politics in Britain from the Nineteenth Century to the Present* (London, 1977).

Weston, Kathleen M. and Lisa B. Rofel, 'Sexuality, Class, and Conflict in a Lesbian Workplace', in *The Lesbian Issue: Essays from 'Signs'*, ed. Estelle B. Freedman, Barbara C. Gelpi, Susan L. Johnson, and Kathleen M. Weston (Chicago, 1985), 199–222.

'When the Gaze is Gay', special section in *FC* 22/2 (Apr. 1986), 31–50.

Whitford, Margaret, *Luce Irigaray: Philosophy in the Feminine* (London, 1991).

Winkler, John J., *The Constraints of Desire: The Anthropology of Sex and Gender in Ancient Greece* (New York, 1990).

Wittig, Monique, *Les Guérillères* (Paris, 1969).

—— *Le Corps lesbien* (Paris, 1973).

—— and Sande Zeig, *Brouillon pour un dictionnaire des amantes* (Paris, 1976).

—— 'Paradigm', in *Homosexualities and French Literature*, ed. George Stambolian and Elaine Marks (Ithaca, NY, 1979), 114–21.

Yingling, Tom, *Hart Crane and the Homosexual Text* (Chicago, 1990).

Zimmerman, Bonnie, 'The Politics of Transliteration: Lesbian Personal Narratives', in *The Lesbian Issue: Essays from 'Signs'*, ed. Estelle B. Freedman, Barbara C. Gelpi, Susan L. Johnson, and Kathleen M. Weston (Chicago, 1985), 251–70.

2. HISPANIC AND LITERARY

Argüelles, Lourdes and B. Ruby Rich, 'Homosexuality, Homophobia, and Revolution: Notes toward an Understanding of the Cuban Lesbian and Gay Male Experience', in *Hidden from History: Reclaiming the Gay and Lesbian Past*, ed. Martin Duberman, Martha Vicinus, and George Chauncey, Jr. (New York, 1990), 441–55.

Bellver, Catherine G., 'The Language of Eroticism in the Novels of Esther Tusquets', *ALEC* 9 (1984), 13–27.

Chacel, Rosa, *Icada, Nevda, Diada* (Barcelona, 1982).

—— *Desde el amanecer* (Barcelona, 1985).

Cummins, J. S., 'Epoca lorquiana: Lorca, Buñuel, Dalí, and Spanish Machismo', *EGR* 1 (1986), 117–24.

—— Review of Mirabet, *Homosexualidad hoy* in *EGR* 2 (1987), 126–9.

Dehennin, Elsa, 'Relato en primera persona: novela autobiográfica versus autobiografía; el caso de Juan Goytisolo', in *Homenaje al professor Antonio Vilanova*, ii (Barcelona, 1989), 149–61.

de la Cova, Joan M., 'What kind of Games are These Anyway? The Metafictional Play and Politics of *Cobra* and *Juan sin tierra*', *RHM* 43 (1990), 206–17.

del Barrio, Ariel, *Dialogismo y novela: el principio dialógico en las novelas de Juan Goytisolo* (Santiago, 1990).

Doblado, Gloria, *España en tres novelas de Juan Goytisolo* (Madrid, 1988).

Epps, Bradley S., 'The Violence of the Letter: Oppression and Resistance in Three Texts by Juan Goytisolo', unpub. Ph.D. diss. (Harvard, 1990).

—— 'The Ecstasy of Disease: Goytisolo, AIDS, and Hispanism', unpub. paper read at Questions of Homosexuality conference, IRS London (June 1991).

Fernández, Josep-Anton, 'Death and the Angel in Lluís Fernàndez's *The Naked Anarchist*', unpub. paper read at Questions of Homosexuality conference, IRS London (June 1991).

FHAR (Frente Homosexual de Acción Revolucionaria), *Documentos contra la normalidad* (Barcelona, 1979).

Forrest, Gene Steven, 'El mundo antagónico de Terenci Moix', *Hispania* 60 (1977), 927–35.

Gámez Quintana, Miguel, *Apuntes sobre el homosexual* (Madrid, 1976).

García Valdés, Alberto, *Historia y presente de la homosexualidad* (Torrejón de Ardoz, 1981).

Gil-Albert, Juan, *Heracles: sobre una manera de ser* (Madrid, 1975).

Gimferrer, Pere, introd. to Terenci Moix, *Mundo macho* (Barcelona, 1990).

Glenn, Kathleen, 'Conversación con Rosa Chacel', *LP* 3 (1990), 11–26.

Gold, Janet N., 'Reading the Love Myth: Tusquets with the Help of Barthes', *HR* 55 (1987), 337–46.

Goytisolo, Juan, *Señas de identidad* (Barcelona, 1976).

—— *Juan sin tierra* (Barcelona, 1977).

—— *Reivindicación del conde don Julián* (Barcelona, 1982).

—— *Reivindicación del conde don Julián*, ed. and annotated Linda Gould Levine (Madrid, 1985).

—— *Coto vedado* (Barcelona, 1985).

—— *En los reinos de Taifa* (Barcelona, 1986).

—— *Marks of Identity*, trans. Gregory Rabassa (London, 1988).

—— *Las virtudes del pájaro solitario* (Barcelona, 1988).

—— *Count Julian*, trans. Helen R. Lane (London, 1989).

—— *Forbidden Territory: Memoirs 1932–56*, trans. Peter Bush (London, 1989).

—— *Realms of Strife: Memoirs 1957–82*, trans. Peter Bush (San Francisco, 1990).

——*Juan the Landless*, trans. Helen R. Lane (London, 1990).

—— 'Juan Goytisolo: La mirada del Islam', interview with Elvira Huelves, *El Mundo* (7 Oct. 1990), 10–11.

—— 'Violencia de Estado y violencia social', *Cambio 16* (24 June 1991), 86.

Guílver, Lubara and Roger de Gaimon, preface to the Spanish trans. of Jean Nicolas, *La cuestión homosexual* (Barcelona, 1978).

Hart, Stephen M., *The Other Scene: Psychoanalytic Readings in Modern Spanish and Latin-American Literature* (Boulder, Colo., 1991).

—— 'Esther Tusquets: Sex, Excess, and the Dangerous Supplement of Language', *Antípodas* 3 (1991), forthcoming.

Institut Lambda, *Perspectives actuals de l'homosexualitat* (Barcelona, 1985).

Karl, Mauricio (pseud.), *Sodomitas: homosexuales políticos, científicos, criminales, espías, etc* (n.p., 1973).

Labanyi, Jo, 'The Construction/Deconstruction of the Self in the Autobiographies of Pablo Neruda and Juan Goytisolo', *FMLS* 26 (1990), 212–21.

Lee Six, Abigail, 'Sterne's Legacy to Juan Goytisolo: A Shandyian Reading of *Juan sin tierra*', *MLR* 84 (1989), 846–59.

—— *Juan Goytisolo: The Case for Chaos* (New Haven Conn., 1990).

—— 'Breaking Rules, Making History: A Postmodern Reading of Historiography in Juan Goytisolo's Fiction', in *History and Post-War Writing* (Amsterdam, 1990).

—— 'Perceiving the Family: Rosa Chacel's *Desde el amanecer*', unpub. paper.

Levine, Linda Gould, 'Reading, Re-reading, Misreading, and Rewriting the Male Canon: The Narrative Web of Esther Tusquets's Trilogy', *ALEC* 12 (1987), 203–17.

—— 'El papel paradójico del Sida en *Las virtudes del pájaro solitario*', in *Escritos sobre Juan Goytisolo: II Seminario Internacional sobre la obra de Juan Goytisolo* (Almería, 1990), 225–36.

Mangini, Shirley, 'Worshipping Mnemosine: The Prose of Rosa Chacel', *LP* 3 (1990), 27–40.

Martin, Marina, 'Juan Goytisolo en deuda con Américo Castro: *Reivindicación del conde don Julián*', *LP* (1989), 211–23.

Martínez Fariñas, Enrique, *Biografía de la homosexualidad* (Barcelona, 1976).

Miglos, Daniele, 'El pequeño mundo de Rosa Chacel', *RFH* 6 (1990), 245–307.

Mirabet i Mullol, Antoni, *Homosexualitat avui* (Barcelona, 1984); trans. *Homosexualidad hoy* (Barcelona, 1985).

Moix, Terenci, *Món mascle* (Barcelona, 1971), Castilian trans., *Mundo macho* (Barcelona, 1990).

—— *Sadístic, esperpèntic, i àdhuc metafísic* (Barcelona, 1976).

—— *El dia que murió Marilyn* (Barcelona, 1984).

—— *El peso de la paja: memorias: el cine de los sábados* (Barcelona, 1990).

—— *Garras de astracán* (Barcelona, 1991).

Molinaro, Nina L., *Foucault, Feminism, and Power: Reading Esther Tusquets* (Lewisburg, Pa., 1991).

Montoya, Baldomero, *Los homosexuales* (Barcelona, 1977).

Nichols, Geraldine Cleary, 'The Prison-House (and Beyond): *El mismo mar de todos los veranos*', *RR* 75 (1984), 366–85.

Núñez, Enrique, *Homoeróticos* (Madrid, 1977).

Ordóñez, Elizabeth J., 'A Quest for Matrilinear Roots and Mythopoesis: Esther Tusquets's *El mismo mar de todos los veranos*' *CH* 6 (1984), 37–46.

Perriam, Chris, 'Reality and the Angels: Luis Antonio de Villena and *La muerte unicamente*', *BHS* 67 (1990), 31–42.

Plaza, Sixto, '*Coto vedado*, autobiografía o novela?' in *Actas del IX Congreso de la Asociación Internacional de Hispanistas*, II (Frankfurt, 1989), 345–50.

Pope, Randolph D., 'La hermandad del crimen: Genet examina a Goytisolo', in *Estudios en homenaje a Enrique Ruiz-Fornells* (Erie, Pa, 1990), 514–18.

—— 'Theory and Contemporary Autobiographical Writing: The Case of Juan Goytisolo', *Siglo XX/20th Century* 8 (1990–1), 87–101.

Porlán, Alberto, *La sinrazón de Rosa Chacel* (Madrid, 1984).

Ramón-Enríquez, José, (ed.), *Los homosexuales ante la sociedad enferma* (Barcelona, 1978).

Ramos, Alicia, 'Texto y contexto en *Reivindicación del conde don Julián* de Juan Goytisolo', *LD* 19 (1989),

Rivas, Héctor Anabitarte and Sanz, Ricardo Lorenzo, *Homosexualidad: el asunto está caliente* (Madrid, 1979).

Rodríguez, Ana, 'El magisterio de Ortega en Rosa Chacel', in *Homenaje al profesor Antonio Vilanova*, II (Barcelona, 1989), 567–77.

Rodríguez, Mercedes M. de, '*Para no volver*: Humor vs. Phallocentrism', *LF* 16 (1990), 29–35.

Roig Roselló, Antonio, *Todos los parques no son un paraíso: memorias de un sacerdote* (Barcelona, 1977).

—— *Vidente en rebeldía: un proceso en la iglesia* (Barcelona, 1979).

Romera Castillo, José, 'Anacronismos lingüísticos con clara intencionalidad literaria en *Nuestro Virgen de los Mártires* de Terenci Moix', *EL* 3 (1985–6), 313–20.

Romero, Héctor R., 'Sexo y escatología en las novelas más recientes de Juan Goytisolo', *Iris* 1 (1989), 177–86.

Sánchez Pascual, Enrique, *Fronteras de la homosexualidad* (Barcelona, 1976).

Sarduy, Severo, 'La desterritorialización', in *Juan Goytisolo*, ed. Gonzalo Sobejano (Madrid, 1975).

Sau, Victoria, *Mujeres lesbianas* (Madrid, 1980).

Servodidio, Mirella, 'Perverse Pairings and Corrupted Codes: *El amor es un juego solitario*', *ALEC* 11 (1986), 237–54.

—— 'A Case of Pre-Oedipal and Narrative Fixation: *El mismo mar de todos los veranos*', *ALEC* 12 (1987), 157–74.

—— 'Esther Tusquets's Fiction: The Spinning of a Narrative Web', in Joan L. Brown (ed.), *Women Writers in Contemporary Spain: Exiles in the Homeland* (Newark, Del., 1991), 159–78.

Smith, Paul Julian, *Writing in the Margin: Spanish Literature of the Golden Age* (Oxford, 1988).

—— *The Body Hispanic: Gender and Sexuality in Spanish and Spanish American Literature* (Oxford, 1989).

—— *Representing the Other: 'Race', Text, and Gender in Spanish and Spanish American Narrative* (Oxford, 1992).

Spadaccini, Nicholas and Jenaro Talens (eds), *Autobiography in Early Modern Spain* (Minneapolis, 1988).

Trujillo, Carla (ed.), *Chicana Lesbians: The Girls Our Mothers Warned Us Against* (Berkeley, Calif., 1991).

Tusquets, Esther, *El mismo mar de todos los veranos* (Barcelona, 1978).

—— *El amor es un juego solitario* (Barcelona, 1979).

—— *Varada tras el último naufragio* (Barcelona, 1980).

—— *Love Is a Solitary Game*, trans. B. Penman (London, 1985).

—— *The Same Sea as Every Summer*, trans. and afterword Margaret E. W. Jones (Lincoln, Nebr., 1990).

Vidal, Marciano, *Homosexualidad: ciencia y conciencia* (Santander, 1981).

Viladrich, Jordi, *Anotaciones al diario de un homosexual comunista* (Madrid, 1977).

Vilaseca, David, 'Homosexuality and the Rejection of the Double in Dalí's Autobiographical Writings', unpub. paper read at the Conference on 'Questions of Homosexuality' at the Institute of Romance Studies in the University of London (June 1991).

Walters, D. Gareth, '"Comprendí. Pero no explico.": Revelation and Concealment in Lorca's *Canciones*', *BHS* 68 (1991), 265–79.

3 HISPANIC AND CINEMATIC

'Almodóvar: bordeando el borde', special feature in *El europeo* 8 (Jan. 1989), 65–87.

Almodóvar, Pedro, 'Pepi, Luci, Bom y otras chicas del montón: guión original' (Madrid, 1981).

—— 'Entre tinieblas: guión original de Pedro Almodóvar' (Madrid, 1982).

—— 'La ley del deseo: guión' (Madrid, 1987).

Andany, Encarnación, 'En defensa de *El diputado*', *La calle* (13–19 Feb. 1979).

Anonymous, interview with Almodóvar on release of *'Pepi, Luci, Bom, Guía del ocio* (3 Nov. 1980).

—— production notes for *¡Atame!* (incl. interview with Almodóvar).

—— review of *El diputado*, *Arriba* (24 Jan. 1979).

—— review of *Los placeres ocultos*, *El pueblo* (19 Apr. 1977).

—— TV preview of *El pico*, *ABC* (11 Aug. 1989).

—— TV preview of *El pico*, *Diario 16* (11 Aug. 1989).

Arderius, Pirula, 'Eloy de la Iglesia: "Aún no hay libertad de expresión"', interview, *Información* (23 Feb. 1978).

Arenas, José, '*El pico*, una película de Eloy de la Iglesia que se presenta polémica', *ABC* (7 Sept. 1983).

Arroyo, José, 'Law and Desire', *Descant* 20/1–2 (1989), 53–70.

Baecque, Antoine de, ' "Pipi [*sic*], Luci, Bom": Pedro Almodóvar joue avec les signes de la pub[licité] sur fond d'instruction sado-maso', *CaC* 437 (1990), 88–9.

Bayón, Miguel, 'No cerrar el pico: el director Eloy de la Iglesia lleva 20 años escandalizando', interview, *Cambio 16* (14 Nov. 1983).

Bosch, Ignasi, '*El pico*: lo viejo y lo nuevo', *Contracampo* 34 (Winter 1984), 52–60.

Bouzet, Ange-Dominique, 'Tournage au bout de la crise de nerfs', location report on *¡Atame!*, *Libération* (9 Jan. 1990).

Brantley, Ben, 'The Wild Man of La Mancha', *Sunday Times Magazine* (18 June 1990).

Cadalso, Isabel, 'Pedro Almodóvar: A Spanish Perspective', *Cineaste* 18/1 (1990), 36–7.

Calvo García, Eduardo, 'Bibí: el sexo de los ángeles', *La calle*, 201 (27 Jan.–2 Feb. 1982), 26–8.

Cardullo, Bert, 'Lovers and Other Strangers' review of *¡Atame!*, *HuR* 43/4 (Winter 1991), 645–53.

Chevallier, Jacques, review of *¡Atame!*, *RC* 461 (1990), 25.

Cirbián, Txerra, 'Almodóvar: "*La ley del deseo* es mi película más madura"', interview, *El periódico* (19 Feb. 1987).

Ciusqui, Noam, 'Pedro Almodóvar: sexo y ganas de divertirse', *Diario de Barcelona* (2 Nov. 1980).

Contel, Raúl, 'Cine de homosexuales', *Cinema 2002*, 56 (Oct. 1979), 54–6.

Crespo, Pedro, Review of *Entre tinieblas* (8 Feb. 1987).

de Cominges, Jorge, 'Los límites de Eloy', *Destino* (3 Aug. 1978).

—— 'Una historia que se permite todas las osadías', *Noticiero universal* (1 Oct. 1983).

de la Iglesia, Eloy, and Gonzalo Goicoechea, 'La acera de enfrente' (working title for *Los placeres ocultos*), script (Madrid, n.d. [1975?]).

—— 'El diputado: título provisional', script (Madrid, 1978).

—— 'Galopa y corta el viento: argumento para una historia cinematográfica escrito por Eloy de la Iglesia y Gonzalo Goicoechea', script outline (Madrid, 1980).

—— 'El pico: guión (título provisional)', (Madrid, 14 Feb. 1983).

De Stefano, George, 'Post-Franco Frankness', *FC* 22 (June 1986), 58–60.

Díaz, Lola, 'Pedro Almodóvar: "Cuando me comparan con Fassbinder me parece una pesadilla"' interview, *Cambio 16* (18 Apr. 1988).

Douchet, Jean, 'L'Amour du cinéma' (on Almodóvar), *CaC* 435 (1990), 52–3.

Egido, Antonio, '*El diputado*, político y homosexual; Eloy de la Iglesia: "Los partidos políticos no deben marginar la libertad sexual"', interview, *El periódico* (19 January 1979).

Evans, Peter W., review of the Eng. trans. of García de Leon and Maldonado, *BHS* 67 (1990), 311–12.

—— 'Almodóvar's *Matador*: Genre, Subjectivity, and Desire', forthcoming in *BHS*.

Fernández, Rafa, 'Pedro Almodóvar: "*La ley del deseo* no es una película de homosexuales"', interview, *Diario 16* (18 Jan. 1987).

Fernández Santos, Angel, 'La ley del exceso', review of *La ley del deseo*, *El país* (11 Feb. 1987).

Fernández Torres, Alberto, review of *Pepi, Luci, Bom*, *Contracampo* 18 (Jan. 1981), 73.

Fernández Ventura, L., 'Eloy de la Iglesia: lo popular y lo político', interview, *Diario 16* (13 Dec. 1977).

Fernando, Carlos, 'Pedro Almodóvar lleva a cabo su antigua aspiración de hacer un film de hermanos', *Diario 16* (1 Sept. 1986).

Forbes, Jill, review of *Mujeres al borde de un ataque de nervios*, *SS* 58/2 (Spring 1989), 135.

Francia, Juan I., and Julio Pérez Perucha, 'Primera película: Pedro Almodóvar', *Contracampo* 23 (Sept. 1981), 5–7.

Galán, Diego, 'Eloy de la Iglesia: la ambición de un cine popular', *Triunfo* (14 Feb. 1979).

—— review of *Pepi, Luci, Bom*, *El País* (30 Oct. 1980).

García de León, María Antonia and Teresa Maldonado, *Pedro Almodóvar: la otra España cañí* (Ciudad Real, 1989).

Guarner, José Luis, review of *El Pico*, *El periódico* (4 Oct. 1983).

—— review of *Entre tinieblas*, *El periódico* (28 Oct. 1983).

Guilliat, Richard, 'Maura the Merrier', interview, *20/20* (June 1989), 70–3.

Harguindey, Angel S., 'Pedro Almodóvar: toma la fama y corre', *El país semanal* (29 Sept. 1984).

Haro Ibars, Eduardo, 'La homosexualidad como problema socio-político en el cine español del postfranquismo', *Tiempo de Historia*, 52 (Mar. 1979), 88–91.

Hidalgo, Manuel, 'Arrojarse a los pies del "caballo"', *Diario 16* (18 Sept. 1983).

Hopewell, John, *Out of the Past: Spanish Cinema after Franco* (London, 1986).

—— *El cine español después de Franco* (Madrid, 1989).

—— 'Prólogo' to García de León and Maldonado, *Pedro Almodóvar* (Ciudad Real, 1989), 13–20.

Izquierdo, Charo, 'Pedro Almodóvar: "Ahora está de moda el placer"', interview, *Dunia* (29 Nov. 1983).

Kinder, Marsha, 'Pleasure and the New Spanish Morality: A Conversation with Pedro Almodóvar', *FQ* (Fall 1987), 33–4.

Leavitt, David, 'Almodóvar on the Verge', *Weekend Guardian* (23–4 June 1990), 12–16.

Llinàs, Francesc [?], '*El diputado* de Eloy de la Iglesia: a por los 300 millones', *La calle* (30 Jan.–5 Feb. 1979).

'Madrid: corte de los modernos', pull-out section in *Tribuna* (18 May 1986).

Mahieu, J. A., review of *Entre tinieblas*, *Fotogramas* (15 Oct. 1983).

Marinero, Francisco, review of *El pico*, *Diario 16* (8 Oct. 1983).

—— Review of *Entre tinieblas*, *Diario 16* (8 Oct. 1983).

Martialay, Félix, review of *El diputado*, *El alcázar* (15 Oct. 1983).

Maso, Angeles (A.M.M.), 'La luz roja a *Los placeres ocultos*: Eloy de la Iglesia no piensa alterar la integridad de su película', *La vanguardia* (15 Feb. 1977).

—— 'Llegó con *El diputado*: Eloy de la Iglesia: "La izquierda ha heredado una moral que no es la suya"', interview, *La vanguardia* (24 Oct. 1979).

—— review of *Entre tinieblas*, *La vanguardia* (23 Oct. 1983).

Méndez-Leite, Fernando, 'Ultimo veto de la censura: *Los placeres ocultos*', *Diario 16* (26 Jan. 1977).

Merck, Mandy, review of *¡Atame!*, *City Limits* (London) (5–12 July 1990).

Montagut, Alberto, 'Batalla para evitar que *¡Atame!* sea declarada "porno"', *El país internacional* (16 Apr. 1990).

Mujeres al borde de un ataque de nervios, press pack (Madrid, 1988).

Murphy, Ryan, 'A Spanish Fly in the Hollywood Ointment: Gay

Director Pedro Almodóvar Refuses to be Tied Up by Censorship', interview, *The Advocate* (19 June 1990), 37–40.

Musetto, V. A., review of *Entre tinieblas*, *New York Post* (6 May 1988).

National Film Theatre, Programme notes to *¡Atame!*, incl. interview with Almodóvar (London, 1990).

Ors, Francisco, 'Sternberg en la cumbre del esplendor homosexual de Hollywood', *Contracampo* 22 (1981), 11–16.

O'Toole, Lawrence, 'Almodóvar in Bondage', *SS* 59/4 (Autumn 1990), 270–3.

Padura, Monty, 'Eloy de la Iglesia: el homosexualismo en el cine', interview, *Catalunya Expres* (19 Oct. 1977).

Pally, Marcia, 'The Politics of Passion: Pedro Almodóvar and the Camp Aesthetic', *Cineaste* 18/1 (1990), 31–5, 38–9.

Peralta, Carel, 'Eloy de la Iglesia: "El PNV tiene un concepto aldeano de la moral"', interview, *Interviú* (30 Oct.–5 Nov. 1985).

Rouyer, Philippe, 'La Prisonnière de l'amour', review of *¡Atame!*, *Positif* 352 (1990), 54–5.

—— review of *Pepi, Luci, Bom*, *Positif* 358 (1990), 79.

Rubio, Andrés F., '"'Atame' equivale a 'te quiero'", dice Pedro Almodóvar de su última película', *El país internacional* (18 Dec. 1989).

Ruiz de Villalobos, '*El pico*: el fabuloso cine tremendista de Eloy de la Iglesia', *Diario de Barcelona* (25 Sept. 1983).

Selo, Gloria, and Emilio Garrido, 'Almodóvar monta un imperio amenazado por sus enemigos', *Tribuna* (5–11 Feb. 1990).

Smith, Paul Julian, review of *¡Atame!*, *TLS* (20–6 July 1990).

Strauss, Frédéric, 'Festival de Berlin: Pedro Almodóvar', interview, *CaC* 430 (1990), 6.

—— review of *¡Atame!*, *CaC* 433 (1990), 88.

Téllez, José Luis, review of *El diputado*, *Contracampo* 1 (April 1979), 51–2.

—— review of *Entre tinieblas*, *Contracampo* 36 (Summer 1984), 108–10.

Thirard, Paul Louis, review of *Entre tinieblas*, *Positif* 336 (1989), 50–1.

Torres, Augusto M., *Cine español 1896–1983* (Madrid, 1983).

—— 'Entre el super 8 y el Oscar' [on Almodóvar], *El país* (30 Apr. 1989).

Trenas, Miguel Angel, 'Con Pedro Almodóvar llegó el escándalo', *La vanguardia* (29 Oct. 1983).

Trueba, Fernando, 'Sexo y política: un coctel que vende', review of *El diputado*, *El país* (27 Jan. 1979).

Umbral, Francisco, 'Almodóvar', *El mundo* (25 Jan. 1990).

Urbistondo, Vicente, 'El triunfo de Almodóvar: forasteros en Hollywood', *El país* (20 Dec. 1988).

Vallina, Isabel 'Homosexuales en cartel', *Interviú* (29 Oct. 1986).

Vallvés, Jordi, 'Pedro Almodóvar presentó ayer en Barcelona su último filme, *¡Atame!*', *Diario 16* (13 Jan. 1990).

Valot, Jacques, review of *Entre tinieblas*, *RC* 445 (1989), 28–9.

—— review of *Pepi, Luci, Bom*, *RC* 465 (1990), 28.

Vecchi, Philippe, 'Accroche-moi', interview with Victoria Abril, *Libération* (23–4 June 1990).

Vega, Javier, Francesc Llinàs, and José Luis Téllez, 'Eloy de la Iglesia', special section in *Contracampo*, 25–6 (Nov.–Dec. 1981), 21–41.

Vidal, Nuria, *El cine de Pedro Almodóvar* (Barcelona, 1988).

Vidal Estévez, M., review of *Gay Club*, *Contracampo* 21 (Apr.–May 1981), 69.

Whyte, Christopher, 'Pedro Almodóvar; Or, Camp and the Limits of Love', unpub. paper read at the Conference on 'Questions of Homosexuality' at the Institute of Romance Studies in the University of London (June 1991).

Index